# VERIFICATION AND VALIDATION FOR QUALITY OF UML 2.0 MODELS

# VERIFICATION AND VALIDATION FOR QUALITY OF UML 2.0 MODELS

BHUVAN UNHELKAR, PhD

WILEY-
INTERSCIENCE

A Wiley-Interscience Publication

JOHN WILEY & SONS, INC.

*Library of Congress Cataloging-in-Publication Data is available.*

ISBN 0-471-72783-0

10  9  8  7  6  5  4  3  2  1

*SONKI*

# Contents

Figures   **xix**

Foreword   **xxiii**

Preface   **xxv**

Acknowledgments   **xxxi**

Glossary of Acronyms and Terms   **xxxiii**

Author Profile   **xxxv**

**1 The Quality Strategy for UML**   **1**

   Chapter Summary   1

   1.1   Modeling and Quality   2
      1.1.1   The Modeling Advantage   2
      1.1.2   Modeling Caveats   2
      1.1.3   Context of Model Quality   3
      1.1.4   Model Quality   4

   1.2   Positioning UML for Modeling   4

   1.3   Quality Aspects of UML   5

   1.4   Understanding Modeling Spaces in Software   7

   1.5   Modeling Spaces and UML   7
      1.5.1   Importance of UML Diagrams to
             Respective Models   8

1.5.2   List of UML Diagrams                                      8
1.5.3   UML Diagrams and Modeling Spaces                          9
1.5.4   Model of Problem Space (MOPS)                            10
1.5.5   Model of Solution Space (MOSS)                           11
1.5.6   Model of Background Space (MOBS)                         12

1.6   Verification and Validation                                14
1.6.1   Quality Models—Syntax                                    15
1.6.2   Quality Models—Semantics                                 17
1.6.3   Quality Models—Aesthetics                                18
1.6.4   Quality Techniques and V&V Checks                        18

1.7   Quality Checks and Skills Levels                           19

1.8   Levels of Quality Checks to UML Diagrams                   20
1.8.1   Syntax Checks and UML Elements
        (Focus on Correctness)                                   21
1.8.2   Semantic Checks and UML Diagrams
        (Focus on Completeness and Consistency)                  22
1.8.3   Aesthetic Checks and UML Models
        (Focus on Symmetry and Consistency)                      22

1.9   Model-Driven Architecture (MDA) and Quality               23

1.10   Prototyping and Modeling Spaces                           23

Discussion Topics                                                24

References                                                       25

2   **Nature and Basics of UML Diagrams**                        27

Chapter Summary                                                  27

2.1   The Nature of UML Diagrams                                 27
2.1.1   Elasticity of UML                                        28
2.1.2   Structural versus Behavioral Nature of
        UML Diagrams                                             28
2.1.3   Static versus Dynamic Nature of
        UML Diagrams                                             29

2.2   Use Case Diagrams                                          30
2.2.1   Nature of Use Case Diagrams                              30
2.2.2   Putting Together a Use Case Diagram                      31

2.3   Activity Diagrams                                          33
2.3.1   Nature of Activity Diagrams                              33
2.3.2   Putting Together an Activity Diagram                     33
2.3.3   Specifications in an Activity Diagram                    34

2.4  Class Diagrams                                                      35
   2.4.1  Nature of Class Diagrams                             35
   2.4.2  Putting Together a Class Diagram                      36
   2.4.3  Specification of a Class                             36

2.5  Sequence Diagrams                                                   37
   2.5.1  Nature of Sequence Diagrams                          37
   2.5.2  Putting Together a Sequence Diagram                  38
   2.5.3  Specifications of a Sequence Diagram                 39

2.6  Communication Diagrams                                              39
   2.6.1  Nature of Communication Diagrams                     39
   2.6.2  Putting Together a Communication Diagram             40

2.7  Interaction Overview Diagrams                                       41
   2.7.1  Nature of Interaction Overview Diagrams              41
   2.7.2  Putting Together an Interaction Overview Diagram     41

2.8  Object Diagrams                                                     41
   2.8.1  Nature of Object Diagrams                            41
   2.8.2  Putting Together an Object Diagram                   42

2.9  State Machine Diagrams                                              43
   2.9.1  Nature of State Machine Diagrams                     43
   2.9.2  Putting Together a State Machine Diagram             44

2.10  Composite Structure Diagrams                                       44
   2.10.1  Nature of Composite Structure Diagrams              44
   2.10.2  Putting Together a Composite
        Structure Diagram                              45

2.11  Component Diagrams                                                 45
   2.11.1  Nature of Component Diagrams                        45
   2.11.2  Putting Together a Component Diagram                46
   2.11.3  Specifications of a Component Diagram               46

2.12  Deployment Diagrams                                                46
   2.12.1  Nature of Deployment Diagrams                       46
   2.12.2  Putting Together a Deployment Diagram               47

2.13  Package Diagrams                                                   47
   2.13.1  Nature of Package Diagrams                          47
   2.13.2  Putting Together a Package Diagram                  48
   2.13.3  Specifications of a Package Diagram                 48

2.14  Timing Diagrams                                                    49
   2.14.1  Nature of Timing Diagrams                           49
   2.14.2  Putting Together a Timing Diagram                   49

2.15    UML's Extensibility Mechanisms                                          50
        2.15.1    Stereotypes                                                   50
        2.15.2    Notes                                                         51
        2.15.3    Constraints                                                   52
        2.15.4    Tagged Values                                                 53

2.16    UML Meta-Models and Quality                                            53

Discussion Topics                                                             55

References                                                                    56


3    Strengths, Weaknesses, Objectives and Traps (SWOT)
     of UML Diagrams                                                           57

Chapter Summary                                                               57

3.1    SWOT Analysis of the UML Diagrams                                       58

3.2    SWOT of Use Case Diagrams                                              59
       3.2.1    Strengths of Use Cases and Use Case Diagrams                   59
       3.2.2    Weaknesses of Use Cases and Use Case Diagrams                  60
       3.2.3    Objectives of Use Cases and Use Case Diagrams                  61
       3.2.4    Traps of Use Cases and Use Case Diagrams                       63

3.3    SWOT of Activity Diagrams                                               65
       3.3.1    Strengths of Activity Diagrams                                 65
       3.3.2    Weaknesses of Activity Diagrams                                66
       3.3.3    Objectives of Activity Diagrams                                66
       3.3.4    Traps of Activity Diagrams                                     67

3.4    SWOT of Classes and Class Diagrams                                      67
       3.4.1    Strengths of Classes and Class Diagrams                        67
       3.4.2    Weaknesses of Classes and Class Diagrams                       68
       3.4.3    Objectives of Classes and Class Diagrams                       69
       3.4.4    Traps of Classes and Class Diagrams                            69

3.5    SWOT of Sequence Diagrams                                               70
       3.5.1    Strengths of Sequence Diagrams                                 70
       3.5.2    Weaknesses of Sequence Diagrams                                71
       3.4.3    Objectives of Sequence Diagrams                                71
       3.5.4    Traps of Sequence Diagrams                                     72

3.6    SWOT of Communication Diagrams                                          73
       3.6.1    Strengths of Communication Diagrams                            73
       3.6.2    Weaknesses of Communication Diagrams                           73
       3.6.3    Objectives of Communication Diagrams                           73
       3.6.4    Traps of Communication Diagrams                                74

3.7    SWOT of Interaction Overview Diagrams                           74

    3.7.1    Strengths of Interaction Overview Diagrams          74
    3.7.2    Weaknesses of Interaction Overview Diagrams         74
    3.7.3    Objectives of Interaction Overview Diagrams         74
    3.7.4    Traps of Interaction Overview Diagrams              75

3.8    SWOT of Object Diagrams                                        75

    3.8.1    Strengths of Object Diagrams                        75
    3.8.2    Weaknesses of Object Diagrams                       75
    3.8.3    Objectives of Object Diagrams                       75
    3.8.4    Traps of Object Diagrams                            76

3.9    SWOT of State Machine Diagrams                                 76

    3.9.1    Strengths of State Machine Diagrams                 76
    3.9.2    Weaknesses of State Machine Diagrams                76
    3.9.3    Objectives of State Machine Diagrams                76
    3.9.4    Traps of State Machine Diagrams                     77

3.10   SWOT of Composite Structure Diagrams                          77

    3.10.1   Strengths of Composite Structure Diagrams           77
    3.10.2   Weaknesses of Composite Structure Diagrams          77
    3.10.3   Objectives of Composite Structure Diagrams          77
    3.10.4   Traps of Composite Structure Diagrams               78

3.11   SWOT of Component Diagrams                                     78

    3.11.1   Strengths of Component Diagrams                     78
    3.11.2   Weaknesses of Component Diagrams                    78
    3.11.3   Objectives of Component Diagrams                    78
    3.11.4   Traps of Component Diagrams                         79

3.12   SWOT of Deployment Diagrams                                    79

    3.12.1   Strengths of Deployment Diagrams                    79
    3.12.2   Weaknesses of Deployment Diagrams                   79
    3.12.3   Objectives of Deployment Diagrams                   80
    3.12.4   Traps of Deployment Diagrams                        80

3.13   SWOT of Package Diagrams                                       80

    3.13.1   Strengths of Package Diagrams                       80
    3.13.2   Weaknesses of Package Diagrams                      81
    3.13.3   Objectives of Package Diagrams                      81
    3.13.4   Traps of Package Diagrams                           81

3.14   SWOT of Timing Diagrams                                        82

    3.14.1   Strengths of Timing Diagrams                        82
    3.14.2   Weaknesses of Timing Diagrams                       82
    3.14.3   Objectives of Timing Diagrams                       82
    3.14.4   Traps of Timing Diagrams                            82

Discussion Topics ........................................................... 82

Note ................................................................................ 83

References ....................................................................... 84

**4   V&V of the Quality of MOPS** .................................. **85**

Chapter Summary .......................................................... 85

4.1    UML Diagrams in MOPS ...................................... 86

4.2    V&V of Use Cases and Use Case Diagrams in MOPS .... 88

    4.2.1    Actors and Use Cases—Initial List ............. 88

    4.2.2    List of Use Case Diagrams ......................... 90

    4.2.3    Describing Client Maintenance Use Case Diagrams .... 91

    4.2.4    Actor–Class Confusion ............................... 95

    4.2.5    Actor Documentation and Quality Checks .... 96

    4.2.6    Describing Policy Creation and Policy Maintenance
            Use Case Diagrams ................................... 100

    4.2.7    Use Case Documentation and Quality Checks .... 103

    4.2.8    Describing the Claims Processing Use Case Diagram .... 113

    4.2.9    Describing the Sales Campaigning Use Case Diagram .... 114

    4.2.10  Syntax Checks for Use Case Diagrams ........ 115

    4.2.11  Semantic Checks for Use Case Diagrams ..... 118

    4.2.12  Aesthetic Checks for Use Case Diagrams .... 120

    4.2.13  Acceptance Testing and Use Case Documentation .... 121

4.3    Quality of Activity Diagrams in MOPS .................. 122

    4.3.1    Describing the AddsClientDetails
            Activity Diagram ..................................... 122

    4.3.2    Describing the CreatesHomeInsurancePolicy
            Activity Diagram ..................................... 124

    4.3.3    Syntax Checks for Activity Diagrams .......... 126

    4.3.4    Semantic Checks for Activity Diagrams ....... 127

    4.3.5    Aesthetic Checks for Activity Diagrams ...... 128

4.4    Quality of Package Diagrams in MOPS .................. 129

    4.4.1    Describing the LUCKY Package Diagram ..... 129

    4.4.2    Syntax Checks for the LUCKY Package Diagram .... 130

    4.4.3    Semantic Checks for the LUCKY Package Diagram .... 131

    4.4.4    Aesthetic Checks for the LUCKY Package Diagram .... 132

4.5    Quality of Classes and Class Diagrams in MOPS ..... 132

    4.5.1    Documenting a Class ................................ 133

    4.5.2    Syntax Checks for Classes ......................... 137

    4.5.3    Semantic Checks for Classes ..................... 138

    4.5.4    Aesthetic Checks for the Client Class ......... 138

| | | | |
|---|---|---|---|
| | 4.5.5 | Describing the ClientDetails Class Diagram | 139 |
| | 4.5.6 | Describing the PolicyDetails Class Diagram | 142 |
| | 4.5.7 | Syntax Checks for Class Diagrams | 142 |
| | 4.5.8 | Semantic Checks for Class Diagrams | 144 |
| | 4.5.9 | Aesthetic Checks for Class Diagrams | 144 |
| 4.6 | | Quality of Sequence Diagrams in MOPS | 145 |
| | 4.6.1 | Describing the CreateClient Sequence Diagram | 145 |
| | 4.6.2 | Describing the CreateClientOnInternet Sequence Diagram | 146 |
| | 4.6.3 | Describing the ApprovePolicy Sequence Diagram | 147 |
| | 4.6.4 | Syntax Checks for Sequence Diagrams | 148 |
| | 4.6.5 | Semantic Checks for Sequence Diagrams | 148 |
| | 4.6.6 | Aesthetic Checks for Sequence Diagrams | 150 |
| 4.7 | | Quality of State Machine Diagrams in MOPS | 150 |
| | 4.7.1 | Describing the Client State Machine Diagram | 150 |
| | 4.7.2 | Describing the Policy State Machine Diagram | 151 |
| | 4.7.3 | Syntax Checks for the ClientStates State Machine Diagram | 152 |
| | 4.7.4 | Semantic Checks for the ClientStates State Machine Diagram | 153 |
| | 4.7.5 | Aesthetic Checks for the ClientStates State Machine Diagram | 153 |
| 4.8 | | Quality of Interaction Overview Diagrams in MOPS | 154 |
| | 4.8.1 | Describing the CreateClient Interaction Overview Diagram | 154 |
| | 4.8.2 | Syntax Checks for Interaction Overview Diagrams | 155 |
| | 4.8.3 | Semantic Check for Interaction Overview Diagrams | 155 |
| | 4.8.4 | Aesthetic Check for Interaction Overview Diagrams | 155 |
| 4.9 | | Validating the Entire MOPS | 156 |
| | 4.9.1 | Use Case to Activity Diagram Dependency and Quality | 156 |
| | 4.9.2 | Use Case to Class Diagram Dependency and Quality | 157 |
| | 4.9.3 | Class to Sequence Diagram Dependency and Quality | 157 |
| | 4.9.4 | Interaction Overview Diagram to Sequence Diagram and Use Case Dependencies | 157 |
| | 4.9.5 | Quality of Documentation Associated with MOPS | 158 |
| | 4.9.6 | Aesthetics of MOPS | 158 |
| 4.10 | | Summary of Quality Checks for MOPS | 158 |
| | | Discussion Topics | 158 |
| | | References | 160 |

**5    V&V of the Quality of MOSS**                                         **161**

Chapter Summary                                                         161

5.1    UML Diagrams in the Solution Space (MOSS)                       161

5.2    Analyzing MOPS for MOSS for a Solution                         163
       5.2.1    Analysis of Use Cases in the Solution Space           163
       5.2.2    Analysis of Business Class Diagrams in the
                Solution Space                                         165
       5.2.3    Analyzing Activity Diagrams in the
                Solution Space                                         165

5.3    Quality of Classes and Class Diagrams in MOSS                  166
       5.3.1    Syntax Checks for Classes in the Solution Space       166
       5.3.2    Semantic Checks for Classes in the Solution Space     170
       5.3.3    Aesthetic Checks for Classes at the Design Level      173
       5.3.4    Describing Class Diagrams in MOSS                     173
       5.3.5    Syntax Checks of Class Diagrams in MOSS              175
       5.3.6    Semantic Checks of Class Diagrams in MOSS            176
       5.3.7    Aesthetic Checks of Class Diagrams in MOSS           177

5.4    Quality of Sequence Diagrams in MOSS                          178
       5.4.1    Describing the Sequence of Submission of a Claim     178
       5.4.2    Syntax Checks for Sequence Diagrams                  180
       5.4.3    Semantic Checks for Sequence Diagrams                181
       5.4.4    Aesthetic Checks for Sequence Diagrams               182

5.5    Quality of Communication Diagrams in MOSS                     182
       5.5.1    Describing the SubmitsClaim
                Communication Diagram                                 182
       5.5.2    Syntax Checks for Communication Diagrams             183
       5.5.3    Semantic Checks for Communication Diagrams           183
       5.5.4    Aesthetic Checks for Communication Diagrams          184

5.6    Quality of Object Diagrams in MOSS                            184
       5.6.1    Describing the Object Diagram for Policy
                and Claim                                             184
       5.6.2    Syntax Checks for Object Diagrams·                   185
       5.6.3    Semantic Checks for Object Diagrams                  185
       5.6.4    Aesthetic Checks for Object Diagrams                 186

5.7    Quality of State Machine Diagrams in MOSS                     186
       5.7.1    Describing an Advanced State Machine Diagram
                for Claim                                             186
       5.7.2    Syntax Checks for State Machine Diagrams
                in MOSS                                               186

5.7.3    Semantic Checks for State Machine Diagrams
in MOSS                                                          187

5.7.4    Aesthetic Checks for State Machine Diagrams
in MOSS                                                          188

5.8    Quality of Timing Diagrams in MOSS                             188

5.8.1    Describing the Timing Diagram for Policy
and Claim in MOSS                                               188

5.8.2    Syntax Checks for Timing Diagrams in MOSS              188

5.8.3    Semantic Checks for Timing Diagrams in MOSS           188

5.8.4    Aesthetic Checks for Timing Diagrams in MOSS          189

5.9    Converting Models into Systems                                189

5.10   Cross-Diagram Dependencies                                    189

Discussion Topics                                                    190

References                                                           192

**6    V&V of the Quality of MOBS                                       193**

Chapter Summary                                                      193

6.1    Working in the Background Space                               194

6.2    UML Diagrams in the Background Space (MOBS)                   194

6.2.1    Layers in Software Architecture
(Functional vs. Infrastructure)                                196

6.2.2    Relating the Functional Slices to
the Infrastructure                                             198

6.3    V&V of Package Diagrams in MOBS                               199

6.3.1    Syntax Checks for Package Diagrams in MOBS            202

6.3.2    Semantic Checks for Package Diagrams in MOBS          202

6.3.3    Aesthetic Checks for Package Diagrams in MOSS         203

6.4    Classes and Class Diagrams in the Background Space           204

6.4.1    Relational Table Representation by Classes            204

6.4.2    Mapping ClientDetails to Relational Tables           205

6.4.3    Describing Active Classes in MOBS                     205

6.4.4    Class and Granularity of Design in the
Background Space                                               207

6.4.5    Assigning Classes to Components                       208

6.5    V&V of Class Diagrams in the Background Space                208

6.5.1    Syntax Checks for Class Diagrams in MOBS             209

6.5.2    Semantic Checks for Class Diagrams in MOBS          209

6.5.3    Aesthetic Checks for Class Diagrams in MOBS         210

6.6    V&V of Robustness through Class Diagrams in MOBS                210
    6.6.1    Extending Class Diagrams to Robustness Diagrams       210
    6.6.2    Robustness through Alternative Sequence Diagrams      211
    6.6.3    Syntax Checks for Robustness Diagrams in MOBS         211
    6.6.4    Semantic Checks for Robustness Diagrams in MOBS       212
    6.6.5    Aesthetic Checks for Robustness Diagrams in MOBS      213

6.7    V&V of Component Diagrams in MOBS                               213
    6.7.1    Syntax Checks for Component Diagrams
        in MOBS                                                213
    6.7.2    Semantic Checks for Component Diagrams
        in MOBS                                                215
    6.7.3    Aesthetic Checks for Component Diagrams
        in MOBS                                                217

6.8    V&V of Composite Structure Diagrams in MOBS                    218
    6.8.1    Syntax Checks for Composite Structure Diagrams        218
    6.8.2    Semantic Checks for Composite Structure Diagrams      219
    6.8.3    Aesthetic Checks for Composite Structure Diagrams     219

6.9    V&V of Deployment Diagrams in MOBS                             219
    6.9.1    Factors Influencing Deployment of Systems             219
    6.9.2    Syntax Checks for Deployment Diagrams
        in MOBS                                                221
    6.9.3    Semantic Checks for Deployment Diagrams
        in MOBS                                                221
    6.9.4    Aesthetic Checks for Deployment Diagrams
        in MOBS                                                221

6.10   Cross-diagram dependencies in MOBS                            222

Discussion Topics                                                    223

References                                                           224

**7   Managing the V&V Process**                                     **225**

Chapter Summary                                                      225

7.1    Processes and UML                                             225

7.2    Understanding the Process and Process Components              226
    7.2.1    A Simple Process Architecture                         226
    7.2.2    A Process Component for V&V of Class Diagrams          227

7.3    Iterations and Increments in a Process                        228
    7.3.1    Iterations and Increments                             228
    7.3.2    Project-Level Iterations                              229

Discussion Topics                                                              230

Note                                                                          230

References                                                                    230

**Appendix A   LUCKY Insurance Case Study**                                   **231**

**Appendix B   UML CASE Tools**                                               **237**

**Appendix C   Summary of Checks for V&V of the Quality of MOPS**             **241**

**Appendix D   Summary of Checks for V&V of the Quality of MOSS**            **251**

**Appendix E   Summary of Checks for V&V of the Quality of MOBS**            **257**

**Appendix F   Templates for Actors, Use Cases and Classes in MOPS**         **263**

**Index**                                                                    **267**

# Figures

**Figure 1.1**  Software modeling spaces and the modeling work of analysis, design, and architecture in them.

**Figure 1.2**  Quality and V&V of models and their mapping to syntax, semantics and aesthetics.

**Figure 1.3**  Application of syntax, semantics and aesthetics.

**Figure 1.4**  V&V checks and quality techniques.

**Figure 1.5**  Syntax, semantics and aesthetics checks verify and validate UML artifacts, diagrams and models.

**Figure 2.1**  Summary of the nature of UML diagrams, depicting their structural versus behavioral characteristics as well as their static versus dynamic nature.

**Figure 2.2**  Nature and basics of a use case diagram.

**Figure 2.3**  Nature and basics of an activity diagram.

**Figure 2.4**  Nature and basics of a class diagram.

**Figure 2.5**  Nature and basics of a sequence diagram.

**Figure 2.6**  Nature and basics of a communication diagram.

**Figure 2.7**  Nature and basics of an interaction overview diagram.

**Figure 2.8**  Nature and basics of an object diagram.

**Figure 2.9**  Nature and basics of a state machine diagram.

**Figure 2.10**  Nature and basics of a composite structure diagram.

**Figure 2.11**  Nature and basics of a component diagram.

**Figure 2.12**  Nature and basics of a deployment diagram.

**Figure 2.13**  Nature and basics of a package diagram.

**Figure 2.14**  Nature and basics of a timing diagram.

**Figure 2.15**  Stereotypes.

**Figure 2.16**  Notes (A, B and C).

**Figure 2.17**  Constraints (A, B).

**Figure 2.18**  Tagged values.

**Figure 2.19**    Practical application of OMG's meta-models to improve the quality of UML diagrams.

**Figure 2.20**    Example of extending the UML meta-model to enforce quality controls.

**Figure 3.1**    SWOT analysis of UML diagrams.

**Figure 4.1**    Primary UML diagrams in MOPS.
**Figure 4.2**    Insurance requirements—list of actors.
**Figure 4.3**    Client maintenance (a) use case diagram.
**Figure 4.4**    Client maintenance (b) use case diagram.
**Figure 4.5**    Client maintenance (c) use case diagram.
**Figure 4.6**    Actor–class confusion.
**Figure 4.7**    Policy creation use case diagram.
**Figure 4.8**    Policy maintenance use case diagram.
**Figure 4.9**    Claims processing use case diagram.
**Figure 4.10**    Sales campaigning use case diagram.
**Figure 4.11**    AddsClientDetails activity diagram.
**Figure 4.12**    CreatesHomeInsurancePolicy activity diagram.
**Figure 4.13**    The LUCKY package diagram.
**Figure 4.14**    Classes Client and Policy.
**Figure 4.15**    ClientDetails–a class diagram.
**Figure 4.16**    ClientDetails–b class diagram.
**Figure 4.17**    ClientDetails–c class diagram.
**Figure 4.18**    PolicyDetails class diagram.
**Figure 4.19**    Creation of client sequence diagram.
**Figure 4.20**    CreateClientOnInternet sequence diagram.
**Figure 4.21**    Approvepolicy sequence diagram.
**Figure 4.22**    Client state machine diagram.
**Figure 4.23**    Policy state machine diagram.
**Figure 4.24**    Interaction overview diagram for CreateClient.

**Figure 5.1**    Primary UML diagrams in MOSS.
**Figure 5.2**    Analysis of the claims processing use case diagram in the solution space.
**Figure 5.3**    Some classes revealed by the SubmitsClaim use case.
**Figure 5.4**    Analyzing the SubmitsClaim activity diagram (for the corresponding use case).
**Figure 5.5**    Upgrading class operations (behavior) by the previous analysis.
**Figure 5.6**    Addition of design-level classes in MOSS (GUI, database, utility, etc.).
**Figure 5.7**    SubmitsClaim basic sequence diagram.
**Figure 5.8**    SubmitsClaim advanced sequence diagram.
**Figure 5.9**    Creating a SubmitsClaim communication diagram.
**Figure 5.10**    An object diagram for Policy and Claim.
**Figure 5.11**    Advanced state machine diagram for Claim in the solution space.
**Figure 5.12**    Timing diagram for Policy and Claim in the solution space.

**Figure 6.1**    UML diagrams in the background space.
**Figure 6.2**    Application- versus infrastructure-based layering in software architecture for the LUCKY insurance system.
**Figure 6.3**    Putting application architecture in the context of the infrastructure (background) architecture.

**Figure 6.4**    Insurance system package diagram.

**Figure 6.5**    Package diagrams as layered frameworks.

**Figure 6.6**    Mapping classes related to Client to the corresponding relational tables.

**Figure 6.7**    Considering active classes, processes and threads in MOBS.

**Figure 6.8**    Granularity of OO designs.

**Figure 6.9**    Assigning classes to components for physical implementation.

**Figure 6.10**    Robustness diagrams for PolicyCreation and ClaimsProcessing processes with <<control>>, <<boundary>> and <<entity>> classes.

**Figure 6.11**    Effect of robustness on the SubmitsClaim sequence diagram.

**Figure 6.12**    LUCKY insurance components, packages and interfaces.

**Figure 6.13**    Insurance system component diagrams.

**Figure 6.14**    An example composite structure diagram for the LUCKY insurance system.

**Figure 6.15**    Deployment diagram for the LUCKY insurance system.

**Figure 6.16**    Web Infrastructure in development and deployment of systems.

**Figure 7.1**    Process wraps around UML.

**Figure 7.2**    Architecture of a process component.

**Figure 7.3**    A process component for V&V of classes and class diagrams in MOPS.

**Figure 7.4**    Iterations and increments (a high-level example).

# Foreword

UML (Unified Modeling Language) has now been in use for several years and is currently coming close to the end of a large-scale review and reformulation resulting this year (2004) in a new major version (2.0). With its previous versions (1.1, 1.3, 1.4 and 1.5), UML has been widely used by business analysts, system designers, system architects and testers. However, despite this increasing usage, many companies are not taking the *best* advantage of UML, and occasionally, individuals have experienced frustration in applying its standards.

Perhaps this is because they have not yet read this book!

In this book, Dr. Unhelkar takes a practical viewpoint in explaining UML, underpinned by a good understanding of the theoretical basis of what makes a *quality* UML model. He introduces a wide range of guidelines to increase and test the quality of UML models in their various guises. UML users now have the chance to benchmark their own models against an experienced modeler's hard-won experience and expertise. Unhelkar has been using and teaching UML to industry (and academic) groups since UML began and has previously published books describing UML. In this book, he views UML from a quality perspective, evaluating the strengths and weaknesses of the diagram suite and then offering tips and guidelines on how to approach the quality verification and validation (V&V) checklists, followed later in the book.

A major element of this book is the SWOT analysis (strengths, weaknesses, objectives and traps). This analysis is done on each UML diagram in turn so that the reader can see both the up- and downsides of each diagram. Very importantly, the traps should be studied since Unhelkar gathers together many of the pitfalls well known to those of us who are using and teaching UML but that never before have been written down and made public. The subsequent V&V is undertaken with three foci: syntax, semantics and aesthetics. The first two are fairly straightforward and can be gleaned from a careful reading of the OMG standard on UML. But nowhere in the standard will you find advice on stylistic use of UML. As the author notes, an aesthetically pleasing diagram can aid understanding. For instance, sensible naming of classes is long established as an aid to communication; conversely, sloppy naming is virtually guaranteed to make a design unusable. While this quality analysis is not quantitative (perhaps Unhelkar's next book will be the metricated version?), this is an important first step toward that achievement. Nowhere else will you find the quality-focussed insights as presented here into how the UML *really* functions.

Another feature of the presentation is the delineation of three viewpoints, termed the model of problem space (MOPS), model of solution space (MOSS) and model of background space (MOBS). These models allow the reader to create frameworks in which, depending on the current life cycle stage (e.g., MOSS rather than MOPS), a different mix and balance of UML diagrams is advocated. Again, most UML books do not emphasize this well but rather offer UML as a one-size-fits-all approach, which in many ways it originally was. This, of course, all hints at process, which keeps creeping in, although this is dealt with in detail elsewhere in another of the author's books.

All of this analysis is held together by a running example of the LUCKY insurance system. This is an excellent vehicle for demonstrating the basic features of UML in early chapters and then for presenting the qualitative quality analysis in later chapters. This means that the reader can see how all the pieces fit together— which is sometimes hard to observe in examples presented in other venues.

The practical checklists are helpful in verifying and validating the UML models well enough to deserve prominence in a software developer's mindset. I hope that this book will facilitate and encourage such a mindset and recommend that the path to this mindset begins with its perusal.

Brian Henderson-Sellers
Director, Centre for Object Technology
Applications and Research
University of Technology, Sydney

# Preface

Only those who detest working on the same thing twice, produce quality!*

## PURPOSE

This book presents reasons and techniques to enhance the quality of software models built using the Unified Modeling Language (UML Version 2.0). While models in general enhance software quality, the quality of the models themselves is rarely scrutinized. This book addresses this lacuna by delving deeply into the verification and validation (V&V) of UML 2.0 models. A simple and practical checklist-based approach gives the UML models the attention and rigor they deserve.

UML is primarily a means to communicate between various parties involved in a software project. It can be used by users and business analysts to specify requirements, by designers to produce solution designs and by architects to produce system architecture for deployment of the software solution. As with most communication mechanisms, the effectiveness of UML depends on its accuracy and standardization together with the prevailing conventions and mutual understanding of its usage within the project. These are some of the aspects of the UML discussed in this book. The discussions start by developing an understanding the nature of UML models and how to create good-quality models, followed by the creation and application of significant checks and cross-checks to these models. These checks, discussed in terms of V&V checks in this work, encompass the syntactic

---

*Source: a lazy brain!

correctness, semantic consistency and completeness and aesthetic symmetry or style of UML-based models.

While UML comprises a suite of diagrams, practically it is helpful to consider these diagrams akin to a suite of tools in a toolbox. Viewing UML as a toolbox permits modelers to choose the right diagrams for the role they must play in the modeling spaces. Subsequently, all of the UML diagrams are discussed in this book according to the modeling spaces in which they are most relevant and effective: use cases, activity and business class diagrams, for example, make perfect sense in creating the model of the problem space (MOPS); advanced class diagrams, advanced sequence diagrams and composite structure diagrams are more relevant in creating the model of the solution space (MOSS) than in the other two modeling spaces; and the model of the background space (MOBS), which deals with the architectural and operational requirements of the system, produces maximum advantage by using the component and deployment diagrams. This distribution of the UML diagrams in the modeling spaces also leads to an appropriate distribution of the V&V checks in the three modeling spaces, making it easy and practical for readers to focus on the UML diagrams and their quality checks corresponding to their respective modeling spaces.

## CONTENTS

This book is divided into seven chapters and six appendices.

Chapter 1 discusses the concept of quality within the context of UML. This chapter also considers quality levels, modeling spaces, syntax, semantics and aesthetic checks, as well as the corresponding skill levels required for the V&V activities. Although this is more than a basic book on UML, it provides sufficient discussion on the nature and creation of the UML diagrams to enable readers to use it as a self-sufficient resource. That discussion, introduced in Chapters 2 and 3, is designed to create good-quality UML diagrams in the first place. Chapter 4 deals with the V&V checks in the problem space as relevant to a business analyst; Chapter 5 deals with quality checks in the solution space, as relevant to a system designer; and Chapter 6 deals with the quality checks in the architectural (background) modeling space, as relevant to system architect. Chapter 7 discusses the process requirements in the context of the V&V techniques discussed in the earlier chapters. Each chapter is supported by Discussion Topics at the end, not only to enable creative discussions, but also to open up potential research directions.

The core V&V chapters of this book—Chapters 4, 5 and 6—are built around a case study based on the author's practical experience in modeling. The problem statement for the case study appears separately Appendix A. Appendix C, D and E summarize the checklists from each of the aforementioned chapters, respectively. Readers keen to practice material from this book may even want to jump ahead and start using these checklists directly in their work. Since UML-based CASE tools play an important part in creating good-quality UML diagrams, their role and selection criteria are mentioned in Appendix B.

# SUMMARY OF CONTENTS

| Chapter | Description |
| --- | --- |
| 1. The Quality Strategy for UML | This chapter discusses the strategic approach to quality. Divides the UML diagrams in terms of relevance and importance in the three modeling spaces: problem, solution and background. Describes the types and levels of quality checks: syntax, semantics and aesthetics. |
| 2. Nature and Basics of UML diagrams | This chapter describes all the UML 2.0 diagrams and their nature (structural versus behavioral versus dynamic). The basics of putting these diagrams together is also discussed from a quality perspective. |
| 3. Strengths, Weaknesses, Objectives and Traps (SWOT) of UML Diagrams | This chapter incorporates a unique feature of this book considered invaluable by many reviewers in understanding the UML diagrams. Discussed here are the strengths and weaknesses (inherent characteristics) of each of the UML diagrams together with their practical (extrinsic characteristics) objectives and traps. |
| 4. V&V of the Quality of MOPS | This chapter undertakes detailed V&V procedures to ensure and enhance the quality of UML diagrams that comprise MOPS. |
| 5. V&V of the Quality of MOSS | This chapter undertakes detailed V&V procedures to ensure and enhance the quality of UML diagrams that comprise MOSS. |
| 6. V&V of the Quality of MOBS | This chapter undertakes detailed V&V procedures to ensure and enhance the quality of UML diagrams that comprise MOBS. |
| 7. Managing the V&V Process | This chapter discusses the process aspect of the V&V undertaken in the previous three chapters. Discussion includes roles and responsibilities, deliverables and activities, and tasks performed during quality assurance. |

This book is also supported by six appendices, as summarized in the following table.

| Appendix | Description |
|---|---|
| Appendix A | LUCKY Insurance System case study problem statement. Forms basis of models in Chapters 4, 5 and 6. |
| Appendix B | Assesment of UML Case Tools |
| Appendix C | Practical checklists summary for MOPS |
| Appendix D | Practical checklists summary for MOSS |
| Appendix E | Practical checklists summary for MOBS |
| Appendix F | Templates for actors, use cases and classes in MOPS |

## Web Support

Relevant parts of this book are made available through the Web site of John Wiley and Sons (www.wiley.com).

## AUDIENCE

This books aims to be an indispensable resource to quality professionals including quality analysts, process consultants, quality managers, test designers and testers. Equally important is the value this material provides to the three central roles in the modeling spaces: business analysts (quality in the problem modeling space), system designers (quality in the solution modeling space) and system architects (quality in the background modeling space). In addition, the philosophical discussions on modeling and quality in Chapter 1, as well as the process discussion in Chapter 7, will be of interest to senior project managers and directors. As a result, the book succeeds in providing practical support in V&V of UML models.

In addition to its practical applicability, this book has a rich academic and research base emanating from a number of enthusiastic and brilliant research associates surrounding the author. The extensive referencing in the relevant chapters, as well as the discussion topics, will be invaluable to students and researchers in quality, modeling and UML.

This is an intermediate to advanced book dealing with the topic of quality and UML. Hence the reader is expected to be familiar with UML and its modeling techniques, as the book does not discuss the basics of UML itself. People responsible for quality assurance will find this work self-sufficient and may even be encouraged, after reading it, to further extend their understanding to UML.

## LANGUAGE

I firmly believe in gender-neuter language. "Person" is therefore used wherever possible. However, in order to maintain simplicity of reading, "he" has been used as freely as "she."

Terms like "programmer" and "quality manager" represent roles, not people. Therefore, these terms do not limit real people like you and me who may transit through many roles in a lifetime or even in a job. Furthermore, we may play more than one role at a given time, such as a business analyst and a part-time academic or a researcher. As a result, the semantics of the theory and examples may change, depending on the role you are playing, and should be kept in mind as you peruse this book.

"We," as used throughout the text, refers primarily to the reader and the author—you and I. Occasionally, "we" refers to the general IT community of which the author is a member. "We" also refers to the teams in which the author has worked. Therefore, although this is a single-author book, you may encounter "we" as a reference by the author to himself, as well as to the IT community.

## WORKSHOP

The practical aspects of UML and the associated V&V activities discussed in this book have been presented and discussed in seminars and conferences. As a result, sufficient material is included here for use in a one- to two-day workshop. Following is a generic outline of a one-day workshop based on this book, which can be extended to a two-day workshop for a complete hands-on discussion of quality, including quality processes (available elsewhere in the UML literature). For the academic community, each chapter in this book can correspond to a three-hour lecture topic, with Chapters 1, 2 and 3 used earlier in the semester to create the UML-based models based on the case study described in Appendix A.

Mapping of the Chapters in This Book to a One-Day Workshop

| Day | Session | Presentation and Discussion Workshop Topic | Relevant Chapters | Comments |
| --- | --- | --- | --- | --- |
| 1 | 9:00–10:30 | Quality strategy. Positioning UML in software projects. Nature of UML diagrams. | 1, 2 | Takes a strategic approach to quality and UML. Discussion on why model quality should itself be improved. Nature and development of basic UML diagrams. Creation of problem, solution and background modeling spaces. |

| Day | Session | Presentation and Discussion Workshop Topic | Relevant Chapters | Comments |
|-----|---------|--------------------------------------------|-------------------|----------|
| 1 | 11:00–12:30 | SWOT of UML diagrams. V&V of UML by business analysts. | 3, 4 | Strengths, weaknesses, objectives and traps (SWOT) of the UML diagrams. Application of V&V quality checks to MOPS. |
| 1 | 1:30–3:00 | V&V of UML by system designers and architects. | 5, 6 | Application of V&V quality checks to MOSS and MOBS. |
| 1 | 3:30–5:00 | Process discussion and case study demonstration and discussion | 7, All | Process supporting the quality approach. Practical demonstration through the case study. |

# Acknowledgments

Following is a list of wonderful people who have helped and encouraged me to produce this quality work. I gratefully acknowledge here their direct and indirect contributions:

| | | |
|---|---|---|
| Dinesh Arunatileka | Darrell Jackson | Rajesh Pradhan |
| Bhargav Bhatt | Alex Jouravlev | Riyed S'duk (Roy) |
| Yogesh Deshpande | Vijay Khandelwal | Prashant Risbud |
| Buddhima DeSilva | Anand Kuppuswami | James Ross |
| Edward D'Souza | Yi-chen Lan | Prince Soundararajan |
| Samir El-Masri | Raj Limaye | Pinku Talati |
| Mark Glikson | Javed Matin | Amit Tiwary |
| Nitin Gupta | Sid Mishra | Asha Unhelkar |
| Vivek Handa | Rahul Mohod | Sunil Vadnerkar |
| Chris Hardy | Chris Payne | John Warner |
| Brian Henderson-Sellers | Shri Prabhat Pradhan (S.D.) | Houman Younessi |

Particularly notable is the assiduous editing of the draft by Roy and Prince and the creation of some of the UML models by Chris in Telelogic's TauG2 CASE tool. Thanks are also due to the staff at Wiley for their excellent support in pursuance of this project. I am also grateful to my family for their support: my wife, Asha, my daughter Sonki Priyadarashani, my son, Keshav Raja, and my extended family, Chinar and Girish Mamdapur.

Finally, this work acknowledges all the organizations whose names and/or tools have been used in this book. Specifically, I acknowledge Telelogic (for TauG2), TogetherSoft (for TogetherControlCenter) and Rational (for ROSE).

## CRITIQUES

This work has been greatly improved by the constructive criticism by the erudite reviewers—both personally known to the author and those at Wiley. A healthy state of affairs exists with the information and communication technology (ICT) world, and particularly in the UML and quality process community, if work of this nature receives criticism. All criticisms have an underlying rationale, and I will be honored to receive them directly from readers. Since your comments will not only enrich my own knowledge and understanding of the quality issues discussed in this book, but will also add to the general knowledge available to the ICT community, I wish to say thank-you to all readers and critiques in advance.

Bhuvan Unhelkar
January 2005
www.unhelkar.com

# Glossary of Acronyms and Terms

| | |
|---|---|
| CBT | Computer-based training |
| CMM | Capability Maturity Model—provides the basis for measuring and comparing the process maturities of various organizations and projects Initiative of the Software Engineering Institute of Carnegie-Mellon University |
| CMS | Content Management System—deals primarily with the contents of a Web site |
| CRC | Class Responsibility Collaborators—a simple technique proposed by Cunningham and Beck in 1989 to help identify classes and their responsibilities |
| CRMS | Customer Relationship Management System |
| ERP | Enterprise resource planning |
| GUI | Graphic user interface |
| ICT | Information and communication technology |
| IIP | Iterative, incremental, parallel—software development life cycle ideally suited for OO development |
| IT | Information technology—increasingly referred to as information and communication technology due to the close relationship of information and communication in today's software world |
| MDA | Model-driven architecture (OMG's initiative) |
| Meta-model | Model of a model that dictates the rules for creation of modeling mechanisms like UML |
| MOBS | Model of background space—created primarily by the business analyst in the problem space using UML notations and diagrams |
| MOF | Meta-object facility |
| MOPS | Model of problem space—created primarily by the system designer in the solution space using UML notations and diagrams |

| MOSS | Model of solution space—created primarily by the system architecture in the background space using UML notations and diagrams |
|---|---|
| OMG | Object Management Group—responsible for unification of modeling notations resulting in the UML |
| OO | Object-oriented—once considered only as a programming technique, OO now permeates all aspects of the software development life cycle |
| UML 2.0 | Unified Modeling Language—result of the effort of a number of well-known methodologists, notably Jacobson, Booch and Rumbaugh; designated by OMG as a de facto software modeling standard (Version 2.0) |
| V&V | Verification and validation |

# Author Profile

Bhuvan Unhelkar (BE, MDBA, MSc, PhD; FACS) has had 23 years of strategic and hands-on professional experience in the field of information and communication technology. Author of eight books, he is also a renowned industrial trainer and presenter in the area of software quality, with a special focus on UML and process. Through MethodScience.com, Bhuvan brings to bear his experience in transforming organizations into high-quality component-based software environments—developing, integrating and implementing projects. Earlier, when affiliated with Dow Jones Markets, he won the prestigious Computerworld Object Developers Award for Best use of the object-oriented approach across the organization. Later he accepted a position with the University of Western Sydney, researching as well as teaching object-oriented analysis and object-oriented design using UML. He is a Fellow of the Australian Computer Society and the convener of their Object-Oriented Special Interest Group, past Mentor Director at www.TiE.org/sydney, and a Rotarian.

Chapter **1**

# The Quality Strategy for UML

Quality—you know what it is, yet you don't know what it is. But that is self contradictory. . . . But some things are better than others, that is, they have more quality. . . . But if you can't say what Quality is, how do you know what it is, or how do you know that it even exists? If no one knows what it is, then for all practical purposes it doesn't exist at all. But for all practical purposes it really does exist. . . . So round and round you go, spinning mental wheels and nowhere finding any place to get traction. What the hell is Quality? What is it?[1]

## CHAPTER SUMMARY

This chapter discusses the underlying concepts of modeling and the effect of verification and validation (V&V) techniques on its quality. After creating an understanding of modeling and its relevance to quality, this chapter describes the toolbox of Unified Modeling Language (UML) diagrams and divides them over the three distinct yet related modeling spaces: problem, solution and background. Following this is a discussion on defining the syntax, semantics and aesthetics checks for V&V of UML models and how their levels and skill sets affect the quality of the project.

[1]From Robert Pirsig's all-time favorite, *Zen and the Art of Motorcycle Maintenance* (http://www. nobigv.tripod.com). For an irresistibly different perspective, read *The Zen Manifesto* (www.osho.com).

*Verification and Validation for Quality of UML 2.0 Models*, by Bhuvan Unhelkar
Copyright © 2005 John Wiley & Sons, Inc.

## 1.1  MODELING AND QUALITY

### 1.1.1  The Modeling Advantage

Modeling enhances quality because it enhances communication. Through modeling, communication becomes efficient and effective. This is so because modeling raises abstraction to a level where only the core essentials matter. The resultant advantage is twofold: easier understanding of the reality that exists and efficient creation of a new reality (Unhelkar, 1999).

The advantage of modeling in understanding complexity is derived from the fact that models *distill* reality. Elements that are not significant in understanding the reality are dropped. Modeling also fosters creativity by focusing on the essentials and ignoring the gory details. This holds true for modeling in many industries such as construction, medicine and transportation. However, the role of modeling is even more important in software development, where it provides the means of understanding existing software systems whose legacy nature renders them extremely complex, as well as in developing and customizing new software systems expected to serve highly demanding customers in constant flux.

Consider, for example, an abstraction of a COBOL application. Modeling assists in understanding that application and the complex environment in which it operates. Creating a model, however brief, is imperative in understanding the traditional legacy application.

Modeling also facilitates smoother creation of the new reality. For example, creating a model of a software system is much easier, cheaper and faster than creating the actual system. Once the concepts are bedded down, they can be adorned with all the additional paraphernalia that makes up the final application. In this process, modeling not only represents what we want, but also educates us in understanding what we *should* want. It is not uncommon to have a user *change* her requirements based on a prototype (type of model) of a system that she has seen. Alterations and additions to the functionality required of the system during early modeling stages are welcome signs, providing significant impetus to the modeling and quality activities within a project. This is because changes during the early modeling stages of a software life cycle are cheaper and faster to incorporate or fix than those introduced later during implementation.

### 1.1.2  Modeling Caveats

Despite the stated and obvious advantages of modeling, there is one singularly important factor that influences the value of a model: *the quality of the model itself.* If the abstraction is incorrect, then obviously the reality eventually created out of that abstraction is likely to be incorrect. An incorrect abstraction will also not reflect or represent the reality truthfully. Therefore, model quality is of immense importance in eventually deriving quality benefits.

Modeling is limited by the following caveats:

- A model, by its very nature, is an abstraction of the reality. The modeler, depending on her needs, keeps parts of the reality that are important to her in a particular situation and leaves out others which may be considered less important. Therefore, the model is not a complete representation of the reality. This leads to the possibility of the model's being subjected to different interpretations.
- Unless a model is dynamic, it does not provide the correct sense of timing. Since the reality is changing, it is imperative that the model change accordingly. Otherwise, it will not be able to convey the right meaning to the user.
- A model may be created for a specific situation or to handle a particular problem. Needless to say, once the situation has changed, the model will no longer be relevant.
- A model is a singular representation of possible multiple elements in reality. For example, a class in software modeling parlance is a single representation of multiple objects. In such cases, a model may not provide a feel for the operational aspects of the system, such as volume and performance.
- The user of the model should be aware of the notations and language used to express the model. For example, when the design of a house is expressed using a paper model, it is necessary for the user to know what each of the symbols means. Nonstandard notations and processes can render a model useless.
- Modeling casually, or at random, without due care and consideration for the nature of the models themselves, usually results in confusion in projects and can reduce productivity. Therefore, formality in modeling is necessary for its success.
- Models must change with the changing reality. As applications and systems change, so should the models if they are to be relevant. Models that are not kept up-to-date can be misleading.
- Processes play a significant role in steering modeling activities. Modeling without considering processes is a potential practical hazard and should be avoided.

Goals, methods and performance are considered the three major aspects of quality by Perry (1991).

### 1.1.3 Context of Model Quality

Where and how should the model quality effort be focused? Firstly, we must understand that model quality is not the only aspect of quality in a project. Model quality exists within the context of other quality dimensions or levels, and these influence each other as well as model quality. In practical UML-based projects, the following levels of quality are listed by Unhelkar (2003):

- *Data quality*—the accuracy and reliability of the data, resulting in quality work ensuring integrity of the data.

- *Code quality*—the correctness of the programs and their underlying algorithms.
- *Model quality*—the correctness and completeness of the software models and their meanings.
- *Architecture quality*—the quality of the system in terms of its ability to be deployed in operation.
- *Process quality*—the activities, tasks, roles and deliverables employed in developing software.
- *Management quality*—planning, budgeting and monitoring, as well as the "soft" or human aspects of a project.
- *Quality environment*—all aspects of creating and maintaining the quality of a project, including all of the above aspects of quality.

### 1.1.4   Model Quality

The aforementioned quality levels play a significant role in enhancing the overall quality of the output of a software project. Most literature on quality, however, focuses on code and data quality. Even when modeling appears in the discussion of quality, it is with the aim of creating good-quality software (data and algorithms). In this book, however, model quality refers to the quality of the software models themselves. Model quality depends on detailed V&V of those models.

In software projects without substantial modeling, code remains the primary output of the developers. In such projects, code emerges from the developer's brain—directly. This, as the history of software development indicates (Glass, 2003), has had disastrous effect on software projects.

Quality-conscious software projects use modeling throughout the entire life cycle. Subsequently, modeling is used not only to create the software solution but also to understand the problem. As a result, modeling occurs in the problem, solution and background (architectural) spaces. The modeling output in such software projects transcends both data and code and results in a suite of visual models or diagrams. While these models go on to improve the quality of the code produced, it is not just their influence on the implemented code that interests us but also their own quality—that is, the quality of the models themselves. There is an acute need to subject the software models themselves to quality assurance and quality control processes. It is important that these models adhere to known standards and are also subjected to stringent quality control. Model quality is all about V&V of the models themselves. The result is not only improved model quality, but also improved communication among project team members and among projects.

## 1.2   POSITIONING UML FOR MODELING

How do we build software models? The ubiquitous flowcharts, followed by the entity relationship (E-R) and data flow diagrams (DFDs), are no longer sufficient to model modern software systems. With the advent of objects and components, Web services and grid computing, and pervasive mobile computing, we need a sophisticated as well as an exhaustive suite of modeling techniques. UML version 2.0 (Object Management Group [OMG]) is specifically advocated as a software *modeling* language for visualization, specification, construction and documentation (Booch et al., 1999). Thus, it is *not* a programming language, although with the recent initiatives involving model-driven architecture (MDA), we are close to using UML as an executable UML language. Thus, overall, UML, together with a programming language for implementation, provides an excellent mechanism to develop software systems.

Furthermore, it is worth noting that UML is not a methodology, but rather a common and standard set of notations and diagrams. These are used by processes in varying ways to create the required models in the problem, solution and background modeling spaces. Therefore, the checklists developed later in this book for V&V purposes are likely to vary, depending on the process; in other words, the V&V checklists will change, depending on the role and the modeling space in which they are applied.

It is also worth mentioning that UML has been (and is being) used effectively in a large range of projects, including:

- New development projects, where systems are designed from scratch and the new business applications are modeled using, for example, UML's use cases and activity diagrams.
- Integration projects, where newer systems—typically Web-enabled systems—are integrated with existing (typically legacy) systems.
- Package implementation, where UML's behavioral diagrams can be used to understand the requirements of the implementation of the customer relationship management system (CRMS) or the enterprise resource planning (ERP) system.
- Outsourcing projects, where UML provides the basis for scoping, delivery and testing.
- Data warehousing and conversion projects, where not only are the data and related information modeled using UML, but the conversion and testing processes also use UML to document the flow.
- Educational projects, where UML can be used for testing concepts, for example for teaching and learning object orientation.

In addition to the above types of projects, UML is being used in small, medium-sized and large projects (Unhelkar, 2003). Due to such wide-ranging applicability of UML, the model quality of UML-based projects assumes great importance. Let us, therefore, consider UML from a model quality perspective.

## 1.3  QUALITY ASPECTS OF UML

UML has four main purposes: visualization, specification, construction and documentation (Booch et al., 1999). Therefore, in investigating the quality of UML models, it is worthwhile to consider how these factors affect, and are affected by, quality.

*Visualizing*—UML notations and diagrams provide an excellent industry standard mechanism to represent pictorially the requirements, solution and architecture. UML's ability to show business processes and software elements visually, spanning the entire life cycle of software development, provides the basis for extensive modeling in software development. UML, through its class representations, can bring the reality (real customers, accounts and transactions in a typical banking system) close to the people working in the solution space by modeling the corresponding Class Customer, Class Account and Class Transaction. The small gap between models and reality, especially in object-oriented (OO) development, improves the quality of visualization. This quality of visualization is enhanced not only by the use of UML as a standard, but also because of the large number of Computer Aided Software Engineering (CASE) tools supporting these visual diagramming techniques. CASE tools in modeling facilitate the work of teams of modelers and prevent syntax errors at the visual modeling level.

*Specifying*—Together with visual representations, UML facilitates the specification of some of its artifacts. For example, specifications can be associated with the actors, use cases, classes, attributes, operations and so on. These UML specifications help enhance the quality of modeling, as they enable additional descriptions of the visual models, enable members of a project team to decide which areas of a particular diagram or element they want to specify, and allow them (through CASE tools) to make the specifications available to all stakeholders. The specifications can be made available in various formats, such as a company's intranet Web page, a set of Word documents or a report.

*Constructing*—UML can also be used for software construction, as it is possible to generate code from UML visual representations. This is becoming increasingly important with the rapidly advancing concepts of executable UML (Mellor and Balcer, 2002) and the MDA initiative (Mellor et al., 2004). A piece of software that is constructed based on formal UML-based modeling is likely to fare much better during its own V&V. Classes and class diagrams, together with their specifications (e.g., accessibility options, relationships, multiplicities), ensure that the code generated through these models is correctly produced and is inherently superior to hand-crafted code (i.e., code without models).

*Documenting*—With the help of UML, additional and detailed documentation can be provided to enhance the aforementioned specifications and visual representations. Documentation has become paramount—not only the type that accompanies the code, but also the type that goes with models, prototypes and other such artifacts. In UML, diagrams have corresponding documentation, which may be separate from the formal specifications and which goes a long way toward explaining the intricacies of visual models.

## 1.4  UNDERSTANDING MODELING SPACES IN SOFTWARE

With the aforementioned four dimensions in which UML promises quality enhancement, it is still vital to remember that UML-based modeling does not happen within a single modeling space. Successful modeling needs to consider the *areas* in which modeling needs to take place. These modeling spaces have been formally considered and discussed by Unhelkar and Henderson-Sellers (2004). This role-based division is shown in Figure 1.1.

This figure depicts the three distinct yet related modeling spaces: problem, solution and background. These role-based divisions form the basis of further quality V&V work with respect to UML models. These divisions provide a much more robust approach to quality modeling, as they segregate the models based on their purpose, primarily whether the model is created to understand the problem, to provide a solution to the problem, or to influence both of these purposes from the background, based on organizational constraints (e.g., stress, volume and bandwidth), and need to reuse components and services.

## 1.5  MODELING SPACES AND UML

The modeling spaces shown in Figure 1.1 can be specifically considered within the context of UML. To ensure the quality of UML-based models and to apply the correct V&V checklists to those models, it is essential to focus on the objectives of the modeling exercise and use the UML-based diagrams that will help the modeler achieve these objectives. Thus, the applicability of UML diagrams differs from

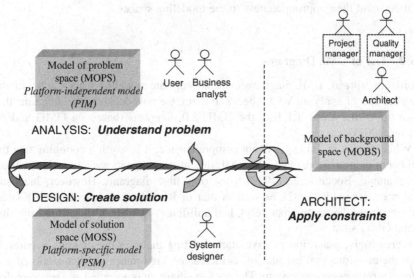

**Figure 1.1**  Software modeling spaces and the modeling work of analysis, design, and architecture in them.

project to project. The intensity of the application of these diagrams in creating the models also differs, depending on the reasons for modeling when creating the diagrams. The purpose for creating the diagrams has a direct bearing on the way they are created, extended, and, of course, verified and validated. The modeling spaces are extremely helpful in clarifying the purpose of modeling, particularly its role.

### 1.5.1 Importance of UML Diagrams to Respective Models

The modeling spaces discussed in the previous subsection were the problem, solution and background spaces. One should expect to encounter these modeling spaces in some form in any modeling exercise. We consider them here specifically in UML-based modeling. For ease of usage and discussion, the three modeling spaces are as follows:

MOPS: model of problem space
MOSS: model of solution space
MOBS: model of background space

These models are shown in their corresponding modeling spaces in Figure 1.1. Also shown in the figure are the various primary roles in the modeling spaces— namely, the user, business analyst, system designer, system architect, project manager and quality manager. Of these roles, the three that work in the modeling spaces to create MOPS, MOSS, and MOBS are the business analyst, the designer and the architect. We now also consider the UML diagrams themselves in order to understand their appropriateness to the modeling spaces.

### 1.5.2 List of UML Diagrams

In order to "spread" UML diagrams in the appropriate modeling spaces, and with the eventual aim of applying V&V checks to them, we now consider the diagrams that make up UML. Table 1.1 lists the UML 2.0 diagrams (based on OMG and on Fowler, 2003).

While the list in Table 1.1 is not comprehensive, it is worth mentioning that the number of diagrams existing in the UML literature even in its earlier versions varies. For example, Booch et al. (1999) listed only nine diagrams. However, Jacobson et al.'s earlier work (1992), as well as that of Rosenberg and Scott (1999), (who list robustness diagrams separately), had a different number of diagrams from that on the OMG's list.

Increasingly, practitioners have started listing the package diagram separately from the class diagram because of its increasing importance in organizational and architectural areas of the system. The package diagram is accepted as a separate diagram in the current UML 2.0 literature. Sometimes the sequence and communication

**TABLE 1.1    UML 2.0 Diagrams**

| UML Diagrams | Represent |
|---|---|
| 1. Use case | functionality from the user's viewpoint |
| 2. Activity | the flow within a Use case or the system |
| 3. Class | classes, entities, business domain, database |
| 4. Sequence | interactions between objects |
| 5. Interaction overview | interactions at a general high level |
| 6. Communication | interactions between objects |
| 7. Object | objects and their links |
| 8. State machine | the run-time life cycle of an object |
| 9. Composite structure | component or object behavior at run-time |
| 10. Component | executables, linkable libraries, etc. |
| 11. Deployment | hardware nodes and processors |
| 12. Package | subsystems, organizational units |
| 13. Timing | time concept during object interactions |

diagrams (as named in UML 2.0, these are the collaboration diagrams of the earlier UML versions) are listed together as interaction diagrams.

The component and deployment diagrams are also referred to as "implementation" diagrams in UML literature. Object diagrams are theoretically treated as independent diagrams in their own right but are often not supported by CASE tools—resulting in their being drawn underneath communication diagrams within CASE tools. While this discussion introduces you to the range of UML diagrams, it is more important to know the diagrams' precise strengths and the purpose for which they can be used rather than focus on the precise list.

### 1.5.3    UML Diagrams and Modeling Spaces

Table 1.1 summarizes the UML diagrams and the modeling aspect of software solutions represented by them. These diagrams have a set of underlying rules that specify how to create them. The rigor of these rules is encapsulated in what is known as the OMG's "meta-model". The meta-model also helps to provide rules for cross-diagram dependencies.

The importance of the meta-model is that it renders the UML *elastic*—it can be stretched or shrunk, depending on the needs of the project. This is discussed further in Chapter 2. Because of the elasticity of UML, the extent and depth to which the UML diagrams are applied in creating models are crucial to the success of projects using UML. Not all diagrams apply to all situations. Furthermore, not all diagrams are relevant to a particular role within a project. As Booch et al. (1999) correctly point out:

> Good diagrams make the system you are developing understandable and approachable. Choosing the right set of diagrams to model your system forces you to ask the right questions about your system and helps to illuminate the implications of your decisions.

Therefore, we must first select the right set of diagrams for a particular modeling space. This is achieved next, followed by a discussion on the right level of application of these models. A series of V&V criteria are then applied to these diagrams in subsequent chapters. While the UML diagrams apply to all modeling spaces, Table 1.2 next summarizes the relative importance of each of the UML diagrams to each of the modeling spaces and major modeling roles within the project. While project team members can work in any of these modeling spaces using any of the UML diagrams, good models are usually the result of understanding the importance of the diagrams with respect to the modeling spaces. This is shown in Table 1.2. As is obvious from this table, modelers are not prevented from using any of the UML diagrams. However, Table 1.2 provides *focus* in terms of using UML diagrams for a particular role within a project. This information can be invaluable in organizing the quality team, as well as in following the process that will verify and validate these diagrams.

The categorization in Table 1.2 ensures a balance between the desire to use everything provided by UML and the need to use only the relevant diagrams as a good starting point for a modeling exercise. Table 1.2 uses the "$*$" rating to indicate the importance and relevance of UML diagrams within MOPS, MOSS and MOBS. A maximum rating of $*****$ is provided for diagrams of the utmost importance to the model in a particular space.

### 1.5.4   Model of Problem Space (MOPS)

Figure 1.1 shows MOPS in the problem space. In UML projects, MOPS deals with creating an understanding of the problem, primarily the problem that the potential user of the system is facing. While usually it is the business problem that is being

**TABLE 1.2   Importance of UML Diagrams to Respective Models (a Maximum of Five $*$ for Utmost Importance to the Particular Space)**

| UML Diagrams | MOPS (Business Analyst) | MOSS (Designer) | MOBS (Architect) |
|---|---|---|---|
| Use case | $*****$ | $**$ | $*$ |
| Activity | $*****$ | $**$ | $*$ |
| Class | $***$ | $*****$ | $**$ |
| Sequence | $****$ | $*****$ | $*$ |
| Interaction overview | $****$ | $**$ | $**$ |
| Communication | $*$ | $***$ | $*$ |
| Object | $*$ | $*****$ | $***$ |
| State machine | $***$ | $****$ | $**$ |
| Composite structure | $*$ | $*****$ | $****$ |
| Component | $*$ | $***$ | $*****$ |
| Deployment | $**$ | $**$ | $*****$ |
| Package | $***$ | $**$ | $****$ |
| Timing | $*$ | $***$ | $***$ |

described, even a technical problem can be described at the user level in MOPS. In any case, the problem space deals with all the work that takes place in understanding the problem in the context of the software system before any solution or development is attempted.

Typical activities that take place in MOPS include documenting and understanding the requirements, analyzing requirements, investigating the problem in detail, and perhaps optional prototyping and understanding the flow of the process within the business. Thus the problem space would focus entirely on what is happening with the business or the user. With the exception of prototyping in the problem space, where some code may be written for the prototype, no serious programming is expected when MOPS is created.

### 1.5.4.1 UML Diagrams in MOPS

As a nontechnical description of what is happening with the user or the business, the problem space will need the UML diagrams that help the modeler understand the problem without going into technological detail. The UML diagrams that help express what is expected of the system, rather than how the system will be implemented, are of interest here. As shown in Table 1.2, these UML diagrams in the problem space are as follows:

*Use case diagrams*—provide the overall view and scope of functionality. The use cases within these diagrams contain the behavioral (or functional) description of the system.

*Activity diagrams*—provide a pictorial representation of the flow anywhere in MOPS. In MOPS, these diagrams work more or less like flowcharts, depicting the flow within the use cases or even showing the dependencies among various use cases.

*Class diagrams*—provide the structure of the domain model. In the problem space, these diagrams represent business domain entities (such as `Account` and `Customer` in a banking domain), not the details of their implementation in a programming language.

*Sequence and state machine diagrams*—occasionally used to help us understand the dynamicity and behavior of the problem better.

*Interaction overview* diagrams—recently added in UML 2.0, these provide an overview of the flow and/or dependencies between other diagrams.

*Package diagrams*—can be used in the problem space to organize and scope the requirements. Domain experts, who have a fairly good understanding not only of the current problem but also of the overall domain in which the problem exists, help provide a good understanding of the likely packages in the system.

### 1.5.5 Model of Solution Space (MOSS)

The solution space is primarily involved in the description of how the solution will be implemented. Figure 1.1 shows MOSS as a model that helps us understand and model the software solution that needs to be provided in response to MOPS. This solution model requires extra knowledge and information about the facilities provided by the programming languages, corresponding databases, middleware, Web application solutions and a number of other technical areas. Thus, MOSS contains a solution-level design expressed by technical or lower-level class diagrams, technical sequence diagrams, detailed state machine diagrams representing events and transitions, designs of individual classes and corresponding advance class diagrams. Object diagrams, communication diagrams and timing diagrams (the recent UML 2.0 addition) can also be occasionally used in MOSS.

***1.5.5.1 UML Diagrams in MOSS*** Because MOSS is a technical description of how to solve the problem, the UML diagrams within MOSS are also technical in nature. Furthermore, even the diagrams drawn in MOPS are embellished in the solution space with additional technical details based on the programming languages and databases. As shown in Table 1.2, the primary diagrams used in MOSS are the class diagrams together with their lowermost details, including attributes, types of attributes, their initial values, signatures of the class operations (including their parameters and return values) and so on. These can be followed by diagrams like the sequence diagrams together with their detailed signatures, message types, return protocols and so on. Modelers may also use the communication diagrams for the same purpose as sequence diagrams. Occasionally state machine diagrams can be used to provide the dynamic aspect of the life cycle of a complex or very important object. Recently introduced timing diagrams show state changes to multiple objects at the same time, and composite structure diagrams depict the run-time structure of components and objects.

## 1.5.6 Model of Background Space (MOBS)

MOBS incorporates two major aspects of software development that are not covered by MOPS or MOSS: management and architecture. As shown in Figure 1.1, MOBS is an architectural model in the background space that influences models in both problem and solution spaces through constraints.

Of the two major aspects of work in the background space, management work relates primarily to planning. Planning deals mainly with the entire project and does not necessarily form part of the problem or solution space. In other words, management work in the background space includes issues from both problem and solution spaces but is not part of either of them. Several aspects of planning are handled in the background by the project manager. These include planning the project; resourcing the project's hardware, software, staff and other facilities; budgeting and performing cost-benefit analysis; tracking the project as it progresses through various iterations; and providing checkpoints for various quality-related activities. These background space activities are related to management work and are briefly discussed, along with other process aspects of quality, in Chapter 7. It is worth repeating here, though, that UML is not a management modeling language, and therefore does not provide direct notations and diagrams to document project plans and resources. The project planning aspect is best to deal with the process techniques as well as process tools (most containing Program, Evaluation & Review Technique [PERT] and Gantt charts and project-based task lists).

Architectural work, on the other hand, deals with a large amount of technical background work. This work includes consideration of patterns, reuse, platforms, Web application servers, middleware applications, operational requirements and so on. This background space also includes issues such as reuse of programs and system designs, as well as system and enterprise architecture. Therefore, work in this space requires knowledge of the development as well as the operational environment of the organization, availability of reusable architecture and designs, and how they might fit together in MOPS and MOSS.

### 1.5.6.1 UML Diagrams in MOBS
The UML diagrams of interest in the background space are the ones that help us create a good system architecture that strives to achieve all the good things of object orientation. For example, reusability, patterns and middleware need to be expressed correctly in MOBS, and UML provides the means to do so. The importance of each of the UML diagrams in the background space is shown in Table 1.2. One should expect a large amount of strategic technical work in the background space that will consider the architecture of the current solution, the existing architecture of the organization's technical environment, the operational requirements of the system (i.e., the technical requirements of the system when it goes into operation, such as disk spaces, memory needs, CPU speeds), the needs of the system in terms of its stress, volume and bandwidth, and so on.

In order to complete the solution, it is necessary to relate the solution-level classes closely to the component diagrams drawn in the background space. These component diagrams contain the .EXEs and .DLLs and are closely associated with the solution-level class diagrams, providing the final steps in the system development exercise before the user runs the application. When run-time components are modeled, they result in composite structure diagrams, which may also be used in the background space to specify and discuss the architecture of a component or a class.

Increasingly, operational issues are being expressed properly using UML diagrams in the background space. UML provides help and support in modeling the operational environment (or deployment environment) of the system by means of deployment diagrams. Furthermore, a combination of component and deployment diagrams can provide a basis for discussions between the architects and designers of the system concerning where and how the components will reside and execute. Using the extension mechanisms of UML, one can develop diagrams that help express Web application architectures, including whether they should be thin-client or thick-client, the level of security needed on each node and the distributed aspects of the architecture, to name only a few issues. These background UML diagrams also have a positive effect on architecting quality (i.e., mapping quality to a good architecture) by providing standard means of mapping designs to existing and proven architectures. For example, an architectural pattern describing thin-client architecture is a much better starting point in terms of quality than designing such a solution from scratch.

## 1.6 VERIFICATION AND VALIDATION

Perry (1991) considers goals, methods and performance to be the three major aspects of quality. These strategic aspects of quality translate operationally into V&V techniques. Verification is concerned with the syntactic correctness of the software and models, whereas validation deals with semantic meanings and their value to the users of the system. V&V are quality techniques that are meant to prevent as well as detect errors, inconsistencies and incompleteness. V&V comprises a set of activities and checks that ensure that the model is correct. Based on Perry's definitions, verification focuses on ascertaining that the software functions correctly, whereas validation ensures that it meets the user's needs. Thus, verification comprises a separate set of activities that ensure that the model is correct. Validation works to ensure that it is also meaningful to the users of the system. Therefore, validation of models deals with tracing the software to the requirements.

Because of the subjective nature of quality, it cannot be easily quantified. However, one simple way to grapple with this subjectivity is to utilize a checklist-based approach as a first step in V&V of the quality aspects of a model. The correctness of the software is verified by a suite of checklists that deal with the syntax of the models, whereas the meaning and consistency of the software models are validated by creating a suite of checklists dealing with semantic checks. Thus, verification requires concrete skills like knowledge of the syntax; validation starts moving toward the abstract, as shown in Figure 1.2. Once augmented with aesthetic checks, this complete suite of checklists provides a quantifiable way of measuring quality, and it can be used as a benchmark for further developing qualitative understanding.

Having discussed the various quality aspects of modeling that are enhanced by UML, we now consider the manner in which these qualities of UML-based

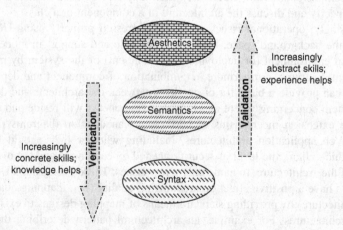

**Figure 1.2**  Quality and V&V of models and their mapping to syntax, semantics and aesthetics.

models can be verified and validated. Some parts of V&V deal with the visual aspects of the model, others with its specification, construction and documentation.

Since UML is a language for visualization, it is appropriate to consider how the quality checks can be applied to UML-based diagrams and models. Therefore, the major part of V&V deals with the visual aspects of the model. This can lead not only to detection of errors in the model (quality checks that ensure validation of the model) but also appropriate quality assurance and process-related activities aimed at the prevention of errors. While recognizing the wide variety of definitions of quality in the software literature, we now start moving toward the basis for creating three types of V&V checks. For V&V of a software artifact, there are three levels of checks: syntax, semantics and aesthetics. These checks have close parallels to the quality approach of Lindland et al. (1994), who created a framework with three axes for quality assessment: language, domain and pragmatics. They translated these axes into syntactic quality, semantic quality and pragmatic quality, providing the theoretical background on which the current quality checks are built. While the syntax and semantic checks outlined here have close parallels to the work of Lindland et al., the aesthetic checks are also discussed by Ambler (2003) under the heading of "styles."

Building further on the framework of Lindland et al. (1994), the understanding of good-quality software modeling results in V&V of software models as follows:

- All quality models should be syntactically correct, thereby adhering to the rules of the modeling language (in our case, UML 2.0) they are meant to follow.
- All quality models should represent their intended semantic meanings and should do so consistently.
- All quality models should have good aesthetics, demonstrating the creativity and farsightedness of their modelers. This means that software models should be symmetric, complete and pleasing in what they represent.

The words "syntax," "semantics" and "aesthetics" are chosen to reflect the techniques or means of accomplishing the V&V of the models. One reason that these words correctly represent our quality assurance effort is that they relate directly to the UML models—especially those models that are created and stored in CASE tools. As a result, their quality can be greatly enhanced by applying the syntax, semantics and aesthetic checks to them. We will now consider these three categories of checks in more detail.

### 1.6.1  Quality Models—Syntax

All languages have a syntax. Latin and Sanskrit have their own syntax, and so do Java, XML and UML. However, two major characteristics of UML differentiate it from the other languages:

- UML is a visual language, which means that it has a substantial amount of notation and many diagram specifications.

• UML is a modeling language, which means that it is not intended primarily to be compiled and used in production of code (as programming languages are)—although the trend toward support for both "action semantics" in UML 2.0 and in MDA, both from the OMG, will likely involve the use of UML in this context in the future.

Needless to say, incorrect syntax affects the quality of visualization and specification, also, although a diagram itself cannot be compiled, incorrect syntax at the diagram level percolates down to the construction level, causing errors in creating the software code.

CASE tools are helpful to ensure that syntax errors are kept to a minimum. For example, on a UML class diagram, the rules of the association relationship, creation of default visibilities (e.g., private for attributes) and setting of multiplicities are examples of how CASE tools help to reduce syntax errors.

In UML-based models, when we apply syntax checks, we ensure that each of the diagrams that make up the model has been created in conformance with the standards and guidelines specified by OMG. We also ensure that the notations used, the diagram extensions annotated and the corresponding explanations on the diagrams all follow the syntax standard of the modeling language.

Figure 1.3 shows a simple example of a rectangle representing a dog. This rectangle is the notation for a class in UML. The syntax check on this diagram ensures that it is indeed a rectangle that is meant to represent animals (or other such things) in this modeling mechanism. The rectangle is checked for correctness, and we ensure that it is not an ellipse or for an arrowhead (both of which would be syntactically incorrect when using UML's notation) that is intended to represent the animal in question. In terms of UML models, a syntax check is a list of everything

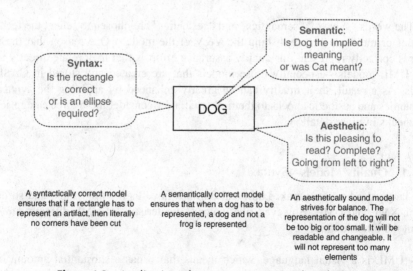

**Figure 1.3**   Application of syntax, semantics and aesthetics.

that needs to be accomplished to achieve the syntax for the diagrams and associated artifacts of UML as laid out by OMG.

Permissible variations on these diagrams in complying with the meta-model can become a project-specific part of the syntax checks. Syntactic correctness greatly enhances the readability of diagrams, especially when these diagrams have to be read by different groups in different organizations in several countries (a typical software outsourcing scenario).

## 1.6.2 Quality Models—Semantics

While one of the qualities enhanced by rigorous syntax checks is the quality of construction (read "compilation"), one cannot be satisfied merely by a program that compiles and executes correctly yet does not consider the manner in which it is interpreted and understood. Such a model, although syntactically correct, would fail to achieve the all-important semantic correctness.

Consider, for example, Figure 1.3. Here, we expect to see a dog represented by a rectangle, with the word "dog" written in it. Writing the word "dog" within a rectangle might be syntactically correct, but it would be semantically wrong if the class Dog is actually representing an object cat (as it is in this example). If the class Dog is specified for an object cat, the meaning of the model is destroyed, however syntactically correct the model may be.

The semantic aspect of model quality ensures not only that the diagrams produced are correct, but also that they faithfully represent the underlying reality represented in the domain, as defined by Warmer and Kleppe (1998). In UML, for example, the business objectives stated by the users should be correctly reflected in the use case diagrams, business rules, constraints, and pre- and postconditions documented in the corresponding use case documentation.

Once again, models in general are not executable; therefore, it is not possible to verify and validate their purpose by simply "executing" them, as one would the final software product (the executable). Consequently, we need to identify alternative evaluation techniques. In this context, the traditional and well-known quality techniques of walkthroughs and inspections (e.g., Warmer and Kleppe, 1998; Unhelkar, 2003) are extremely valuable and are used more frequently and more rigorously than for syntax checking.

Another example of such techniques, for instance as applied to use case models in UML, is that we anthropomorphize[2] each of the actors and use cases and act through an entire diagram as if we were the objects themselves. We can insist that testers walk through the use cases, verify the purpose of every actor and all use cases, and determine whether they depict what the business really wants. This is the semantic aspect of verifying the quality of a UML model, supplemented, of course, by the actual (non-UML) use case descriptions themselves (e.g., Cockburn, 2001).

---

[2]Personify—by assuming that the actors are alive and conducting a walkthrough/review with business users, developers and testers.

### 1.6.3   Quality Models—Aesthetics

Once the syntax and the semantics are correct, we need to consider the aesthetics of the model (e.g., Ambler, 2003). Very simply, aesthetics implies style. Often, while reading a piece of code, one is able to point out the style or programming and hence trace it to a specific programmer or a programming team. Although the code (or, for that matter, any other deliverable) may be accurate (syntactically) and meaningful (semantically), difference still arises due to its style. The style of modeling has a bearing on the models' readability, comprehensibility and so on. One example of a factor that affects style is granularity (discussed in detail in Chapter 6). In good OO designs, the level of granularity needs to be considered, as it strongly affects understandability (Miller, 1956). For example, in Figure 1.3, how many rectangles (classes) are there on a diagram (as against the previous two checks: "Is that a class notation?" and "What is the meaning behind this class?")? It is, of course, possible that a system with 10 class diagrams, each with 10 classes and numerous relationships, may accurately represent a business domain model—although such large numbers should be regarded as a warning (e.g., Henderson-Sellers, 1996). In another example, one class diagram may have 20 classes (not wrong from a UML viewpoint, but ugly) and another class diagram may have only 1, albeit an important and large one. This aesthetic size consideration is studied in terms of the granularity of the UML models, as described by Unhelkar and Henderson-Sellers (1995), and requires a good metrics program within the organization to enable it to improve the aesthetics of the model. Such a model will then offer a high level of customer satisfaction, primarily to the members of the design team but also in their discussions with the business enduser(s).

### 1.6.4   Quality Techniques and V&V Checks

The three aspects of quality checks—syntax, semantics and aesthetics—should not be treated as totally independent of each other. A change in syntax may change the meaning or semantics of a sentence or diagram. While syntax is checked minutely for each artifact, an error in syntax may not be limited to the error in the language of expression.

This also happens in UML, where syntax and semantics may depend on each other. For example, the direction of an arrow showing the relationship between two classes will certainly affect the way that class diagram is interpreted by the end user. Similarly, aesthetics or symmetry of diagrams facilitates easier understanding (e.g., Hay, 1996), making the semantics clearer and the diagrams more comprehensible to their readers.

This brings us to the need to consider the various traditional quality techniques of walkthroughs, inspections, reviews and audits in the context of the V&V checks of syntax, semantics and aesthetics, as shown in Figure 1.4.

*Walkthroughs*—may be performed individually, and help weed out syntax errors (more than semantic errors).

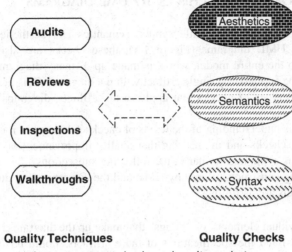

**Quality Techniques**          **Quality Checks**

**Figure 1.4**  V&V checks and quality techniques.

*Inspections*—are more rigorous than walkthroughs, are usually carried out by another person or party, and can identify both syntax and semantic errors.

*Reviews*—increase in formality and focus on working in a group to identify errors. The syntax checks are less important during reviews, but the semantics and aesthetics start becoming important.

*Audits*—formal and possibly external to the project and even the organization. As a result, audits are not very helpful at the syntax level, but they are extremely valuable in carrying out aesthetic checks of the entire model.

## 1.7  QUALITY CHECKS AND SKILLS LEVELS

As shown in Figure 1.2, while the syntax can be verified by anyone who has sufficient knowledge of UML, the semantics of each of the UML diagrams and the models that these diagrams describe need a little more experience. It is therefore important to include the users in all quality checks and to encourage them to participate in all quality walkthroughs, inspections and playacting (anthropomorphizing) in verifying the semantics of each of the models. The UML experience here fully supports the participatory role of the user envisaged by Warmer and Kleppe (1998).

The aesthetic aspect of model quality requires a combination of knowledge and experience. In ensuring the aesthetics of the UML models created, we require knowledge not only of UML and of the business, but also of the CASE tools and the environment in which they have been used. We need experience with more than one project before we can successfully apply the aesthetic aspect of model quality to the UML model.

## 1.8  LEVELS OF QUALITY CHECKS TO UML DIAGRAMS

Levels of checks mean that while syntax, semantics and aesthetic checks are applied to the UML diagrams (Figure 1.5), these checks are also applied in various ways to the entire model, which is made up of many diagrams. Alternatively, they can be applied to a single artifact within a diagram. Thus, it is not necessary to have all types of checks that apply to all artifacts, diagrams and models produced.

However, this understanding of the levels of checks is helpful in focusing on the intensity of the checks and in ensuring that quality improvement efforts are well balanced. This is explained further in the following subsections.

The modeling constructs offered by UML and the corresponding quality checks at the three levels are as follows:

a. The individual elements, or "things" that make up the diagrams. The artifacts (or things) and the specifications of these artifacts should have the syntax, semantics and aesthetics checks applied as far as possible. This comprises "ground-level" or highly detailed checking. In these checks, the syntax of the artifacts is checked most intensely.

b. The UML diagrams and the validity of their syntax, semantics and aesthetics. This is the equivalent of a "standing view" of the model being verified and validated, with an intensive check of the semantics of diagrams.

c. A combination of interdependent diagrams called a "model". The V&V of the entire model, made up of the relevant UML diagrams, their specifications, and so on, includes syntax, semantics and aesthetics checks. This is the "bird's-eye view," allowing checks of symmetry and consistency, resulting in aesthetic quality checks being applied most intensely.

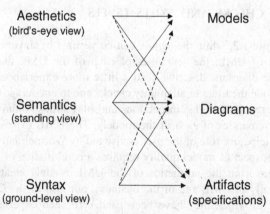

**Figure 1.5**   Syntax, semantics and aesthetics checks verify and validate UML artifacts, diagrams and models.

It is not necessary to apply all types of checks to all of the artifacts, diagrams and models produced.

### 1.8.1 Syntax Checks and UML Elements (Focus on Correctness)

When we say that we want to apply syntax checks to a use case diagram, what exactly do we mean? Are we checking the use case itself and its specification, or are we checking whether the "extends" relationship arrow in a use case diagram is pointing correctly to the use case being extended? This question leads us to expand our V&V effort to levels beyond just one diagram.

In syntax checks, we are looking at the ground-level view of the models. This includes the artifacts and elements of UML, as well as their specifications and documentation. Furthermore, when we check the syntax of these elements, we focus primarily on the correctness of representation as mandated by UML. Therefore, during syntax checks the semantics, or the meaning behind the notations and diagrams, are not the focus of checking.

For example, consider a class diagram that contains Car as a class. The syntax check of the correctness of this artifact would be something like this:

- Is the Car class represented correctly by attributes and operations?
- Do the attributes have correct types and do the operations have correct signatures?
- Is the Car class properly divided into three compartments?
- Is the Car class compilable? (This syntax check will apply in the solution space.)

In UML terms, when we start applying syntax checks to a use case diagram, we first apply them to the artifacts or elements that make up the diagram, such as the actors and the use cases. In a class diagram, these basic syntax checks apply to a class first and whatever is represented within the class. Since these artifacts are the basic building blocks from which the diagrams and models are created in UML, checking them in terms of correctness of the UML syntax is the first thing that should be done in any quality control effort.

This syntax check for an element or artifact is followed by a check of the validity of the diagram itself. Here we do not worry about whether, say, the specifications of the use case itself follow a standard and whether the use case semantically represents what it is meant to represent. Instead of focusing on one element at this level, we inspect the entire diagram and ensure that it is syntactically correct.

If these syntax checks for the elements and the diagrams that comprise them are conducted correctly, they ensure the correctness of the UML diagrams. As a result, the intensity of syntax checks will be reduced when the entire model is checked.

### 1.8.2   Semantic Checks and UML Diagrams (Focus on Completeness and Consistency)

Semantic checks deal with the meaning behind an element or a diagram. Therefore, this check focuses not on the correctness of representation but on the completeness of the meaning behind the notation. In the example of the Car class considered above, the semantic check for the model of Car would be: "Does the Car class as named in this model actually represent a car or does it represent a garbage bin?" It is worth noting here that should a collection of garbage bins be named as a Car class, so long as it has a name, an attribute and operation clearly defined, the UML syntax checks for the Car class will be successful. It is only at the semantic level that we can figure out that something is wrong because in real life the name Car does not represent a collection of garbage bins.

Because the meaning of one element of UML depends on many other elements and on the context in which it is used, therefore, semantic checks are best performed from a standing-level view of the UML models. This means that we move away from the ground-level check of the correctness of representation and focus on the purpose of representation. Needless to say, when we stand up from the ground (where we inspect the syntax), a lot more become visible. Therefore, it is not just one element on the diagram but rather the entire diagram that becomes visible and important. Semantic checks, therefore, become more intense at the diagram level rather than just at an element level.

Taking the Car example further, semantic checks also deal with consistency between diagrams, which includes, for example, dependencies between doors and engine and between wheel and steering. In UML terms, while a class door may have been correctly represented (syntactically correct) and may mean a door (semantically correct), the dependencies between door and car, or between door and driver (or even between door and burglar), will need a detailed diagram-level semantic check. This check will also include many cross-diagram dependency checks that extend the semantic check to more than one diagram. Semantic checks also focus on whether this class is given a unique and coherent set of attributes and responsibilities to handle or whether it is made to handle more responsibilities than just Car. For example, do the Driver-related operations also appear in Car? This would be semantically incorrect. Thus, semantic checks apply to each of the UML diagrams intensely, as well as to the entire model.

### 1.8.3   Aesthetic Checks and UML Models (Focus on Symmetry and Consistency)

As noted in the preceding two subsections, the correctness and completeness of UML elements and the corresponding individual diagrams are ensured by applying detailed syntax and semantic checks to them. The aesthetic checks of these diagrams and models add a different dimension to the quality assurance activities, as they deal not with correctness or completeness but rather with the overall consistency and symmetry of the UML diagrams and models. They are best done with a birds-eye view of the model. Because these checks occur at a very high level, far more is visible—not just one diagram, but many diagrams, their interrelationships, and their look and feel. This requires these aesthetic checks to be conducted at certain "check-points," where a certain amount of modeling is complete. Therefore, aesthetic checks also require some knowledge and understanding of the process being followed in the creation of the models and the software (briefly discussed in Chapter 7). The process ensures that the aesthetic checks are applied to the entire model rather than to one element or diagram.

In UML terms, the aesthetic checks of the Car class involve checking the dependency of Car on other classes and their relationships with persistent and graphical user interface (GUI) class cross-functional dependencies. This requires cross-checks between various UML diagrams that contain the Car class as well as checks of their consistency. Furthermore, aesthetic checks, occurring at a birds-eye level, focus on whether the Car class has too many or too few attributes and responsibilities. For example, if the Car class has too many operations, including that of "driving itself," the entire model would become ugly. Thus, a good understanding of the aesthetic checks results in diagrams and models that do not look ugly, irrespective of their correctness.

Finally, aesthetic checks look at the entire model (MOPS, MOSS, MOBS or any other) to determine whether or not it is symmetric and in balance. If a class diagram in a model has too many classes, aesthetic checks will ensure redistribution of classes.

Thus we see that, together, the syntax, semantic and aesthetic checks ensure that the artifacts we produce in UML, the diagrams that represent what should be happening in the system, and the models that contain diagrams and their detailed corresponding documentation are all correct, complete and consistent.

## 1.9 MODEL-DRIVEN ARCHITECTURE (MDA) AND QUALITY

MDA (OMG, 2004) is the latest initiative by the OMG to create an application architecture that is reusable in developing applications. The purpose of MDA is to provide the basic infrastructure and leave developers free to concentrate on solving application problems. MDA enables developers to look at the challenges of requirements modeling, development, testing and portability of deployed systems. MDA provides the basis for this effort and, at the same time, helps to increase the reusability of architecture by separating specification of the system's operation from the details of the way that the system uses the capabilities of its platform. The MDA initiative depends strongly on UML. Some authors bring the initiative close to the discussion of executable UML (see Fowler, 2003). The key components of MDA are the computation independent model (CIM), platform independent model (PIM) and platform specific model (PSM). PIM and PSM are effectively in the problem and solution spaces, as shown in Figure 1.1.

## 1.10 PROTOTYPING AND MODELING SPACES

An introduction to the concepts of quality would not be complete without mentioning prototyping. A prototype is a type of model, and it is advisable to use it in conjunction with the UML models to achieve overall good quality in the project. Prototypes can be created in each of the three modeling spaces to validate and verify the requirements as well as extract complete and correct requirements. Here are some brief comments on the nature of prototypes in each of the three modeling spaces.

MOPS has its own prototype, which is called the "functional prototype." This contains the user interface prototype. An example of using the prototype in MOPS is the use of the class responsibility collaborator (CRC) technique in requirements modeling. Each of the cards representing the classes can be used in role-playing a use case and the domain-level classes and their responsibilities extracted. Another well-known example of a prototype in MOPS is a "dummy" executable of a system, using screens and displaying their look, feel and navigation. Functional prototypes can thus be used to set the expectations of both users and management. By showing what a system can and cannot do early in MOPS, it is possible to reiterate the objectives and the scope of the system.

The prototype in MOSS is that of the technology. This implies testing programming languages and databases. While the MOPS prototype need not be an executable, the one in MOSS probably would. For example, a technical prototype would have an example Java class created that would be made to run on a potential client machine. The prototype would also experiment with running a small application on a server by trying various languages, like Java and C++, to handle the server-side capabilities. Potential reuse through patterns and reusable components is also facilitated by the technical prototypes created in MOSS.

Prototypes in the background space would test architectural requirements such as bandwidth and operating systems. Some aspects of performance, volume, stress, security and scalability would also be managed between the prototypes, MOSS and MOBS.

The architectural prototype could be the same prototype created in the solution space to explore how well the overall architecture of the system fits in with the rest of the system's and the organization's environment. Unlike the prototype in the problem space, this prototype would usually be an executable piece of software that experiments with various components, databases, networks and security protocols, to name but a few.

## DISCUSSION TOPICS

1. What is the importance of modeling in enhancing the quality of software projects? How is the importance of modeling different in enhancing the quality of the software models themselves?

2. What are the limitations of modeling? What rules should we adhere to when using modeling in software projects?

3. What are the various levels of quality, and how does model quality fit into these quality levels?

4. How does modeling help in projects where there is a large amount of existing legacy code (integration, creating models of existing applications)?

5. Describe the three suggested modeling spaces within software and how they relate to UML-based modeling.

6. What are the different aspects of quality enhanced by UML?

7. Discuss the important UML 2.0 diagrams in MOPS.

8. Discuss the important UML 2.0 diagrams in MOSS.

9. Discuss the important UML 2.0 diagrams in MOBS.

10. What is verification and validation? Discuss the difference between the two.

11. How does the aesthetic aspect of quality models differ from their syntax and semantic aspects?

12. What is an appropriate quality technique to verify syntax?

13. What is an appropriate quality technique to verify semantics?

14. What is an appropriate quality technique to verify aesthetics?

15. In addition to the knowledge of UML, what else is needed in ensuring the semantic quality of UML?

16. How is prototyping helpful in modeling? Discuss this with respect to the three modeling spaces and the models created there.

17. What is MDA? How does it relate to the three modeling spaces?

# REFERENCES

Ambler, S. *UML Style Guide*. Cambridge: Cambridge University Press, 2003.

Booch, G., Rumbaugh, J., and Jacobson, I. *The Unified Modelling Language User Guide*. Reading, MA: Addison-Wesley, 1999.

Cockburn, A. *Writing Effective Use Cases*. Boston, MA: Addison-Wesley, 2001.

Fowler, M. *Patterns of Enterprise Application Architecture*. Reading, MA: Addison-Wesley Professional, 2003.

Glass, R. *Facts and Fallacies of Software Engineering*. Reading, MA: Addison-Wesley, 2003.

Hay, D.C. *Data Model Patterns: Conventions of Thoughts*. New York: Dorset House, 1996.

Henderson-Sellers, B. *Object Oriented Metrics: Measures of Complexity*. Upper Saddle River, NJ: Prentice Hall, 1996.

Jacobson, I., Christerson, M., Jonsson, P. and Övergaard, G. *Object-Oriented Software Engineering: A Use Case Driven Approach*. Reading, MA: Addison-Wesley, 1992, pp. 524.

Miller, G. "The Magical Number Sever, Plus or Minus Two: Some Limits on our Capacity for Processing Information," *The Psychological Review*, 63(2), 1956, pp. 81–97.

Mellor, S.J., and Balcer M.J. *Executable UML: A Foundation for Model Driven Architecture.* Reading, MA: Addison-Wesley, 2002.

Mellor, S., Scott, K., Uhl, A., and Weise, D. *MDA Distilled: Principles of Model-Driven Architecture.* Reading, MA: Addison-Wesley, 2004.

Lindland, O.I., Sindre, G., and Sølvberg, A. "Understanding Quality in Conceptual Modeling," *IEEE Software* (March 1994), 42–49.

OMG. OMG Unified Modeling Language Specification, Version 1.4, September 2001. OMG document formal/01-09-68 through 80 (13 documents) [online]. Available at http://www.omg.org (2001).

OMG, Model Driven Architecture Initative; accessed 2004.

Perry, W. *Quality Assurance for Information Systems.* MA: QED Information Sciences, 1991.

Rosenberg, D., and Scott, K. *Use Case Driven Object Modelling with the UML.* Reading, MA: Addison-Wesley, 1999.

Unhelkar, B. *After the Y2K Fireworks.* Boca Raton, FL: CRC Press, 1999.

Unhelkar, B. *Process Quality Assurance for UML-Based Projects.* Boston: Addison-Wesley, 2003.

Unhelkar, B., and Henderson-Sellers, B. "ODBMS Considerations in the Granularity of Reuseable OO Design," *Proceedings of TOOLS15 Conference*, C. Mingins and B. Meyer, eds. Upper Saddle River, NJ: Prentice-Hall, 1995, pp. 229–234.

Unhelkar, B., and Henderson-Sellers, B. "Modelling Spaces and the UML," *Proceedings of the IRMA (Information Resource Management Association) Conference*, New Orleans, 2004.

Warmer, J., and Kleppe, A. *The Object Constraint Language. Precise Modeling with UML.* Reading, MA: Addison-Wesley, 1998.

# Chapter 2

# Nature and Basics of UML Diagrams

Fire, invariably, goes up and water comes down! The nature of things is such![1]

## CHAPTER SUMMARY

This chapter describes all the UML 2.0 diagrams in terms of their nature (structural versus behavioral and static versus dynamic). It also discusses the basics of these diagrams and how they are put together. Understanding the nature and applicability of the UML diagrams, discussed here using some basic examples, provides the necessary groundwork for techniques of V&V that are applicable to these models. Finally, the chapter briefly considers UML's extensibility mechanisms and UML's meta-model, which provide elasticity to UML.

## 2.1 THE NATURE OF UML DIAGRAMS

The wide range of UML diagrams provides flexibility and applicability to modelers in the problem, solution and background spaces. At the same time, the width and breadth of these diagrams challenges modelers to select the right diagrams for the right task. This requires an understanding of the UML diagrams in terms of their structural versus behavioral nature as well as their static versus dynamic nature.

[1]Source: Unknown.

*Verification and Validation for Quality of UML 2.0 Models*, by Bhuvan Unhelkar
Copyright © 2005 John Wiley & Sons, Inc.

In discussing the nature of these diagrams, it is important to note that they are not independent, standalone diagrams. In fact, in our later attempts at V&V of these models, we also consider their interconnectedness and their dependencies at both the syntactic and semantic levels. Furthermore, these diagrams, and the artifacts within them, are also augmented by their corresponding specifications and documentation, resulting in greater information than is provided by mere visual means.

### 2.1.1   Elasticity of UML

As described in the previous chapter (Table 1.1), UML, through its 13 diagrams, provides the primary mechanism for visual communication in software projects. These diagrams provide versatility to UML, enabling it to be used in projects of various sizes and types, as well as by persons playing different roles within the projects. In practice, UML can be expanded to cover major aspects of a large project, including functional scoping, architecture and design. It can also be shrunk and applied to a relatively small area of a project that is of high importance or top priority. Thus, in practice, UML is elastic.

This elasticity of UML is not merely the result of having a suite of diagrams to choose from. Instead, the UML diagrams themselves are underpinned by OMG's meta-model, which, as discussed later in this chapter, is the model of a model providing the ground rules for creation of an instance of UML. This frees the users (modelers) of UML to extend the language to suit their purpose—provided that it adheres to the meta-model.

The elasticity of UML is further enhanced by the fact that some of its key mechanisms also allow it to be extended and enriched. Modelers routinely apply these extensibility mechanisms to create diagrams that meet their particular objectives. These mechanisms, with their quality connotations, are discussed toward the end of this chapter.

Finally, the specifications associated with the UML 2.0 modeling elements (e.g., specifications associated with a use case or a class) can also be customized to suit the objectives of the model. These specifications and their associated diagramming elements are also discussed here for the appropriate diagrams.

Given the range and versatility of UML and the availability of its 13 diagrams in the three modeling spaces, it is imperative to understand the basic and applied nature of these diagrams. We will now discuss this subject.

### 2.1.2   Structural versus Behavioral Nature of UML Diagrams

A structural model describes how things are organized or composed. A behavioral model describes how they function or behave. For example, consider a small prototype (model) of a door. The model, containing the door, its frame, hinges, latches and locks, represents its structural organization. Now consider a brief set of instructions attached to the model door that describes how the door can be opened, closed and locked. Those instructions represent the behavioral aspect of the door.

Note, however, that both the structure and the description of the door are devoid of time dependency. This can be easily understood when we consider information that is *not* provided in the aforementioned model. For example, the precise time when the door will be opened or closed, how long it will take to open it, how long it will remain open or shut and precisely which actions/activities will change the states of the door are pieces of information not provided by the behavioral description (but rather by the dynamic description, discussed later).

What is true for the door is also true for the UML diagrams. Some diagrams are very good at describing the way business entities are organized; others describe the system's behavior or functionality in practice. For example, use case diagrams are considered behavioral by many, but they are static in the sense that they are *not concerned with time*. Even activity diagrams, which provide excellent means of depicting behavior, do not contain messages and states that are time-dependent.

Figure 2.1 shows a summary of the nature of UML 2.0 diagrams. This division of the diagram suggests its *major* characteristics. It is not a watertight compartmentalization. For example, the use case diagram is shown as behavioral in nature in Figure 2.1, but some practitioners argue that use case diagrams show the structure of the requirements. It is best to avoid such discussions of technicality and instead focus on the *bent* of these diagrams, as is done here.

### 2.1.3  Static versus Dynamic Nature of UML Diagrams

Figure 2.1 divides the UML 2.0 diagrams based on another important characteristic: *temporal dependency*. When we consider time-based dependency between elements

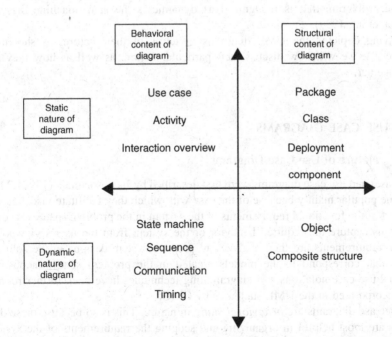

**Figure 2.1**  Summary of the nature of UML diagrams, depicting their structural versus behavioral characteristics as well as their static versus dynamic nature.

on a diagram, that model can be considered dynamic. A dynamic model displays the various states of the elements and the messages that cause such state changes. However, when a dynamic model is *frozen in time*, it becomes static.

Considering the door example further, if a model represents a door that is held open, then that representation is a static model. Something is *happening* and, at the same time, what is happening is *frozen in time*. Both structural and behavioral aspects of a model, described in the previous subsection, are important in creating a static model. For example, in the static model of a door being held open, the structural aspect of the door is also utilized. This structural information deals with understanding the location of the handle, its distance from the frame and perhaps the maximum angle to which it can be opened. Similarly, the behavioral description of the door may be helpful in indicating how the door is held open—perhaps by using a door stopper or a foot. Thus, the structural and behavioral aspects of a model can be used in representing the static snapshot of the model. This static snapshot contains the concept of time, but that time is frozen.

The dynamic nature of a model not only has a concept of time, but that time is also changing. A model that shows how the door can change its state from open to closed reflects the dynamic aspect of modeling. A dynamic model may comprise a number of static models. Alternatively, a dynamic model can be thinly sliced into many pieces, each representing a snapshot or a time-based static model. The most appropriate dynamic model in a software environment is an executable prototype. In terms of UML, such a dynamic model may be realized in the future through executable UML and MDA. However, currently, in terms of the UML diagrams, the only diagram that is recognized as dynamic is the state machine diagram (Booch et al., 1999).

Having depicted the UML diagrams in terms of their nature, as shown in Figure 2.1, we will now discuss their particular nature, as well as how they are put together.

## 2.2  USE CASE DIAGRAMS

### 2.2.1  Nature of Use Case Diagrams

Use cases and use case diagrams were first described by Jacobson et al. (1992). They became popular mainly because of the ease with which they facilitate visualization of most of the functional requirements of the system in the problem space. Use case diagrams capture the required behavior of the system from the user's viewpoint. Visual requirements are then analyzed to produce system designs in the solution space that correspond to the models created in the problem space. Jacobson's original use case notations and diagramming techniques have been further refined and incorporated in the UML standards by OMG.

Use case diagrams are *behavioral-static* in nature. This is so because these diagrams are most helpful in organizing and scoping the requirements of the system in the problem space. Note, though, that the behavioral aspect of the requirements

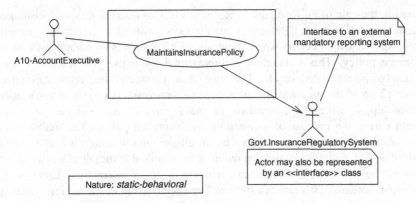

**Figure 2.2** Nature and basics of a use case diagram.

is not obvious in the use case diagrams but, instead, is delegated to the textual documentation within the use cases and accompanying activity diagrams. For example, while it is possible to see, in Figure 2.2, that there is an interaction between the actor and the system, it is not possible to see what sort of interaction it is; those details are documented *within* the use case specification. Because of the descriptive nature of the interactions documented within a use case, the use case diagram is considered behavioral.

Consider Figure 2.2 in greater detail. As is apparent, this figure does not describe a flow or a process. While the use cases (e.g., MaintainsInsurancePolicy) themselves represent the manner in which the user will use the system, the use case diagram needs additional annotation, description and notes to make the process it represents understandable to the reader. By simply looking at the diagram, the reader is unable to decipher the sequence in which use cases will be executed. Aesthetically good use case diagrams are usually arranged in such a manner that readers can get some idea of the process flow. However, drawing such diagrams depends on the dexterity of the modeler rather than on a specification provided by UML itself. Thus, a use case diagram itself is static (there is no concept of a time sequence, a "then"), showing organization of the requirements rather than any dynamic aspect of the system behavior.

This nature of the use case diagram is a potential source of confusion for people who have data flow diagramming (DFD) experience and who are new to UML. The intuitive interpretation of the arrowheads on the use case diagrams as a sequence of use cases is incorrect. As use case diagrams indicate, none of the three allowable relationships between two use cases represent the concept of time or dependency.

### 2.2.2 Putting Together a Use Case Diagram

Figure 2.2 shows a typical use case diagram that represents maintenance of an insurance policy. Although deceptively simple, this diagram carries substantial information from the problem space. First of all, it shows an important user of the system in the role of an `Account Executive`. Considering a typical insurance system, this `Account Executive` interacts with the system in various ways—one of which occurs when she deals with all aspects of maintenance of an insurance policy. This interaction is represented by a use case called 'Main tainsInsurancePolicy'. The line that connects the actor `Account Executive` to the use case `MaintainsInsurancePolicy` is an association relationship showing the interaction of the `Account Executive` with the system during the process of maintaining an insurance policy. The maintenance of a policy is a use case represented by an ellipse, and although it is not visible on the diagram, that ellipse contains within it (or is linked to the) detailed documentation of the use case, including, in particular, a set of interactions between the `Account Executive` and the system. The specification of the `MaintainsIn surancePolicy` use case may also, optionally, contain pre- and postconditions. One of the postconditions might be that whenever any maintenance is done on the insurance policy, an update is sent to a `Govt.InsuranceRegulatorySys tem`. This external system is shown as another actor in Figure 2.2, and an arrowhead is used to indicate that the `Govt.InsuranceRegulatorySystem` is the receiver of the message (not its initiator). Appearance of this "interface actor" representing another system is quite common, especially in large and legacy integration projects. In these projects, the system being built will interface with legacy systems, external agencies and databases. Requirement modelers and system designers will be concerned with interfacing to these external systems rather than building their internal details.

### 2.2.2.1 Describing a Use Case Specification

Putting together a good use case diagram involves less than half of the work done in specifying the requirements. It is equally important, if not more so, to document each of the use cases that appears in the use case diagram in a succinct but complete manner. A typical use case documentation template used in practice is shown in Chapter 4, together with a documented example.

Some of the important things to be documented in a use case include the name and description of the use case and, more important, the text or the interactions. In the approach suggested by Constantine and Lockwood (1999), these use cases can be documented as essential versus concrete. An essential use case would describe the essential behavior of the system but not how it will be implemented. For example:

Account Executive intends to maintain a policy and the system responds by asking questions.

The concrete version of the same use case would include the exact details used in maintaining a policy and the exact contents of the questions. For example:

Account Executive enters policy number, policy details and policy type of a particular policy, and the system responds by asking for related customer details and a password.

Thus use case specifications can be more elaborate or they can be briefly described in a few sentences. In either case, as seen above, they can be an abstract generic description or a precise description of how the user will use the system.

As noted by Booch et al. (1999) in their discussions of forward and reverse engineering, "use case describes how an element behaves, not how that behavior is implemented, so it cannot be directly forward or reverse engineered," (p. 239). This statement is sufficient proof of the nature of use case documentation; it is not meant to follow a set template pedantically. A common piece of information encountered in practice is "Use cases don't cause systems to crash." Therefore, good-quality use case documentation should be less code-like, and more readable and descriptive.

Finally, use cases should be documented, keeping in mind that this documentation provides valuable input for the creation of test designs and test cases.

## 2.3 ACTIVITY DIAGRAMS

### 2.3.1 Nature of Activity Diagrams

As shown in Figure 2.1, activity diagrams are static-behavioral. Compared to use case diagrams, activity diagrams are capable of documenting the flow within a use case or within a system. An important characteristic of activity diagrams is their ability to show dependency between activities. This dependency, however, is not based on a precise concept of time; therefore, activity diagrams are not considered dynamic (such as, for example, sequence diagrams). The sense of timing is restricted to showing how one activity follows another. Furthermore, because of their ability to show multiple threads—through forks and joins—activity diagrams also show what happens *simultaneously* in the system. Therefore, these diagrams provide an excellent mechanism to model business processes.

Activity diagrams are meant to show any flow or process in the system. This makes them capable of being used to model processes

- at the business process level
- within a use case
- occasionally between use cases

This diagram does precisely what the use case diagram does not: it shows dependency or flow between two entities in a process. Therefore, the activity diagram, as shown in Figure 2.3, is far more readable from the user's viewpoint than the use case diagram.

### 2.3.2 Putting Together an Activity Diagram

Figure 2.3 is an activity diagram that represents the process of making an insurance proposal. The diagram starts with the pseudo "start" activity, followed by the activity `'AcceptHomeInsuranceProposal'`. After this activity is completed, the flow

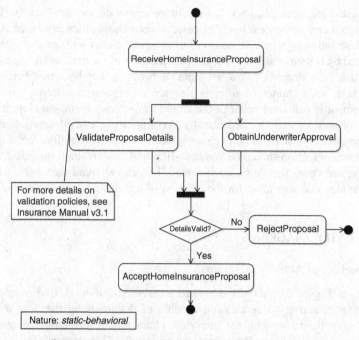

**Figure 2.3**    Nature and basics of an activity diagram.

within this activity diagram reaches a sync point. The activities after the sync point are split into two threads, one dealing with validation of the proposal details called 'ValidateProposalDetails' and the other with obtaining the underwriter's approval, 'ObtainUnderwriterApproval'. Note how these two activities, if conducted sequentially, would take much longer than they would if conducted in parallel. When the two activities are conducted in parallel, as shown in Figure 2.3, time is saved. However, note that the time taken by each of these two activities conducted in parallel may be different. For example, ValidateProposalDetails may take only half an hour, but ObtainUnderwriterApproval may take a day. It is only when both of these activities, with different time frames, are complete that the next activity can start. Completion of both of these activities at a point in time is shown by the horizontal joining bar. This forking and joining of an activity diagram facilitates good-quality workflow or process documentation.

In Figure 2.3, the horizontal bar representing the join is followed by a decision point indicating the two potential ways in which the decisions can go. Either the insurance proposal is valid, in which case the cover commences, or it is invalid and the cover is rejected.

### 2.3.3 Specifications in an Activity Diagram

An activity diagram may optionally have a description, which can also be called its "specification." The activity diagram can contain descriptions of the flow and additional notes, as well as stereotypes. An activity diagram can be put together to describe pictorially the text within the use case. However, it is a generic diagram and therefore describes the flow within the use case in a generic fashion. Activities themselves can be further specified in terms of their pre- and postconditions.

## 2.4 CLASS DIAGRAMS

### 2.4.1 Nature of Class Diagrams

Class diagrams are highly structural and static in nature. As shown in Figure 2.4, the class diagram is modeling the structure of the system and has no behavioral content. Class diagrams show business-level classes as well as technical classes derived from the implementation language (e.g., Java or C++). In addition to showing the classes, class diagrams show the relationships between them. The entire description of the classes (or "entities," as they may be called in the problem space) and their relationships with each other is static. No dependency is shown in this diagram and no concept of time.

By reading a class diagram, it is not possible to ascertain any behavioral aspect of the system. Exceptions to this statement are elements like notes and constraints

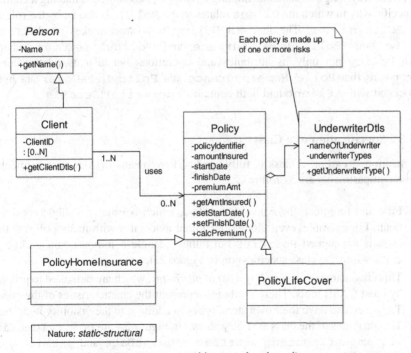

**Figure 2.4** Nature and basics of a class diagram.

(see the discussion of extensibility mechanisms later in this chapter), which may show some dependency in an extremely limited fashion.

### 2.4.2 Putting Together a Class Diagram

Figure 2.4 shows a typical class diagram. It contains various classes, their relationships and their multiplicities. For a typical simple insurance application, these classes (or business entities) are Person, Client, Risk (UnderWriterDtls), Policy, PolicyHomeInsurance and PolicyLifeCover.

Firstly, look at the inheritance relationship between class Client and class Person. Client is shown as inheriting from Person. This relationship has connotations of reuse as well as quality. Also, two types of policies are shown inheriting from an abstract policy. Policy itself is made up of a set of attributes and operations. The entire 'Underwriter Details' and its related attributes and operations have been factored out and shown as a separate class on its own. The Policy class contains underwriter details, and therefore the relationship is that of aggregation. Because the aggregation is shown as an unfilled (or white) diamond, it indicates that underwriter details can be shared by many policies.

The basic relationship between Client and Policy is that of association. This relationship indicates that the Client class will use details of the Policy class, as well as provide details to the Policy class. The Client can relate to the Policy in various ways (e.g., as someone holding a policy versus someone making a claim). A specific way in which the Client relates to the Policy is shown by the role of the Policyholder. The fact that Policy is abstract makes no difference because both PolicyHomeInsurance and PolicyLifeCover inherit from Policy not only its attributes and operations but also its relationships. This means that PolicyHomeInsurance and PolicyLifeCover are both associated with a Client and both contain Underwriter Details.

### 2.4.3 Specification of a Class

As mentioned earlier, a class is fully specified by means of four compartments. These compartments are as follows:

- First and foremost, the *name* of the class, which is usually a single common noun. For example, even though one client associates with many policies, the class is not named Policies but rather a single common noun, Policy, as shown in the class specification in Figure 2.4.
- This class name is followed by a *list of attributes*, which are defaulted to private by most CASE tools. These attributes represent the characteristics of the class. They can also have their own stereotypes in addition to the visibility indicator. The attributes of the class Policy shown in Figure 2.4 are policyIdentifi er, amountInsured, startDate, finishDate and premiumAmt, all of which are prefixed by a (-), indicating that they are all private attributes.

- The third compartment of the class is *operations*. During business analysis, these operations also represent the behavior of the class. In the solution space the operations are carried and implemented by means of methods or functions. The operations for the Policy class shown in Figure 2.4 are getAmtInsured(), setStartDate(), setFinishDate() and calcPremium().

- The fourth compartment is meant to document, the *responsibilities*. Responsibilities can be plain English statements; hence they can be documented using manual techniques like CRC (Cunningham et al., 1999) cards. Eventually, responsibilities are translated into combinations of attributes and behaviors and placed in the second and third compartments of the class specifications. The difference between behavior and responsibility can be further clarified by means of the Car example. A Car has the behavior of driving, honking, and braking. However, these behaviors of car will be applied in different ways, depending on the responsibility of the car. A Car with responsibility for transporting patients will have a distinctly different use of brakes and horn than, say, a car responsible for responding to an emergency call. The way in which the behavior of a police Car responsible for reaching a crime scene is put together will be different from the behavior of a car transporting patients—although both types of cars can drive, honk and brake!

### 2.4.3.1 Specification of a Class Diagram
Class diagrams may occasionally have some description associated with them that provides additional explanation. However, the level of detail in the specifications provided for each class may vary. Furthermore, such specifications may be restricted to the classes and may not be provided for the class diagram. In the problem space, though, description of a class diagram can be provided separately, in a textual document, instead of placing it alongside a class diagram created within a CASE tool.

## 2.5 SEQUENCE DIAGRAMS

### 2.5.1 Nature of Sequence Diagrams

Sequence diagrams have been popular ever since Jacobson et al. (1992) introduced them as a means of documenting behavior within use cases. In their earlier usage, sequence diagrams were also called "scenario diagrams," for they represented pictorially a scenario (or an instance) within a use case. Because of their practical ability to show what is happening in a use case, sequence diagrams are popular with both business analysts and system designers. Furthermore, each of the steps within a use case can also appear on a sequence diagram as a note or a narration.

Rumbaugh et al. (1999, p. 87) describe a sequence diagram as a two-dimensional chart. The vertical dimension is the time axis, which runs from the top to the bottom of the diagram. The horizontal dimension shows the classifier roles that represent the individual objects collaborating with each other. The sequence diagram thus shows the interactions among the collaborating objects between two given points in time. Therefore, to understand the nature of a sequence diagram, we have to consider its behavioral content. In addition, since the sequence diagram does have some concept of time, it is more dynamic than most other UML diagrams.

By reading sequence diagrams, one gets to know the detailed interaction between actors and the system, or between collaborating objects, *within a given time block.* However, information on what happened before the interaction started and what will happen after it is completed is not shown on the sequence diagram. While messages shown on the sequence diagram can have pre- and postconditions, these conditions are not directly visible on the diagram. Despite this limitation, the time appearing on this diagram is far more precise than that on the activity diagram. It is possible to show what happens between two messages, and it is also possible to ascertain what happens *as time progresses.* Therefore, sequence diagrams are considered dynamic-behavioral in nature.

Sequence diagrams are able to show not only how a particular behavior is carried out but also which objects and actors are involved in carrying it out. As a result, the concept of time as well as dependencies between objects is introduced in these diagrams. Thus, a sequence diagram is dynamic, compared with, say, an activity diagram or a use case diagram. For a given time frame, a sequence diagram shows exactly how the messages will flow between the actor and the system and between the collaborating objects of the system. More important, the sequence diagram shows the exact sequence of messages rather than just what the messages between two objects will be.

### 2.5.2   Putting Together a Sequence Diagram

Figure 2.5 shows the actor `Account Executive` sending a message to the `aPolicy` (object), which belongs to the class `PolicyHomeInsurance`. The message sent is `'ValidatePolicyDetails'`, and this message starts the sequence. Once the `policy` object receives this message, it sends a message to a `aClient` object saying `'getClientDetails'`. Note that this `aClient` is an object belonging to the class `Client` and is quite different from the actor client trying to access the system. Once the `Client` validates the details of the client, the `Policy` object then sends the message to itself `'basicInterna lValidation()'`—now validating the details of the client with respect to the policy. This is followed by another message which is sent by the `aPolicy` object to the `UnderwriterDetails` asking it to `'obtainUnderwriter Approval'` for this policy. Finally, the `Account Executive` is able to `'approvePolicyCover'`.

Steps describing the sequence appear on the left side of the diagram as text or notes. As stated earlier, what happens before we enter this sequence (e.g., who created `aPolicy` and when) and what will happen after this sequence is exited is not shown on this diagram. If necessary, another sequence diagram may be appended to it.

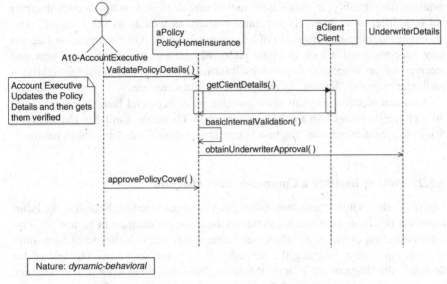

**Figure 2.5** Nature and basics of a sequence diagram.

Finally, note that two objects belonging to the same class can be shown as two separate objects on this diagram. For example, if aPolicy needs to send a message to bPolicy (not shown in Figure 2.5), then both of these policy objects can be shown as separate objects on a sequence diagram. This is also true of two messages using the same method at different points in time.

### 2.5.3 Specifications of a Sequence Diagram

A sequence diagram itself may not have detailed specifications of its own. However, the elements on the diagram, such as the messages, have their own specifications. These specifications describe the pre- and postconditions of the message and can indicate additional constraints on the execution of the messages. Because each element of the sequence diagram is an "instance element," it has a corresponding class or method, and it is that class or method that will have the detailed specifications and documentation. Notes can and should be added to the sequence diagrams to clarify them further. Entry of these specifications is facilitated by most CASE tools, although their format may differ, depending on the CASE tool being used.

## 2.6 COMMUNICATION DIAGRAMS

### 2.6.1 Nature of Communication Diagrams

A communication diagram (also known as a "collaboration" diagram in previous versions of UML) shows how objects collaborate with each other to satisfy a required functionality. It shows information similar to that on a sequence diagram but in a different manner. Its structural content, as well as its static nature, does not change significantly from that of a sequence diagram. A communication diagram may be considered a tool to show pictorially all the messages being sent and received by an object. This provides information on how heavily (or lightly) a particular object is "loaded" in the execution of a sequence.

A communication diagram shows a suite of objects, and how they are related through their messages, in a particular sequence. Therefore, similar to the sequence diagram, a communication diagram is considered dynamic-behavioral in nature.

### 2.6.2   Putting Together a Communication Diagram

Figure 2.6 shows how a communication diagram is put together. Note that, the information in this diagram is similar to that in the sequence diagram in Figure 2.5. This communication diagram still shows the same actor, `AccountExecutive`, initiating a sequence by sending the message `validateDetails`. The rest of the details in the diagram are exactly the same. Note that by looking at this diagram, one gains an understanding of the load on `aPolicy` object. Two messages are

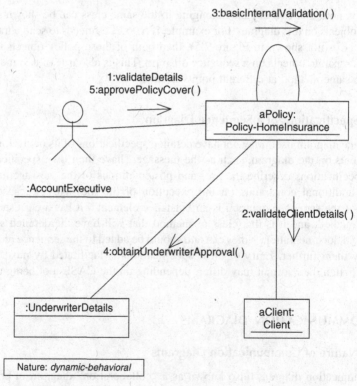

**Figure 2.6**   Nature and basics of a communication diagram.

coming in and two going out. This object sends one more message to itself—
3:basicInternalValidation(). When extended to a large, complex set of
interactions, this diagram can help redistribute the load on a particular object and
thereby improve the quality of the design.

## 2.7 INTERACTION OVERVIEW DIAGRAMS

### 2.7.1 Nature of Interaction Overview Diagrams

Interaction overview diagrams, as their name suggests, provide a high-level overview of the interactions within the system. Since those interactions are best depicted
using sequence (or, alternatively, communication) diagrams, interaction overview
diagrams contain a reference to sequence diagrams. However, unlike sequence
diagrams, where it is not possible to show an if-then-else situation, an interaction
overview diagram enables this situation to be shown. This brings the interaction overview diagram closer to the activity diagram. Thus, overall, the interaction
overview diagram is considered behavioral but static in nature.

### 2.7.2 Putting Together an Interaction Overview Diagram

Figure 2.7 shows an interaction overview diagram. Note that this diagram starts like
an activity diagram, with the start state shown as a filled dot. This is followed by a
reference "ref" to an InquirySequence, which is a sequence diagram of the
same name. However, any other diagram, such as another activity diagram or
even a use case can be referenced here. Based on the type of inquiry sequence
being executed, there is a division of the flow between two other sequences—
HomeInsurancePolicy and LifeInsurancePolicy. These could also
be sequence diagrams or use cases representing the course of action for home insurance policies versus life insurance policies. Both of these sequences meet at the
second decision point, and the interaction overview ends.

## 2.8 OBJECT DIAGRAMS

### 2.8.1 Nature of Object Diagrams

An object diagram shows, at a particular point in time, the *structure* of the various
objects as they relate to each other. Because object diagrams show what is happening in the system at a particular point in time, they are considered more dynamic
than the class diagrams. However, they are not totally dynamic, as they do not
show any *change* in the system based on time. While time is there—as a snapshot—it is not changing. These diagrams are suspended in time—showing what
happens in terms of relationships between objects either in main memory or as a
mechanism to express and discuss multiplicities on a whiteboard. Thus, the object
diagram is highly structural, with no behavioral content. It is also more static than

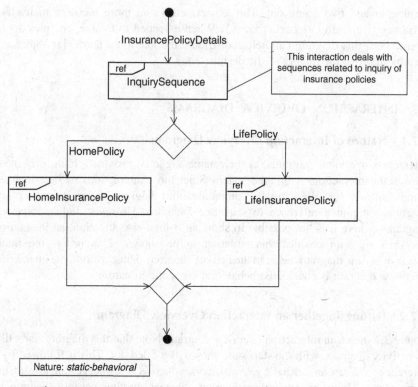

**Figure 2.7**    Nature and basics of an interaction overview diagram.

dynamic. However, whatever dynamism is attributed to object diagrams is due to the fact that they are drawn with respect to a particular point in time.

## 2.8.2    Putting Together an Object Diagram

In Figure 2.8 an object diagram is shown that links a client object called `aClient` with three `Policy` instances. In a corresponding class diagram we would have shown the `Client` class associating with a `Policy` class. In an object diagram, though, we are able to show exactly how many policies a client will associate with. In Figure 2.8, we see `aClient` associating with `aPolicy`, `bPolicy` and `cPolicy` because this particular client has three policies with the insurance company. If another object diagram were drawn for `bClient` where that client had only two policies, then `bClient` would be shown linked with only two policy objects (not shown on Figure 2.8).

Object diagrams provide an ideal mechanism to discuss on a whiteboard how objects link with one another and how the multiplicities shown on a class diagram will occur when the application is executed (a snapshot of an instant of time). An object diagram thus helps express the requirements in greater detail, especially

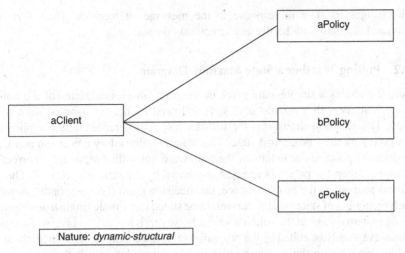

**Figure 2.8**  Nature and basics of an object diagram.

when an object has complicated links with many others objects. This ability of object diagrams to show objects and links is different from showing the messages between various objects on a communication diagram. A communication diagram shows the flow of messages and their sequence. An object diagram has no concept of flow and does not show messages; it only shows links, and those too have no dependencies. As a result, object diagrams are considered dynamic-structural in nature.

## 2.9  STATE MACHINE DIAGRAMS

### 2.9.1  Nature of State Machine Diagrams

An object belonging to a class can be in various states, and so can an entire system. A state machine diagram is used to indicate the various states in which an object, a use case or an entire system can be. When used to show system states, it is important to note that it is the "instance version" of the system that can be shown on an object diagram.

The nature of the state machine diagram is considered dynamic-behavioral. In fact, many authors consider this dynamic nature of the state machine diagram ideal for major real-time modeling exercises (Douglass, 1999, 2003). It has its origins in state transition diagrams of the Simula language of the 1960s, where simulation of machine tools or the trajectory of a rocket were major applications of the simulating models (Jacobson et al., 1992). Like its precursor (the state transition diagram of Simula), the state machine diagram of UML has the ability to represent time precisely and in a real-time fashion. "What happens at a certain point in time?" is a question that is answered by this diagram. Because of the dynamic nature of state machine diagrams, they are ideal for modeling real-time systems. These diagrams also show the entire behavior of one object—depicting the life cycle of an object as it changes its state in response to the messages it receives. Thus, this is a behavioral diagram with hardly any structural content.

### 2.9.2 Putting Together a State Machine Diagram

Figure 2.9 shows a simple state machine diagram for various states of the policy object. It starts with a pseudo start state followed by the Proposed state for a policy. This diagram shows that the insurance system is recording the application for a policy by the Proposed state. This state is followed by a decision point. At this decision point, if the details of the policy are not sufficient, or are incorrect or incomplete, then the policy is rejected, as shown by the state Rejected. During business analysis in the problem space, this decision point (i.e., the condition under which branching of states will occur) might be stated in a simple English description. During system design in the solution space, however, it has to be a precise condition that can eventually be coded by the programmer. If the condition is satisfied, the state machine branches to the Accepted state. Note though that it is the same object policy that is following a different suite of states (or a different path) in its life cycle. Once the policy is accepted, it moves into the state Paid, during which the payment of a premium (Payment message) continues to reach the policy object again and again—ensuring that the policy continues to remain in its current state of Paid.

## 2.10 COMPOSITE STRUCTURE DIAGRAMS

### 2.10.1 Nature of Composite Structure Diagrams

Composite structure diagrams are architectural in nature, fitting well with the modeling requirements in the background space. They are able to decompose an object or a

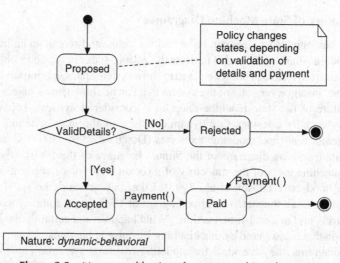

**Figure 2.9** Nature and basics of a state machine diagram.

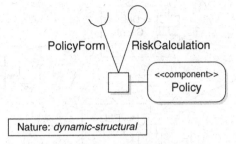

Figure 2.10   Nature and basics of a composite structure diagram.

component at run-time and show the various interfaces and realizations linked to that object, as shown in Figure 2.10. These diagrams show run-time scenarios including the structure of the run-time components. As a result, their nature is dynamic-structural, similar to object diagrams.

### 2.10.2   Putting Together a Composite Structure Diagram

Figure 2.10 shows a very simple composite structure diagram that depicts the run-time scenario of the Policy component. The Policy component is related to two other interfaces, namely, PolicyForm and RiskCalculation. As will be obvious to requirements modelers, the Policy component at run-time will have to depend on the RiskCalculation interface, which it will use to calculate the premiums. However, when it comes to displaying the information, it will be PolicyForm that will depend on the Policy component for the information to be displayed.

## 2.11   COMPONENT DIAGRAMS

### 2.11.1   Nature of Component Diagrams

Component diagrams are static structural in nature. They show the structure of the system as it is implemented, but they do not show the behavior of the system in operation. These diagrams also do not have the concept of time and are therefore not dynamic. Component diagrams only show where the classes and various other logical artifacts will eventually be realized (or coded) into final executables. A component diagram is thus a pictorial representation of the final executables or linked libraries that contain the code of the system.

Examples of components include COM+ objects, Enterprise Java beans, executables, linked libraries of linked objects and so on. Booch et al. (1999, p. 350) clarify the meaning of a component further by indicating its possible stereotypes—executable, library, table, file and document. Thus, a component becomes a physical representation of—mainly—a collection of classes.

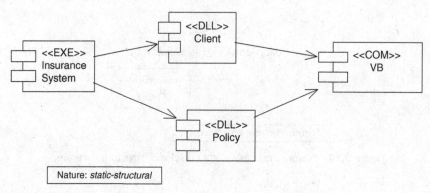

**Figure 2.11**    Nature and basics of a component diagram.

Components, like classes, can also reside in packages, and components also have interfaces.

### 2.11.2  Putting Together a Component Diagram

As shown in Figure 2.11, a basic component diagram has components and dependencies. Additionally, it may have interfaces, but they are not shown in this figure. The dependency relationship in Figure 2.11 indicates how the insurance system executable depends on two linked libraries, Client and Policy. These two libraries, in turn, depend on a Visual Basic (VB) COM library. This dependency also indicates that the Policy and Client components will need the VB library for either compilation or build—or even for their execution. Note again that there is no concept of time in this diagram.

### 2.11.3  Specifications of a Component Diagram

While a component usually has only its name on the component diagram, the UML allows additional compartments to be drawn to provide further details of a component. These additional compartments or pieces of information on a component could be direct values or constraints applicable to a component or may simply be a detailed path name of the component. Component diagrams themselves may simply have a description providing further explanatory notes or information on how the components have been put together. Therefore, compared with a use case specification or a use case diagram, a component diagram may have a relatively less organized or less structured specification.

## 2.12  DEPLOYMENT DIAGRAMS

### 2.12.1  Nature of Deployment Diagrams

Deployment diagrams are also structural and static in nature. However, these diagrams are the only "hardware" diagrams in UML. They show how processing

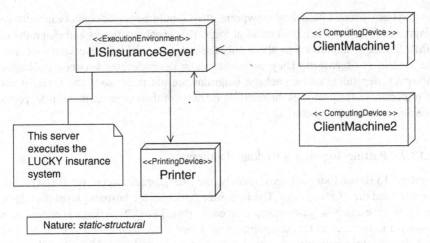

Figure 2.12 Nature and basics of a deployment diagram.

nodes are organized to enable deployment of software systems, as well as the components that will be executed on these nodes. As hardware diagrams, deployment diagrams provide a valuable basis for communicating hardware-related decisions. Thus, they allow consideration of the operational requirements of a system by enabling discussion of the capacity of the nodes, their ability to handle speed and volume, and the manner in which the executables will be deployed across the network.

### 2.12.2   Putting Together a Deployment Diagram

Figure 2.12 shows a basic deployment diagram, with a Server machine or processor and two Client processors. Furthermore, the Server is shown related to the Printer, another physical device. A more sophisticated deployment diagram will contain additional devices, such as the local network (LAN) or the Internet or a dial-up modem or a combination of all of these. Many UML-based CASE tools provide variations on these basic notations by extending them. For example, a printer is represented in some CASE tools by a printer icon rather than by a node with a printer labeled on it. While extending the notations to represent physical devices improves the readability of these diagrams, inconsistencies can be introduced.

## 2.13   PACKAGE DIAGRAMS

### 2.13.1   Nature of Package Diagrams

Package diagrams are static structural in nature, providing an excellent means of organizing the requirements in the problem space. They represent primarily a large, cohesive part of a system and, hence, may also be considered as representing a subsystem. From a modeling viewpoint, they should be considered organizational diagrams. A package is a collection of logically cohesive artifacts and diagrams of UML. Package diagrams thus show only the top view—a bird's eye view—of how the system is organized. They may also show dependencies between packages. However, dependencies on package diagrams are not mandatory and are also not as important as the packages themselves. Because of their organizational role, package diagrams have no behavior.

### 2.13.2    Putting Together a Package Diagram

Figure 2.13 shows four packages, namely, the `BusinessLogic`, the `Database`, the `GUI` and the `COM` package. The first three packages are business-level packages, and they have a two-way dependency on each other. The `COM` package is generic and is shown separately on this diagram, without any relationship. This does not mean that there is no relationship between `COM` and other packages. However, the `COM` package is generic and applies to all other packages in this system. Whenever relationship between packages is expressed, it indicates that the classes and components within a package will be using classes and components from other packages. Even without such explicit dependency, the diagram provides valuable information on how the system is organized.

### 2.13.3    Specifications of a Package Diagram

Specifications and associated documentation for a package depend on the needs of the system. At times, packages may not have separate documentation, as they are representative of a logical collection of use cases and classes—which have their

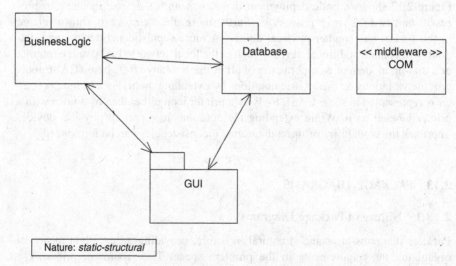

**Figure 2.13**    Nature and basics of a package diagram.

own specification and documentation. However, because packages are assigned to teams where many people will be dealing with one package, it is always very helpful to have some explanatory documentation for the package. This documentation can then be linked to the package shown within a CASE tool or it may be kept separately as a high-level description of the package. The documentation for a package can include information such as the nature of the package (e.g., technical, business, third party or reusable), assignment of the package to a corresponding team, and possibly further details on leveling of packages.

## 2.14  TIMING DIAGRAMS

### 2.14.1  Nature of Timing Diagrams

Timing diagrams are dynamic behavioral in nature, depicting the states of an object and the state changes at precise points in time. These diagrams are derived from the timing diagrams used in engineering to show state changes to an object. While a similar purpose is achieved by state machine diagrams, timing diagrams can show multiple objects and their corresponding states *at the same time*.

### 2.14.2  Putting Together a Timing Diagram

Figure 2.14 shows an example of a timing diagram. It shows the two states of a light bulb object—on and off. More important, it shows the exact point at which the state change is occurring and how long the object will remain in the on state (in this case, it is shown by the constraint {5 mins}) before returning to the off state. It is possible to show multiple objects in this diagram with their corresponding states and state changes. A comparison of state changes and dependencies between these state changes can be very interesting from a real-time modeling perspective. However, due to lack of CASE tool support, these diagrams have not been used extensively in practice.

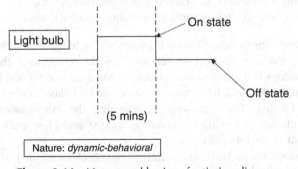

**Figure 2.14**  Nature and basics of a timing diagram.

## 2.15 UML'S EXTENSIBILITY MECHANISMS

The creators of UML envisaged its potential for wide-ranging applicability (perhaps more than they themselves could think of!). Therefore, in addition to the suite of UML diagrams discussed earlier, UML has the ability to extend itself. These methods are called the UML's "extensibility mechanisms." They include

- Stereotypes
- Notes
- Tagged values
- Constraints

These mechanisms can be applied to all diagrams and to most elements within the diagrams. They play a crucial role in classifying, organizing and providing additional information on the diagrams. This obviously has a bearing on the quality of the diagrams and the ability of the diagrams to express the semantics. We consider these four mechanisms especially from the point of view of quality.

### 2.15.1 Stereotypes

Stereotypes are "types of types" or "meta-types." This means that they can be used to classify almost all elements in UML. While they are mostly optional, they promote understanding of the diagrams by enabling a first-level grouping. Thus, by referring to a stereotype, it is possible to understand whether a particular element shown on a diagram is technical or business, whether it is a hardware device or software, or whether it belongs to a team of designers or business analysts.

In Figure 2.15 the notation for a stereotype is shown as double arrowheads (<< >>, also called "guillemots"). These double arrowheads are used to classify some example elements of UML as follows:

- Use cases (<<functional>>, other possibilities being <<technical>>)
- Classes (<<entity>>, compared to, say, <<boundary>> or <<controller>>)
- Node, being stereotyped as <<device>>
- Actors which themselves stereotype <<interface>> classes, representing <<user>> here. (Other example types being <<nonhuman>>, etc.)

Some stereotypes are mandatory—such as the <<include>> and <<extend>> stereotypes for use case-to-use case relationships. In other cases, the stereotype for the relationships is implicit in the symbol or icon used to represent that relationship. For example, the <<inheritance>> stereotype in a class-to-class relationship need not be labeled. The arrowhead representing the inheritance relationship between two classes makes that relationship unique and clear even without the stereotype label of <<inheritance>>.

Because extensions to UML are permitted, some elements in UML may have their own icons rather than labeling the elements with corresponding stereotypes.

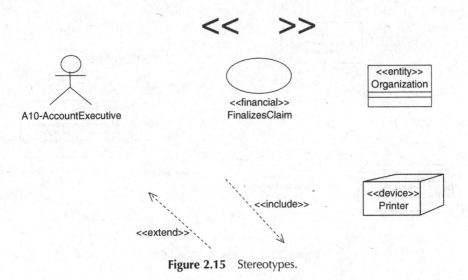

**Figure 2.15** Stereotypes.

However, care should be taken in creating and applying icons, as widely varying icons may impede readability of the diagrams—especially when readers are unfamiliar with the icons or notations used.

### 2.15.2 Notes

Notes are an excellent descriptive means of clarifying UML diagrams and providing further explanations of dependencies between elements of a UML diagram. This is very helpful, especially in structural static diagrams, where it is difficult to show dependencies. Notes are represented by a rectangle with a dog-eared corner.

Notes in a UML diagram are similar to comments in a well-written program. A few lines of comments in program source code go a long way toward explaining the rationale behind a difficult and/or complex piece of code. Similarly, judicious notes on a UML diagram can provide a lot of information and explanation that can help the reader of the diagram understand the deeper implied meaning behind the diagram.

Notes can contain textual comments, but may also contain graphics, detailed descriptions, links to Web pages, references to other documents and so on. Furthermore, notes themselves can be stereotyped to facilitate their grouping. This grouping or stereotyping of notes may depend on their purpose and the way they are used.

Figure 2.16A shows a note containing a text comment providing additional explanation wherever it is used. This note has also been stereotyped as <<comment>> rather than being used to express a dependency between two uses cases. Figure 2.16B shows another example of a note that describes how the actor Client will behave differently once it is an InternetClient. Figure 2.16C relates to a use case and an actor. Both have a precondition that needs to be satisfied, and that precondition is expressed easily and visibly by a note. Quality, especially of

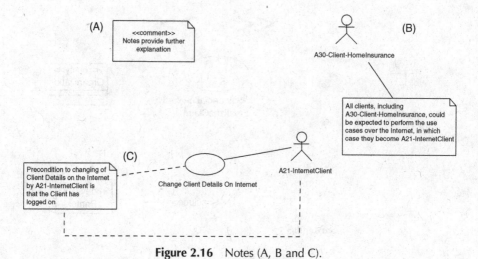

**Figure 2.16**   Notes (A, B and C).

MOPS, directly benefits from the use of notes, as users are able to explain things that would otherwise be difficult to clarify or would be misinterpreted.

### 2.15.3   Constraints

A constraint is an additional rule that the modeler can assign to the diagram to provide special significance to the whole diagram or some element(s) of it. Figure 2.17A shows a constraint on the actor-use case relationship. This constraint is that the CollectsClaimInformation use case will be {iteratively exe cuted}—implying that other use cases like, say, RegisterClaim will be executed followed by additional execution of CollectInformation. Another

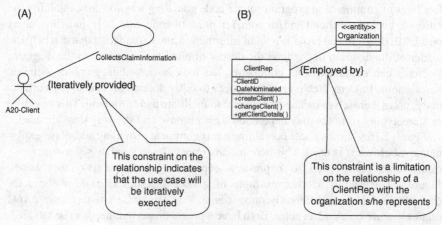

**Figure 2.17**   Constraints (A, B).

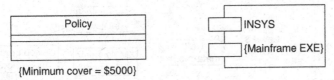

**Figure 2.18**  Tagged values.

example of a constraint, shown in Figure 2.17B, is in the class-to-class relationship. This constraint shows that the class ClientRepresentative relates to an Organization class in the capacity of an {employee}.

### 2.15.4  Tagged Values

Tagged values enable us to extend UML by allowing modelers to create new properties for the existing and standard modeling elements. For example, in Figure 2.18, a Policy class has a tagged value indicating that minimum Policy coverage is for $5000. This means that every time Policy is referred to within an insurance system, it will have a minimal cover for $5000 irrespective of any other business logic. Another example of tagged value is shown on the component INSYS in Figure 2.18. This tag indicates that every time the INSYS executable is run, it will do so on the mainframe.

## 2.16  UML META-MODELS AND QUALITY

Improving the quality of UML diagrams has one more dimension that may not be available to modeling techniques that are not based on the rigors of a meta-model: OMG's four-level meta-model architecture. Of the four levels, Level 2, which is a comprehensive meta-model for UML, has caused significant debate among modeling thinkers and authors of software modeling. Meta-models play a vital role in enhancing the quality of UML, for they lay down the basic rules of modeling that are binding on the developers and extenders of UML and the CASE tool vendors. Meta-models are more like barriers on a freeway. They work to *prevent* fundamental modeling errors rather than merely correct them. Also, most well-known CASE tools comply with the UML meta-model, enabling a certain standard across the industry. Needless to say, this has had a major impact in improving communication and, thereby, quality.

Figure 2.19 shows how that facility can be used to create a meta-model, how that meta-model, in turn, provides rules for creation of a model, and eventually how this model controls the quality of the instances. This is possible because the meta-model provides the rigors and rules that the diagrams have to abide by; and it is those meta-model rules, rather than specific notational standards, that the diagrams have to comply with, enabling CASE tool vendors to develop UML-based modeling tools (discussed in Appendix B) to suit the roles that will be using the tools.

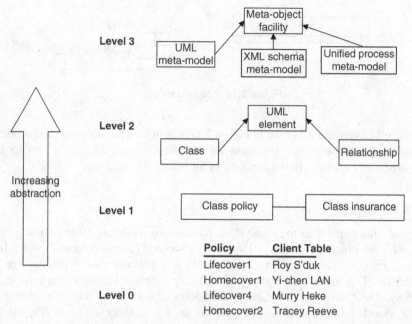

**Figure 2.19**    Practical application of OMG's meta-models to improve the quality of UML diagrams.

The Level 2 UML meta-model (see Figure 2.19) describes the rules that govern the relationships between elements on the diagram as well as among various diagrams. For example, the UML meta-model can state that class specifications have attributes and operations. This sets the rule for the relationship between a class and its corresponding attributes and operations. This rule simply ensures that it is a class that contains attributes and not the reverse, as such, and any CASE tool that wants to provide the facility for class diagrams will have to conform to this rule.

Meta-models enable UML to be extended in its visual representation (notations and diagrams) so long as it conforms to the UML meta-model. It is then left up to the users of UML to implement the extensions to it, guided by the objectives of the project. Although all UML-based CASE tools comply with the diagramming requirements of OMG, some tools are more conducive to sketching UML diagrams in the problem space, whereas others are more technical in nature and appropriate for the solution space.

A further extension to this level of modeling, and mixing it with the concrete modeling Level 1, was presented at TOOLS31 in Nanjing, China, by Lauder and Kent (1999). In recounting their experience in a paper titled "Two-Level Modelling," they state:

> The second realization was that it is possible to model directly from the UML meta-model without being constrained by the limits of the standard syntax, and this has the potential to enhance the richness of a model significantly. (p. 108)

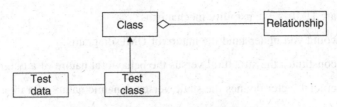

Read at the meta-model level, this diagram states
the rules for a class. It states that a
class has relationships. The rules can be
further extended to mandate that a test class is
derived from a class. A test class would use test data.
Note that this is not a level 1 class diagram.

**Figure 2.20**  Example of extending the UML meta-model to enforce quality controls.

The richness of the meta-model can and should be used to enhance the quality of the individual models. Take the case of a class diagram. At Level 1, this diagram represents the business entities within the problem domain, which are then enhanced in the solution domain by language-level classes. At Level 2, the meta-model level, we draw a class diagram that does *not* represent any business entities but instead represents the class and its relationships.

This is shown in Figure 2.20, where a class is shown having an aggregation relationship with `Relationship`. This meta-model is further extended to indicate that a test class is derived from a class. This is equivalent to extending the rules that put the UML elements of a class together to ensure that whenever a test class is created for unit testing of a class, that test class is derived from the class. This rule can be stated as "A test class is derived from the class it will test." Furthermore, this test class is shown as associated with a test data class, as shown in Figure 2.20. While the test class and test data are both types of classes, this "combination of UML users" thinking and the OMG standard meta-model can lead to creative quality assurance work—as shown in this example. This is equivalent to creating a pattern for quality. To an extent, pattern-based thinking extends the meta-models for particular projects.

## DISCUSSION TOPICS

1. Where can UML be applied or used?

2. Why is UML considered elastic?

3. What are the caveats in applying the elasticity of UML?

4. How does one balance the visual modeling capabilities and specification and documentation capabilities of UML?

5. What is a meta-model? How does it contribute to the elasticity of UML?

6. List the UML diagrams and describe each one briefly.

7. What are UML's extensibility mechanisms?

8. How would you understand the nature of UML diagrams?

9. What constitutes the structural versus the behavioral nature of a diagram?

10. What crucial factor defines the static versus dynamic nature of a diagram?

11. Why is a use case diagram considered behavioral rather than dynamic in nature?

12. Which UML diagram is considered dynamic yet structural in nature?

13. What is a stereotype?

14. What are the major modeling spaces in software that can use UML?

15. What are the two most important diagrams in creating MOPS? Why?

16. What are the two most important diagrams in creating MOSS? Why?

17. What are the two most important diagrams in creating MOBS? Why?

## REFERENCES

Booch, G., Rumbaugh, J., and Jacobson, I. *The Unified Modelling Language User Guide.* Reading, MA: Addison-Wesley, 1999.

Beck, K., and Cunningham, W. "Languages and Applications," *Proceedings of Conference on OO Programming Systems.* New Orleans, LA: ACM Press, NY, 1989, pp. 1–6.

Constantine, L., and Lockwood, L. *Software for Use: A Practical Guide to the Models and Methods of Usage-Centered Design.* Reading, MA: Addison-Wesley, 1999. See also www.foruse.com.

Douglass, B.P. *Doing Hard Time: Developing Real-Time Systems with UML, Objects, Frameworks and Patterns.* Reading, MA: Addison-Wesley, 1999.

Douglass, B.P. *Real-Time Design Patterns: Robust Scalable Architecture for Real-Time Systems.* Reading, MA: Addison Wesley Professional, 2003.

Jacobson, I., Christerson, M., Jonsson, P., and Övergaard, G. *Object Oriented Software Engineering: A Use Case Driven Approach.* Reading, MA: Addison-Wesley, 1992.

Lauder, A., and Kent, S. "Two-Level Modelling," *Technology of OO Languages and Systems, (TOOLS 31)*, J. Chen, J. Lu, and B. Meyer, eds. Nanjing, China: IEEE Computer Society, 1999, pp. 108–117.

Rumbaugh, J., Jacobson, I., and Booch, G. *The Unified Modelling Language Reference Manual.* Reading, MA: Addison Wesley Longman, 1999.

Chapter **3**

# Strengths, Weaknesses, Objectives and Traps (SWOT) of UML Diagrams

A sword is strong in severing, and a needle in stitching. Role reversal renders both weak![1]

## CHAPTER SUMMARY

This chapter discusses the characteristics of the UML diagrams in terms of their inherent strengths and weaknesses and their objectives and traps in practice—the SWOT analysis of UML diagrams. The chapter builds on the previous chapter and creates a deeper understanding of the UML diagrams from a quality viewpoint. As a result, modelers are able to understand and use the subset of diagrams that is relevant to their roles in the problem, solution and background modeling spaces.

As noted in the previous chapters, UML has an expansive suite of diagrams that can help modeling in projects of varying types and sizes. It was also mentioned that proper usage of the UML diagrams is akin to selecting the right tool from a toolbox for the right job. This understanding is reinforced in this chapter by a detailed understanding of the characteristics of UML diagrams. Armed with full knowledge of the nature, ingredients, basics (as discussed in Chapter 2) and characteristics of all the UML diagrams (as discussed in this chapter), the modeler has already advanced a long way in his quest for quality.

[1]Source: Unknown.

---

*Verification and Validation for Quality of UML 2.0 Models*, by Bhuvan Unhelkar
Copyright © 2005 John Wiley & Sons, Inc.

## 3.1  SWOT ANALYSIS OF THE UML DIAGRAMS

Characteristics of the UML diagrams are divided into two groups: intrinsic and extrinsic. UML diagrams have some basic or *intrinsic* characteristics that they exhibit irrespective of the type or size of the project in which they are used. These intrinsic characteristics of the diagrams are both their strengths and their weaknesses. UML diagrams also have *extrinsic* characteristics, which become important when these diagrams are applied in creating practical models. These extrinsic characteristics are dependent not only on the modeling spaces in which the diagrams are used, but also on the type of project in which they are applied. It is therefore possible that a diagram that provides a lot of value to one modeler and is extremely important in one modeling space may not be of much relevance to a different modeler in a different modeling space. The relevance can shift even with different project types and project sizes. For example, a use case diagram in a data warehousing project will not provide the same advantages of quality and relevance as in, say, a new development project. Thus, the extrinsic characteristics of the UML diagrams are derived from the particular objectives of the project in which the diagrams are used.

The study of the intrinsic and extrinsic characteristics of UML diagrams has been dubbed SWOT analysis (Figure 3.1). Following is a description of what is included in SWOT analysis.

- Strengths—intrinsic strengths of the diagram represented by the reason for having that diagram in UML. The strength of the diagram remains the same irrespective of the modeling space, roles of people, and type and size of the project.
- Weaknesses—intrinsic weaknesses of the diagram that are due primarily to the lack of modeling capabilities of that diagram, irrespective of the modeling space, roles of people, and type and size of the project.

| | Strengths | Weaknesses |
|---|---|---|
| **Intrinsic** | Strengths represent the intrinsic (inherent) positive characteristics of the diagrams irrespective of where they are used. | Weaknesses represent the intrinsic (inherent) negative characteristics of the diagram irrespective of where they are used. |
| | **Objectives** | **Traps** |
| **Extrinsic** | Represent the purpose of the diagram in practical modeling in the modeling spaces. | Represent the problems/traps encountered in usage of the diagram in the modeling spaces. |

**Figure 3.1**  SWOT analysis of UML diagrams.

- Objectives—extrinsic *usage* or purposes of the diagram when applied in a particular modeling space. The objectives can also change, depending on the project size and type. Objectives help narrow the focus of the UML diagrams in application, thereby capitalizing on their practical value in the context of a project.
- Traps—problems faced by practitioners when they start using the UML diagrams in projects. Obviously, the traps also vary, depending on the project characteristics. While the traps in using UML diagrams are known to many practitioners, those trying out UML for the first time find that the traps in using the diagrams usually become apparent *after* the modelers have tried them out in projects. Upfront knowledge of these traps is very helpful in focusing the project team's effort to improve the quality of these diagrams. This is because such knowledge not only helps users avoid these traps, but it also clarifies further the objectives of the diagrams.

In the remainder of this chapter, we undertake SWOT analysis of the UML diagrams by approaching each diagram from the point of view of its inherent strengths and weaknesses followed by its objectives and traps with reference to projects of various types and sizes. This provides a solid basis for the syntax, semantics and aesthetic checks of these UML diagrams described in the next three chapters (for each of the modeling spaces and their models—MOPS, MOSS and MOBS, respectively).

## 3.2 SWOT OF USE CASE DIAGRAMS

### 3.2.1 Strengths of Use Cases and Use Case Diagrams

One of the important strengths of a use case diagram is its ability to model the actor (role, as per Fowler, 2003). The actor demonstrates clearly to the user—who is involved in specifying requirements—where he exists in the context of the software system. The actor also plays a crucial role in enabling the business analyst to understand and document the user's requirements. In addition, the actor helps users to express their requirements in greater detail. Once the users see themselves represented on the use case diagram, they find it easier and more attractive (expressive) to explain what they want from the system and how they plan to use it. This involvement of users at a very early stage of the development life cycle is one of the major contributions of use case diagrams in software projects.

By their very nature, use case diagrams facilitate discussions among various parties involved in requirements modeling. The business analysts, users and designers of the system are able to see pictorially the structure of their system. Such visual representation is of immense value to the information architect in creating the system architecture.

Use cases and use case diagrams help to organize the requirements. The notation for a use case represents a cohesive set of interactions between the user and the system. By simply referring to a use case, a complex set of interaction can be accessed easily, thereby simplifying the discussions.

Use cases document complete functional requirements. Thus, for projects using use cases and use case diagrams, no separate functional requirements document is needed, although additional operational and interface requirements or additional details such as mathematical formulas may be placed in a separate document.

The three relationships of include, extend and generalize between use cases provide means to extend and reuse requirements. This ability of use case diagrams to enable reuse and extension of requirements is one of their major strengths. Actors can also be generalized in use case diagrams. The ability to show pictorially an abstract actor that deals with the most common users of the system is a major strength of use case diagrams.

Use cases facilitate tracing of requirements. By providing well-organized documentation of the requirements, a use case creates a trace for a particular requirement throughout the system. This is very helpful in creating and executing acceptance tests by the user.

Use case diagrams also provide an excellent mechanism to document the context of the system. By creating a system boundary, it is possible to clearly visualize what is inside the system as compared with external entities in the system, including the users.

Use case diagrams provide high-level workflow *across* the boundary of the system. This creates an understanding of the major internal and external functionalities of the system.

Use case diagrams form the basis for creation and documentation of use cases. Therefore, they also help identify major components, objects and functions of a system.

### 3.2.2    Weaknesses of Use Cases and Use Case Diagrams

Use cases themselves have no formal documentation standard. This leads to confusion and debates on what comprises a good use case. Most projects proceed on the basis of a predetermined standard for documenting use cases (one such template is provided in Chapter 4). However, this lack of standards creates an opportunity for modelers and project managers to develop their own standards, as well as their own interpretation of what needs to be documented.

As discussed in detail in the previous chapter, use cases are not intrinsically object-oriented. Use cases appeared on the software modeling scene through their original use in object-oriented modeling by Jacobson, as mentioned in Chapter 2. However, they are not an ideal mechanism to model design-level constructs in the solution space (where object orientation plays an important role).

The meaning behind the association or communication relationship between the actor and the corresponding use case is not clear. If the actor initiating the use case is a human actor, then the convention is to show an arrowhead pointing to the use case. However, if the use case represents a series of interactions between the actor and the system, the arrowhead on the association between the actor and the use case does not make sense. The same confusion can exist in the relationship between a use case and a corresponding actor representing an interface to an external system.

Use case-to-use case relationships are also not precise, leading to confusion. For example, generalization between use cases will be imprecise, as there are no well-defined attributes and operations in a use case. The other two relationships, include and extend, may also be confusing, as at times it is possible to visually represent the requirements with either of the two relationships.

While use cases themselves document business processes, use case diagrams do not exhibit any sequential flow and do not depict any dependency. Thus use case diagrams are not an ideal mechanism to show the flow between different entities within the system.

Use cases and use case diagrams do not have a granularity standard. Therefore, sometimes, use cases are written as huge descriptive documents, preventing the modelers from capitalizing on the reusable and organizational aspects of use case modeling. Alternatively, too brief a description results in a large number of minuscule use cases, making them less comprehensible and manageable.

### 3.2.3 Objectives of Use Cases and Use Case Diagrams

The main objective of a use case diagram is to visualize how the user (represented by the actor) will interact with and use the system. This is done by showing the actor associating with one or more use cases and, additionally, by drawing many use case diagrams. The rest of the objectives follow from this main objective.

The main objective of the use case (compared to a use case diagram) is to document a process within the system. This is the documentation (content) of the functional requirement of the system. "Almost all the value of use cases lies in the content, and the diagram is of rather limited value" (Fowler, 2003, p. 100).

Use case diagrams can be used by the project manager to scope the requirements. The system designer (or architect) can use them to start creating her model in the solution space. For an interesting discussion on the relevance of use case modeling to the various stakeholders in the project, see Armour and Miller (2001).

An important purpose of use case diagrams is to help schedule development. A comprehensive list of use cases in a use case diagram helps the users, together with the business analyst and the project manager, to decide which use case(s) to include in the initial iteration of the development cycle. Without the techniques of use cases, the standard descriptive requirements would require more time and effort in their scoping and prioritization.

Prioritization and scheduling of use cases also provide a means of risk reduction by enabling users and business analysts to provide reasons for their priorities. Based on a mutually agreed-upon ranking system, users can specify the most important and/or high-risk use cases, which would be included in the scope of the first iteration.

Use cases can be very helpful in producing proof of concepts. Developers can start coding prototypes from use cases, get the users involved at an early stage by means of feedback and create great interest among the users. Use cases can also be used to develop a close relationship between the user and the developer.

Use case diagrams can help project managers estimate time and budgets for the project. While not always accurate, this method of estimating time and budgets based on the number of use cases to be developed, their complexity and their priority is far better than estimating without them. An initial scoping exercise can reveal the approximate number of use cases to be developed. Figures for the time and budgets needed to develop a use case can be acquired from past projects (if the organization has a history of using UML) or from industry sources. Based on this understanding of the time and effort needed to develop a use case, and the total number of use cases based on the initial scoping exercise, reasonable estimates for time and budgets for the entire project can be developed. As the organization—and the industry—matures in its use of UML, the margins in estimations will become more accurate. However, unless the use cases are granularized and/or drilled down, it becomes difficult for the project manager to make estimations based on a high-level use case.

Use cases and use case diagrams also provide excellent support in package implementation projects. The challenge for use case diagrams used in package-based projects is huge. As most package-based projects already come with their own business rules, the challenge for use cases is to define requirements for already existent objects. Here is where use cases can be very helpful in defining the outcome of customizable package-based software. Although one should be careful while reengineering business processes, the basic principles of process-based business processes must be kept in mind; otherwise, the result is an unwieldy process with a very weak foundation—a recipe for disaster. In these projects, major work is required in specifying the requirements (as the solution package will already contain most of the code). Use case diagrams provide an ideal mechanism to document the requirements in MOPS.

Documentation of the use case provides means for creating activity diagrams. The documentation of the flow within the use case can also be influenced and improved by the activity diagram(s) drawn for a use case. Furthermore, specifications and documentation of use cases provide a rich source of information for the identification of business entities. These business entities can be put together in a suite of class diagrams, providing vital information in MOPS. Sequence diagrams can also be created for scenarios within a use case, enabling complete documentation of the requirements in text and in visual forms.

Documentation of a use case can provide most of the functional description of the system's requirements. This documentation includes the name and number of the use case, its pre- and postconditions, the list of actors associated with the use case and, most important, the text of the use case (which describes the basic course of action by interacting with the system), the alternate flows, the exception flows and the constraints. This is discussed in greater detail, with examples, in Chapter 4.

### 3.2.3.1 E-Commerce Applications
E-commerce applications are different from the normal client-server-type applications, particularly in the way they are accessed. An Internet-based e-commerce application could be accessed by any

person from any location. This requires the business analyst to understand all the possible types of end users who will be accessing the system.

The architecture of the e-commerce system must also consider unknown hardware, operating systems and operational environments, which otherwise would have been under the control of the system administrators. Use cases and use case diagrams facilitate the capture of requirements in these situations because of their ability to model actors and document interactions. By conducting walkthroughs of use cases and use case diagrams, it is possible to ascertain these operational requirements, which can then be documented separately in operational specifications.

***3.2.3.2 Use Cases and Contract Management*** Use cases enable better understanding of the project requirements, especially when the parties involved in development are geographically and culturally dispersed. This is true for outsourced projects, where the requirements are specified in a location distant from the one where the actual development will take place. Outsourced projects have a far greater need for accurate specification of requirements, as two separate organizations and many parties are involved in development. Furthermore, if maintenance is part of the contract, it is essential to document the requirements visually through use cases. For example, a high-risk or crucial use case will have to be maintained in the system at an appropriately high level of priority. This requires the outsourced partner to understand the use case, maintain it and charge for it according to its importance. Commonly accepted and easily understandable notations are far better than long-winded descriptions as a basis for outsourcing contracts. Thus, because of the acceptance of UML standards, use cases provide an excellent rationale for outsourced projects.

***3.2.3.3 Education and Use Case Diagrams*** Use cases instill discipline in students learning the skills of business analysis. They also inform programming students that although the eventual aim of this modeling is to produce code, that code is not the only thing happening in a quality-conscious software project. Furthermore, use cases highlight how the actual activity of coding happens later in the software development life cycle. Students learn that earlier activities in a project deal with understanding the problem, and that it is important to understand the problem properly and formally without rushing to develop a solution. Analysis of a well-documented use case is another learning experience, as the business entities discovered are based on the requirements specified, and not casually placed in the business class diagrams.

### 3.2.4 Traps of Use Cases and Use Case Diagrams

Use cases do not cover nonfunctional (operational) requirements, although they may allude to them. Hence, one of the major traps of use cases and use case diagrams is to assume that all requirements have been documented in them. The operational aspects of the system (such as speed, security, volume and performance) cannot be easily documented in a use case model.

Each use case shown on a use case diagram represents a set of interactions between the actor and the system. This interaction is documented *within* a use case—in its appropriate documentation. Initial adopters of use case diagrams tend to ignore the associated documentation and remain at the diagram level. This is a trap that should be avoided by producing documentation associated with the use cases.

For larger projects, where writing of "remaining" use cases in the last scheduled package and the development of the first may happen in parallel, it is helpful to keep provisions in use case writing for changes that occur due to the influence of solutions development. If use cases are finalized in a single attempt, with no provision for changes, this will lead to an inferior requirement.

Since one of the main objectives of use case diagrams is to model the problem space, any attempt to use these diagrams in solution and architectural spaces will lead to confusion within the project and should be avoided. Use cases and use case diagrams should be used as requirements modeling techniques, not as system design techniques.

Attempting to code directly from use cases is a major trap in practice and should be avoided. More often than not, developers are eager to get hold of use cases and try to produce code directly from them. This can lead to confusion, because without proper business class diagrams (and eventually system class diagrams), the development effort will not be precise and focused. Use cases should lead to good class diagrams, from which the coding activities should be carried out. Use cases should not be used directly for coding.

People with DFD experience tend to draw use case diagrams containing a *flow*. The relationships of include and extend in use case diagrams actually represent an encapsulated form of requirements, not a flow within the system. If there is a genuine need to represent a flow, activity diagrams should be used instead of use case diagrams. Any flow *inside* a use case is also better represented by the activity diagrams attached to the use case.

An important trap to avoid in creating use case diagrams is to draw them in such a precise and pedantic fashion that there is an association line going from every actor to every use case on the diagram. Such diagrams tend to look like a spider's web. This trap can be avoided by drawing many use case diagrams, each focused on a particular subject area. Since it is possible for a use case and an actor to appear in more than one use case diagram, it is acceptable to draw more than one such diagram, focusing on a particular area of the requirements, rather than cluttering a single diagram with all of the actors and use cases.

Creating a project plan based on use cases is a well-known trap for project managers attempting UML-based development for the first time. Use cases to class mapping will be a many-to-many mapping. Solution-level classes are modeled and coded in the solution space. Therefore, programmers should be assigned the solution-level classes and components—not the use cases. If the project plan is created based on use cases, it will soon be embroiled in the unenviable situation of two programmers trying to check out a single class because the two use cases assigned to them have functionality that needs to be coded in the same class. Thus, programmers should not be assigned use cases.

Attempting to model "batch processing" applications with use cases is another trap that should be avoided. This is because batch applications (e.g., applications that deal with performing calculations in the background or printing bank statements overnight) do not have the same interactions between actors and the system that other applications (particularly Web applications) have. Using use cases to model what is happening in the background of the system will not provide a good model.

Other than indicating where the user interfaces will be, use cases cannot handle in great detail the user interface aspect of the system. Therefore, use cases should not be used for detailed usability designs. However, use cases can be used to verify the usability designs.

While use cases can be used to develop prototypes, these prototypes should not evolve into the final solution. Converting prototypes into final solutions may lead to a suboptimal design.

Using use case diagrams in an intense data warehousing and/or data conversion application is not recommended. This is because these data-intense applications have far more structural elements in their designs than behavioral elements. Use cases, as a mechanism to document behavioral aspect of the system, are unable to do the job that, say, a class diagram showing relational tables can do. Therefore, use cases should not be used extensively in applications that need mostly data modeling. Instead, class diagrams should be considered in greater detail for this type of modeling.

## 3.3 SWOT OF ACTIVITY DIAGRAMS

### 3.3.1 Strengths of Activity Diagrams

Activity diagrams model the flow within the system. This is because they are like flowcharts and are behavioral-static in nature. Thus, one of the major strengths of activity diagrams is their ability to show flows within a use case or among use cases and also in the entire system. Activity diagrams complement use case diagrams by visually showing the *internals* of a use case.

Activity diagrams are able to show multiple flows happening simultaneously within the system. This, as discussed in Chapter 2, is accomplished by means of the forks and joins (derived from the sync points) on the activity diagrams. "An activity graph is like a traditional flow chart except [that] it permits concurrent control in addition to sequential control—a big difference" (Fowler, 2003). This difference between an activity diagram and a flowchart is one of the major strengths of the activity diagram.

Another important concept shown on an activity diagram (which is different from a flowchart) is that of partitions. Partitions neatly categorize activities within the activity diagram based on dependencies among activities and their cohesiveness. They also provide an opportunity to document not only the flow but also the role that is responsible for that flow.

Activity diagrams acts as a bridge between use case and sequence diagrams. This enables the text-based documentation of the use cases to be shown pictorially in activity diagrams. At the same time, activity diagrams also enable a high-level view of what happens at the object level in sequence diagrams.

Notes, appropriately appearing on the activity diagrams, enable easier reading and understanding of the diagrams for users with no technical background. Explanations of the activities, their dependencies and the decisions points all provide excellent user-level documentation. Activity diagrams have also been used in training users new to a system.

### 3.3.2   Weaknesses of Activity Diagrams

Activity diagrams have no structural characteristics, and they do not provide direct information on how the system or the requirements are organized and prioritized.

Activity diagrams represent use case behavior pictorially. However, they do not usually give a complete picture of the system. For large and complex use cases, multiple activity diagrams are required. The inability of activity diagram to view the full requirements of the system at a glance is their weakness.

Activity diagrams depict process flow. Therefore, they should be used whenever there is a need to show dependencies between activities. If used for organizational purposes, they will lose the value they add to the requirements model.

### 3.3.3   Objectives of Activity Diagrams

Activity diagrams, like flowcharts, show the flow of a process. Therefore, they are ideal for documenting use cases and system flows in practice. This ability of activity diagrams to visually model a use case is important in new development as well as package implementation projects, where requirements in the problem space need to be modeled in greater detail than in other types of projects.

Activity diagrams are easily understood by people new to UML. Therefore, at times, it is easier to start a requirements modeling workshop with an activity diagram. This is especially true if users participating in workshops are new to the concept of modeling.

Activity diagrams can provide documentation on the use of a system. Therefore, they can be inserted in user manuals and help files. In such cases, notes to explain the diagrams should be used in abundance.

Activity diagrams can also be used in business process engineering, where they document the existing business processes followed by the reengineered processes.

Activity diagrams are also used in documenting processes themselves. For example, a software development process can be documented using a series of activity diagrams (see Unhelkar, 2003, on process documentation with activity diagrams).

Since activity diagrams show multiple threads, they can be used to optimize both business and system processes. This is because, through multiple threads, a group of processes running in parallel can be captured and modeled. Once modeled, they can be refined and optimized.

### 3.3.4 Traps of Activity Diagrams

Activity diagrams can become very complicated if every aspect of the process is documented within the same diagram. Therefore, when documenting a large and complex use case, it is recommended that two or three activity diagrams be drawn.

Activity diagrams in the earlier versions of UML had their origins in and links to state machine diagrams. Therefore, modelers confused the activity diagrams with state machines. This trap can be avoided by keeping in mind that activities are not states. Similarly, modelers experienced with DFDs should avoid the trap of considering activity diagrams as a type of DFD.

The scope of an activity diagram is within a use case or a business process. Different *types* of processes cannot be shown on a single activity diagram. Attempts to do so will lead to unwieldy activity diagrams.

Although activity diagrams are used in the solution space, unless a system is multithreaded and multitasked, activity diagrams do not add great value in this space.

Modelers are prone to assume that the activity flow within the activity diagram includes time lines. However, activity diagrams do not display times and hence are not considered dynamic.

## 3.4 SWOT OF CLASSES AND CLASS DIAGRAMS

### 3.4.1 Strengths of Classes and Class Diagrams

Class diagrams, by their very nature, are very strong, structural, static representations. As a result, they are able to represent not only the entities in MOPS but also the implementation classes in MOSS, as well as third-party and reusable classes in the background space. A major strength of class diagrams is, therefore, their ability to show the structure of a problem or solution.

Class diagrams were used earlier to model the problem exclusively (e.g., in the earlier Booch and OMT methods). The result was creation of a business domain model (BDM) using classes and class diagrams. In UML, it is still possible to use classes to represent business entities. Thus, a major strength of class diagrams is to represent business entities structurally in MOPS.

Class diagrams provide a modeling construct that is closest to coding. The attributes and operations provided in the classes are a "first cut" of the code. UML CASE tools can easily create class templates from class diagrams, depending on the language of implementation. Thus, class diagrams provide a ready basis for code generation in the solution space.

Classes, with their attributes and operations, are excellent means to incorporate good object-oriented principles such as encapsulation and polymorphism. The "private" attributes and "public" operations, for example, provide means for the modelers to ensure that classes are encapsulated.

Classes without their operations or responsibilities are entities, as represented in E-R diagrams. In other words, classes with only their attributes are entities. These entities easily represent the database tables. Therefore, another strength of class diagrams is their ability to represent relational database schemas in UML format.

Multiplicities on a class diagram are also helpful in relational database modeling. Depending on the multiplicities on an association between two classes, primary and foreign keys can be created and assigned to classes. This is further clarified in Chapter 6, where class designs are mapped to relational tables.

Class diagrams, through their relationship of inheritance, facilitate reuse. Reuse can improve productivity but, more important, it can improve quality. Therefore, one of the strengths of class diagrams is their ability to enhance quality and productivity through reuse.

Stereotyping of class diagrams is also an important mechanism to provide a proper architecture. GUI classes, entity classes and controller classes should be properly classified in order to ascertain which classes fit into which particular type. This is definitely an architectural decision or is influenced by the architect. There are also other types of classes, like data, helper or global classes, which should all be stereotyped correctly in order to improve understanding and readability—and eventually the quality of these class diagrams. This provides a major strength in terms of the ability to "cast" classes into relevant stereotypes to enhance the architecture. These stereotypes can also be used to enhance the requirements. In addition to class stereotyping, stereotyping of operations and attributes is allowed, but this should be done either later in the life cycle, during modeling of the solution space, or not done at all.

### 3.4.2   Weaknesses of Classes and Class Diagrams

Class diagrams do not have any dynamics. They have no concept of time. Therefore, they are only able to represent how the system is structured and what its relationships are. There is no opportunity to model an if-then-else scenario on a class diagram. Thus, class diagrams are extremely weak when it comes to modeling the dynamic-behavioral aspect of the system.

The class-to-class relationships of aggregation and variations of aggregation (composition) continue to create confusion in practical modeling exercises. This is because aggregation has many variations that do not have corresponding notations in the current UML. For example, within the aggregation relationship, the unfilled versus filled diamond on the aggregation relationship represents shared versus non-shared aggregation, respectively. This difference between the two types of aggregation is still being debated. As suggested in the section on putting together a class diagram in Chapter 2, the difference in the two types of aggregation in the problem space can be avoided in practice.

Multiplicity, as shown on class diagrams, can also sometimes lead to confusion. For example, in an aggregation relationship, the multiplicity shown on the diamond side of the aggregation can create misunderstanding, as the aggregator side of the relationship should, by default, be 1 to satisfy a whole-part relationship.

### 3.4.3 Objectives of Classes and Class Diagrams

The objective of class diagrams is to represent—in one or more views—various business entities and their relationships in MOPS. In MOSS, class diagrams provide the solution model, which is very close to implementation.

Class diagrams provide detailed design including reusable classes in the solution space. Thus class diagrams are meant to provide a means of discussion during later stages of formalizing the problem space as well as throughout the solution space.

Classes and class diagrams are meant to represent entities that are derived by analyzing the use cases and problem statements in MOPS. Therefore, the objective of class diagrams is to take the modeling within use cases to the next level of formality and detail.

Class diagrams enable creation of good relational database models. This is because they map very well to relational tables. This ability of classes to map to tables can provide immense value to class diagramming in data warehousing projects.

Class diagrams, when related to sequence diagrams, are able to document messages as methods. This is further discussed in the section on cross-diagram dependencies between the class and sequence diagrams in Chapter 4.

Through inheritance, class diagrams provide the prime mechanism to enable class-to-class reuse—an important facet of the modeling work in the background space.

### 3.4.4 Traps of Classes and Class Diagrams

Class diagrams are often used at the wrong level, causing confusion and major errors. For example, when a business analyst is discussing with end users the major business entities in the system, it is *inappropriate* to introduce concepts of polymorphism or multiple inheritance into the discussion.

Class diagrams at the highest level or in MOPS should be used only to represent major business entities, followed by their attributes and responsibilities. In the solution space, class diagrams can contain a full list of all classes including the implementation-level classes. These classes will also be fully defined in terms of their initial values, the signatures of their operations and their visibility. These features are not used in the solution space, where the class diagrams are not complete and do not provide sufficient value to the programmer who is assigned that particular diagram. Thus it is important to keep the purpose or objective of the diagram in mind when it is being drawn or used.

Code generation from class diagrams can be helpful but can also be a trap. In iterative and incremental development, it is important to note that code generation during each iteration may not be helpful and can have undesirable consequences. It should also be kept in mind that in UML class diagrams, the same class diagram can be shown with some of its features hidden; for example, attributes and operations can be hidden. Showing the right features to the right audience is extremely important. If that is not done, then the audience will not understand the relevance of the diagram. For example, an end user shown all the features, including visibility, will not consider the diagram relevant and may find it too complicated to understand.

On the other hand, a programmer who is shown or given a class diagram without the visibility features will code according to his fancy. It is therefore important to make good use of CASE tools in showing or hiding visibilities and providing the right level of features to the right person.

Reverse engineering or creating class models from relational databases should be done carefully, ensuring that such classes contain only the database functionalities in their operations. If the operations or the responsibilities section of the classes contain business logic, this will lead to the trap of mixing functional behavior with database behavior. In such cases, where the responsibilities of the classes that represent relational tables also include business logic, the architecture of the system will be semantically and aesthetically wrong. Ideally, all the business logic should be in the middleware or on the server side.

Using classes to model tables may mean that the concepts of object orientation are not faithfully maintained in such diagrams. This is not to say that such class diagrams are incorrect. What is meant here is that if class diagrams are used to model tables, then most of the object-oriented fundamentals—like inheritance and encapsulation—will not make sense.

## 3.5   SWOT OF SEQUENCE DIAGRAMS

### 3.5.1   Strengths of Sequence Diagrams

The sequence diagram shows a time line of events that happen in the system. Therefore, a sequence diagram is a time-based representation of messages in the system.

Since the sequence diagram is dynamic, it shows exactly what happens when a particular flow through a use case or an activity thread in an activity diagram is executed. By its nature, the sequence diagram is capable of showing a time-based sequence of actions or events.

A sequence diagram also shows a set of collaborating objects, in addition to showing the messages that pass between them. It is thus an ideal snapshot of what happens. Occasionally it is called a "scenario" because it shows objects (instead of classes) on the diagram. The sequence diagram is thus an example representation of what happens in the use case rather than a generic representation.

As an "instance diagram," a sequence diagram is also capable of showing multiple objects belonging to the same class on the diagram. For example, a sequence diagram can contain two or more claim objects (aClaim and bClaim) belonging to class Claim. We are unable to show two such objects derived from the same class on a class diagram.

Sequence diagrams can also show the same message being passed between two or more objects more than once. For example, if aPolicy object sends a message called 'verifyClaim' to aClaim, then, after a few more messages, the same message, verifyClaim, can be sent to aClaim again. The ability of sequence diagrams to display multiple objects, multiple messages and messages passed to the same objects provides some of the dynamic strengths of the diagram.

From a programmer's perspective, a normal flow of events is shown in a sequence diagram, whereas the exception cases may not be shown at all or may be described as text on the diagram. Occasionally, it may be shown on a separate diagram. The programmer is then able to review all these sequence diagrams and their notes, and get a comprehensive picture of what she has to build. Thus, sequence diagrams provide a pictorial dynamic representation of the sequence of messages in a system and, thereby, provide valuable input to the programmer.

### 3.5.2 Weaknesses of Sequence Diagrams

A sequence diagram, as a snapshot between two time frames, is in a way incomplete. It is not meant to show a complete process or flow, which is documented within a use case from start to stop. Therefore, it should not be used for complete process documentation.

Sequence diagrams are also not structural in nature and therefore are unable to show any structural relationships between classes. Thus, although sequence diagrams can be used to identify missing classes, they cannot be used to identify precise structural relationships between classes.

Although they show behavior in a temporal sequence, sequence diagrams are not pure dynamic diagrams. This is because they show messages exchanged during a particular time or period but are unable to show changes to the state of the object or changes to the values of the attributes of an object.

It is difficult to show an if-then-else or a for-next condition on sequence diagrams. Therefore, these diagrams should not be used to depict such scenarios.

The sequence diagram is able to represent only a single flow or thread within a process. Multiple threads require multiple sequence diagrams for appropriate modeling. However, there is still no relationship *between* two sequence diagrams. (This weakness of sequence diagrams has now been obviated with the advent of interaction overview diagrams in UML 2.0, which can show multiple threads as well as if-then-else scenarios encompassing many sequence diagrams.)

### 3.5.3 Objectives of Sequence Diagrams

Sequence diagrams are used wherever there is a need to show messages between a set of collaborating objects. This ability to show collaborating objects and the message flow between them is a major purpose of sequence diagrams.

Sequence diagrams explain to the programmer in the solution space when and where data need to be stored in the database. They also model the "when and what" of displaying fields on a Web page or perform functions such as developing client side scripts.

Another important purpose of the sequence diagram is to uncover missing objects and messages. By drawing a sequence diagram even on a whiteboard or using pencil and paper, a business analyst can ascertain missing objects and thereby missing classes.

Sequence diagrams are also used to show a scenario within a use case and therefore a user story. This means that a sequence diagram can show pictorially what a user describes as an example. It provides a mechanism to build storyboards. Thus, an additional objective of the sequence diagram is to provide a visual mechanism to build storyboards with the users.

Technically, the message signatures of sequence diagrams provide information in terms of parameters to be passed by one object to another. These message signatures also provide information on return values of those messages.

Sequence diagrams explain to the programmer when data need to be stored in the database and when it is merely necessary to display fields on a Web page or perform functions such as developing client side scripts. Not all data shown on a screen need to be stored in a database.

These diagrams can be used in a variety of projects to model message passing to external systems and databases. In practice, many patterns are documented using sequence diagrams (database interface pattern), providing a basis for new sequence diagrams with enhanced quality.

### 3.5.4   Traps of Sequence Diagrams

One of the major traps of sequence diagrams is an attempt to complete the diagram—that is, to show every possible sequence, as well as an entire sequence from creation of objects to their destruction.

Attempting to show if-then-else scenarios can create confusion within sequence diagrams. Even if notes are added to the diagram, they will not be able to represent these optional executions. This is a trap in practice.

Creating a sequence diagram to model each exception or alternative scenario will lead to numerous sequence diagrams with generally similar information. This trap can be avoided by adding notes to the diagrams explaining the exceptions or alternative flows.

Inappropriate level of usage of sequence diagrams is another trap. Like most UML diagrams entered using a CASE tool, the sequence diagram can also be switched on and off at varying levels. Attempting to keep all features of the diagram on is a trap and should be avoided in practice. For example, "focus of control," which is a major aspect of sequence diagrams, may not add much value at a very high business analysis level. Trying to show such things as focus of control or creation and destruction of objects should be avoided in high-level, first-cut or MOPS level of work. Experience has shown that attempting to draw a complete sequence of a particular use case or activity diagram within a sequence diagram can lead to a massive and at times unreadable diagram.

Return values of a message signature are mostly implicit in the message signature. Therefore, in most cases, it is not necessary to show the return values of a message on the sequence diagram. However, those trying out sequence diagrams for the first time tend to show the return values of a message by a separate arrow. For example, if a `Policy` object sends a message `IdentifyPolicy` to a `Claim` object, the return value (of, say, a policy number indicating the policy to which this claim belongs) need not be shown separately, as it is implicit in the parameter list of `IdentifyPolicy`. If it is shown separately, it constitutes a return protocol, which needs to be shown by a dotted arrow. Instead, early modelers tend to use the same message arrow for a return value. This trap should be avoided.

Finally, although technically it is possible and at times attractive to code by inspecting a sequence diagram, it is advisable to consider both sequence and class diagrams simultaneously when coding is attempted. Coding directly from sequence diagrams is a trap that should be avoided.

## 3.6 SWOT OF COMMUNICATION DIAGRAMS

### 3.6.1 Strengths of Communication Diagrams

As mentioned in the discussion of the nature of the communication diagram in the previous chapter, this diagram provides another view of the information captured in a sequence diagram. It has the same relatively dynamic nature as the sequence diagram. However, some designers working in the solution space are more comfortable with this view than with the sequence diagram. The communication diagram also shows object-to-actor and object-to-object relationships in terms of message passing. Furthermore, the communication diagram can also provide additional information (e.g., mandatory numbering of messages) that may be helpful to designers. These are some of the strengths of the communication diagram.

### 3.6.2 Weaknesses of Communication Diagrams

Communication diagrams do not show the sequence in a time-bound fashion, as sequence diagrams do. Therefore, numbering of messages on communication diagrams is mandatory. This can increase the effort needed to read and maintain these diagrams.

### 3.6.3 Objectives of Communication Diagrams

The objectives of a communication diagram are the same as those of a sequence diagram: to show objects and messages passing between them. An additional purpose of this diagram is to show a visual loading of an object. This happens because we are able to visualize the messages going in and out of an object, resulting in a metrics like the fan in (ratio of the number of messages coming into a class to the total number of messages) and fan out (ratio of the total number of messages going out of a class to the total number of messages).

Because communication diagrams can show, in a single view, the amount of load on an object, they provide valuable visual information during the testing phase. Through communication diagrams, objects with likely heavy load can be identified and appropriate load testing preparations done. This can also help project managers modify their project plans with regard to extra load testing that needs to be done on certain classes. This is possible because the communication diagram shows directly the number of relationships a class or an object has with other classes.

### 3.6.4   Traps of Communication Diagrams

If a project team tries to use both communication and sequence diagrams in order to model the same sequence of messages, it will lead to unnecessary complication that should be avoided. Therefore, those who prefer communication diagrams (such as people used to earlier collaboration and object diagrams) should decide upfront on their use and adhere to it throughout the solution domain and the background architectural domain. It may not be advisable for business analysts to use these diagrams in the problem space.

## 3.7   SWOT OF INTERACTION OVERVIEW DIAGRAMS

### 3.7.1   Strengths of Interaction Overview Diagrams

The primary strength of interaction overview diagrams arises from the fact that they are able to show the dependencies between various sequences within the system. Therefore, they are like a flowchart or an activity diagram, where the activities are replaced by references to sequences. Those sequences can be sequence diagrams or use cases. Interaction overview diagrams strengthen the modeling effort in the problem space by enabling display of conditions and multiple threads on the diagrams.

### 3.7.2   Weaknesses of Interaction Overview Diagrams

Interaction overview diagrams may have weaknesses similar to those of activity diagrams. This is because they are similar to activity diagrams and are meant to model the flow in the system, but at a much higher level of granularity. Interaction overview diagrams may not be able to show instance-level modeling and should not be used for that purpose.

### 3.7.3   Objectives of Interaction Overview Diagrams

Because these diagrams are new to UML 2.0, their objectives in practice still need to be fully understood. However, being similar to activity diagrams, they show the normal and alternative flows of sequences within the system through a combined overview of flowchart and references to sequence diagrams. Similarly, they may also reference use cases, providing a high-level view of the overall flow within the system. Because of these abilities, the interaction overview diagram, may eventually become the "context diagram" for the system.

### 3.7.4 Traps of Interaction Overview Diagrams

As overview diagrams, interaction overview diagrams should be used sparingly. Excessive modeling using these diagrams can lead to confusion between them and activity diagrams.

Referencing to other diagrams within the interaction overview diagrams is also not clearly stated or understood in practice. Hence, there may be confusion as to what is being referenced (sequence diagram, communication diagram, use case?) within the interaction overview diagram.

## 3.8 SWOT OF OBJECT DIAGRAMS

### 3.8.1 Strengths of Object Diagrams

An object diagram shows objects (at run-time) and how they are linked. Therefore, this diagram provides a powerful mechanism to show the run-time behavior of the system, particularly in the memory, at a given point in time.

Object diagrams show visually the multiplicities on a class diagram. As noted in the previous chapter, a multiplicity of greater than one will be represented by more than one object in the object diagram.

### 3.8.2 Weaknesses of Object Diagrams

There is no concept of behavior or dependency in object diagrams. Therefore, these diagrams are unable to show a sequence of actions. They cannot provide a mechanism to model the changing scenarios in the system.

There is no support specifically for these diagrams in any of the popular UML-based CASE tools discussed in Appendix B.

### 3.8.3 Objectives of Object Diagrams

The ability of object diagrams to show how objects are linked with each other can be used to visually model multiplicities on an association or aggregation relationship. Object diagrams facilitate showing multiple objects separately on an object diagram (compared to a class diagram, where they are shown as a single class). Object diagrams are helpful in verifying the business rules and constraints on class diagrams.

Since object diagrams show links between objects. They can also be used to discuss the action to take when a particular link is broken. For example, if a Policy linked to a `Client` is deleted, that particular link between `Policy` and `Client` *and all of its dependencies* should be neatly removed from the memory. This is also called "garbage collection." An object diagram can help ensure that once objects are deleted, they do not leave links hanging in the system, as these links will continue to chew up memory and cause the system to crash.

### 3.8.4   Traps of Object Diagrams

Object diagrams have limited modeling capacities. Using object diagrams on their own in a detailed modeling exercise is a trap that should be avoided. Object diagrams do not have the same comprehensive notations that other diagrams have. Therefore, they should only be used along with other diagrams.

## 3.9   SWOT OF STATE MACHINE DIAGRAMS

### 3.9.1   Strengths of State Machine Diagrams

As discussed in terms of their nature, state machine diagrams are the only truly dynamic UML diagrams that show the life cycle of an object. Thus, the strength of state machine diagrams is that they show the various states in which an object can be and the transitions that occur when an object changes its state.

These diagrams also show the conditions (guard conditions) under which the transition occurs, as well as the direction of the transition.

Additionally, these diagrams are capable of showing nesting as well as historical states, which enables modeling of more complicated life cycles.

### 3.9.2   Weaknesses of State Machine Diagrams

State machine diagrams are drawn only for a single object of a class. Therefore, if two objects belonging to the same class under different guard conditions follow different states, both suites of state changes cannot be shown on the same diagram. Furthermore, although decision points are allowed on state machines, they are not ideal for representing multiple objects.

### 3.9.3   Objectives of State Machine Diagrams

State machine diagrams are ideal for modeling real-time systems or real-time aspects of a system. In the problem space, they are ideally suited to show the states and changes to states pictorially, rather than the traditional way of documenting these situations by using a two-column table with states and flags to indicate how a states will change and how it will be stored.

These diagrams are extremely valuable in projects where there is a need to document a large number of state changes to objects (including objects representing business entities). Therefore, these diagrams may play a more important role in a project dealing with newer developments and package implementation than in a project on, for example, data warehousing.

With their ability to show a full cycle of an object, these diagrams are very helpful in clarifying many business and system issues.

### 3.9.4 Traps of State Machine Diagrams

State machine diagrams give an impression of a flow, but they should not be used like a flowchart. States indicate values of attributes of an object and should not be confused with the process flow happening at a business level (e.g., at a use case or activity diagram level).

Going overboard with nesting and history states, especially during business analysis, can lead to overly complicated state machine diagrams and is one of their major traps.

Finally, although UML syntax can show a message going out of the state machine or out of a state of an object, this should be done with care, for this leads to the trap of showing many objects or more than one object on the diagram.

## 3.10 SWOT OF COMPOSITE STRUCTURE DIAGRAMS

### 3.10.1 Strengths of Composite Structure Diagrams

Composite structure diagrams, as discussed in terms of their nature and creation in Chapter 2, are dynamic-structural. Their core strength lies in their ability to show *run-time* decomposition of a class or a component. Earlier, in the absence of these diagrams, object diagrams were used to show these run-time links between objects. Composite structure diagrams make this task much easier and also more elaborate. These diagrams show relationships between the run-time components and their interfaces that need to be realized or interfaces that are being used.

### 3.10.2 Weaknesses of Composite Structure Diagrams

Composite structure diagrams do not embody behavioral characteristics of the system. Therefore, they are akin to a snapshot of the system.

### 3.10.3 Objectives of Composite Structure Diagrams

Composite structure diagrams show the relationships between a run-time component and its interfaces. Therefore, they are valuable in the solution space as well as in the background/architectural space. They can be used to show how classes or components have been instantiated and, once in memory, how the corresponding objects are linked with each other. Thus, the primary objective of these diagrams is to provide an architectural view of various components and interfaces at run-time. This view also includes information such as the amount of load and complexity on a class/component at run-time. These diagrams require the modeler to be aware of the solution environment such as language, databases and deployment of the system. Multiple composite structure diagrams can and should be drawn in order to investigate the run-time architecture of the system.

### 3.10.4   Traps of Composite Structure Diagrams

These diagrams should be used only in the solution and/or background modeling space. Their usage in the problem space should be totally avoided. The diagrams display a run-time characteristic of the system. However, they have no provision to express pre- and postconditions. Therefore, ignoring these conditions related to the diagrams is a trap to be avoided during modeling.

## 3.11   SWOT OF COMPONENT DIAGRAMS

### 3.11.1   Strengths of Component Diagrams

As discussed in terms of its nature, the component diagram shows the executables (physical release) of a system. Since it deals with implementation-level issues, it is also called an "implementation" diagram (the other implementation diagram being the deployment diagram). These diagrams show components as well as their interfaces. These multiple interfaces provide the basis for a good and flexible design. By looking at a component diagram, it is possible to ascertain which components will be over- and/or underloaded and thereby distribute their load. In a distributed environment, it is important to decide the processors and nodes on which the components will execute. Component diagrams are also able to facilitate reuse, especially when third-party components are involved in the architecture of the system.

### 3.11.2   Weaknesses of Component Diagrams

Components represent large and cohesive collections of classes. Therefore, component diagrams are unable to show the "finer" concepts of object orientation like encapsulation or polymorphism.

The definition of components changes, depending on the user of the components. Therefore, components have been used to represent structured programs, relational databases and linked libraries. Unless components are formally stereotyped, component diagrams tend to be confusing.

### 3.11.3   Objectives of Component Diagrams

The primary object of component diagrams is to map components to classes and "realize" the classes by making them executable. Component diagrams do this by providing interfaces for a good, reusable design that also improves the quality.

These diagrams remain primary architectural diagrams that are used by architects and senior designers in assigning classes and their realization to components. Component diagrams also assist in making decisions to create and distribute various types of executables, libraries and DLLs.

### 3.11.4 Traps of Component Diagrams

Components without properly defined interfaces will not be usable. This is because without a proper interface, even if the component has the ability to perform a function, it is not possible to send or receive a message from the component.

Changing interfaces is a major trap in the usage of components. Once the interfaces to a component are defined, it is important to keep them as stable as possible. Rapidly changing component interfaces will be unable to provide the advantages of iterative and parallel development.

Circular dependencies between components, in which one component depends on another component, which, in turn depends on the first component, can lead to bad architecture. In practice, though, component diagrams do end up with partially circular dependencies. Architects who are not aware of the possibilities of circular dependencies may create either a bad architecture or, at the other extreme, a pedantic architecture that will be difficult to maintain.

Components that do not have a corresponding node on which they exist and are executed should be investigated further in detail. While not an error, it is important to cross-check components that do not have a corresponding hardware mapping. This is, of course, true only of executable components (not design-level components).

## 3.12 SWOT OF DEPLOYMENT DIAGRAMS

### 3.12.1 Strengths of Deployment Diagrams

The deployment diagram is the only hardware diagram in UML. It shows nodes, processors and links. Therefore, its strength is its ability to visualize the hardware and the deployment aspect of the software system.

As a hardware diagram, the deployment diagram can also be helpful in modeling the effect of operational requirements. For example, the requirements related to performance and volume can be shown as constraints on the hardware nodes depicted on this diagram.

Together with the component diagram, the deployment diagram helps show the responsibilities of hardware nodes in terms of component execution.

### 3.12.2 Weaknesses of Deployment Diagrams

Since UML itself does not dictate the notations for the nodes and processors of the deployment diagram, it is left up to the CASE tool vendors to create and map their

icons to the elements on this diagram. This has led to a wide variety of usually different deployment diagrams.

There is no dynamicity or time dependency on deployment diagrams. Hence,
changes to the architecture/deployment based on increasing transaction volume,
for example, cannot be shown on these diagrams.

### 3.12.3    Objectives of Deployment Diagrams

The primary objective of deployment diagrams is to show where and how components are deployed and where will they be executed.

The Deployment diagram also shows nonfunctional requirements specifications
by indicating, through notes and constraints, the speed, volume and stress that a
processor will be required to handle.

### 3.12.4    Traps of Deployment Diagrams

Detailed architectural discussions and modeling should not be left up to this single
simple diagram. A more detailed diagram should be drawn separately for architectural
and deployment needs. Also, a simple deployment diagram without proper use of
notes and stereotypes will lead to confusion and inadequate architectural modeling.

## 3.13    SWOT OF PACKAGE DIAGRAMS

### 3.13.1    Strengths of Package Diagrams

Package diagrams provide an excellent mechanism to organize the entire system
development process. This is because package diagrams, through the package
element, represent a subsystem.

Since a package diagram shows the organization of the system at the highest
level, it is the most convenient diagram in terms of assigning project teams to
subsystems during the development process. With most popular CASE tools, it is
possible for a project team member to "check out" a package, work on it, and
then "check it back in." This ensures that no conflicting updates are done by different
designers and different teams of modelers working on the same model. Because of
the importance of package diagrams, they are treated as separate diagrams—
compared to previous releases of the UML, where they were not considered separate
diagrams.

While dependency is the most popular relationship shown between packages, it
should be noted that there is no pressing need to show a relationship on a package
diagram. Each diagram can simply show packages and can provide a bird's-eye view
of the overall system.

Package diagrams can be leveled within the UML. This means that a package can
have levels of other packages within it. This can facilitate organization of the
system, as well as assignment of responsibilities to various team members.

A package diagram is static. Therefore, any additional dynamic or behavioral information that needs to be shown on the package diagram will have to be added as notes. Occasionally, stereotypes and colors are used to differentiate packages that are being developed inhouse from those that are produced by a third party or were developed in earlier projects. Packages may be color-coded to indicate their stage of development, their maturity and the stage of their iteration. However, use of colors in modeling should be done with caution, as not all CASE tools and people are comfortable with this practice.

### 3.13.2 Weaknesses of Package Diagrams

Package diagrams cannot show the detailed implementation-level modeling that can be shown with class and component diagrams. Packages are also unable to show any dynamicity. The only relationship between two packages is that of dependency. As a result, there is not much sophistication in assigning relationships between packages on a package diagram.

### 3.13.3 Objectives of Package Diagrams

A package diagram, as discussed in terms of its nature in Chapter 2, can be used to create and document subsystems in MOPS. The same concept of subsystems can be taken further in MOSS, and again, package diagrams can be used to model subsystems in these modeling spaces.

Packages are meant to show the way in which a system is divided into subsystems. A domain expert or a project manager with a few years of experience can come up with a fairly accurate package diagram up front. Arriving at the highest-level package diagram first and then decomposing it into lower-level diagrams is called a "top-down" approach to creation and assignment of packages to teams. For people with less experience in modeling or in UML-based project management, a much better method is a "bottom-up" approach. Here a substantial number of use cases are documented and put together in a use case diagram first; then these use cases are put together in various subsystems or packages.

After an organization has undertaken several UML projects, packages can also play a substantial role in reuse and can increase both productivity and quality. This is because reusable chunks of requirement and design can be directly imported or provided in new package diagrams by simply showing the old packages in the new diagram.

### 3.13.4 Traps of Package Diagrams

Using packages as a technical modeling mechanism is a trap of package diagrams. Therefore, even if packages are to be used to show reusability, that should be done at an organizational level rather than at a technical level. Relationships on a package diagram tend to confuse rather than add value. Therefore, using detailed relationships on a package diagram in MOPS should be avoided.

## 3.14  SWOT OF TIMING DIAGRAMS

Being new to the UML 2.0, timing diagrams do not provide us with an opportunity to evaluate them in practice. Therefore, this section is theoretical in nature, and the opportunities and traps are merely educated guesses.

### 3.14.1  Strengths of Timing Diagrams

The strengths of timing diagrams are:

- Ability to show states of an object
- Clearly show the time constraints in terms of state change
- Potential to show multiple objects and their state changes in one view

### 3.14.2  Weaknesses of Timing Diagrams

The weaknesses of timing diagrams are:

- Inability to show events/transitions
- Inability to show any technical details on the diagram

### 3.14.3  Objectives of Timing Diagrams

Timing diagrams can show multiple objects and their relative state changes in a single view, providing much better comprehension of comparative state changes.

The constraints on timing diagrams should show precise time laps between state changes. As a result, preconditions and postconditions for a state change can be easily represented on these diagrams.

### 3.14.4  Traps of Timing Diagrams

Timing diagrams are new to UML and have not been used extensively in practice. As a result, not much is known about their potential traps. However, lack of sophisticated notations to support events and transitions appears to be a potential problem in practice.

## DISCUSSION TOPICS

1. What is a SWOT of UML diagrams?

2. What is the major philosophical difference between strengths and weaknesses as compared with objectives and traps?

3. Why should the SWOT of class diagrams include a separate discussion on classes?

4. Why should the SWOT of use case diagrams include a separate discussion on use cases?

5. Why is there no significant difference between the SWOT of a sequence diagram and a communication diagram?

6. Why are sequence and communication diagrams also called interaction diagrams?

7. Why are component and deployment diagrams also called implementation diagrams?

8. Why are robustness diagrams not a separate type of diagram in UML? Which UML diagram are they based on?

9. An object diagram shows links between objects in memory. Why, then, is it more static than dynamic?

10. What are the two important extensibility mechanisms of UML?

11. Are there situations where stereotyping should be avoided? When and where?

12. What is the difference between stereotyping the include relationship on a use case diagram and an inherits relationship on the same diagram?

13. What role does a CASE tool play in good UML-based modeling?

14. What are the issues in using a CASE tool in working with three modeling spaces?

15. What are the five most important criteria in selection of CASE tools for UML-based modeling? Why?

## NOTE

The idea of performing a SWOT analysis on UML diagrams originated in queries arising in practice on the nature and application of UML diagrams. While the original and well-known SWOT analysis conducted for businesses provides the strengths, weaknesses, opportunities and threats, UML usage revealed that the strengths and weaknesses provided the intrinsic characteristics of the diagrams, whereas the practical application of these diagrams required an understanding of the objectives of the diagrams and the traps in using them. It was more relevant to consider objectives and traps, rather than opportunities and threats, in application of the diagrams. Thus evolved the current SWOT of the diagrams discussed in this chapter.

# REFERENCES

Armour, F., and Miller, G. *Advanced Use Case Modelling*. Upper Saddle River, NJ: Addison-Wesley, 2001, p. 75.

Fowler, M. *UML Distilled*, 3rd Edition. Boston: Addison-Wesley Professional, 2003.

Rumbaugh, J., Jacobson, I., and Booch, G. *The Unified Modelling Language Reference Manual*. Reading, MA: Addison Wesley Longman, 1999, p. 81.

Unhelkar, B. *Process Quality Assurance for UML-Based Projects*. Boston: Addison-Wesley, 2003.

# Chapter 4

# V&V of the Quality of MOPS

When you model something, you create a simplification of reality so that you can better understand the system you are developing.[1]

## CHAPTER SUMMARY

The business analyst, together with the user, is responsible for the creation of MOPS. This chapter outlines a checklist-based strategy that can be used by these persons for V&V of the UML diagrams in MOPS, including use case, activity, class, sequence, package and interaction overview diagrams. The chapter briefly discusses each of the relevant MOPS diagrams, followed by V&V syntax, semantics and Aesthetic checks, as discussed in Chapter 1. These quality checks are built on the understanding of these UML diagrams and their SWOT, as developed in Chapters 2 and 3.

---

[1]Booch, G., Rumbaugh, J., and Jacobson, I., *The Unified Modelling Language User Guide*. Reading, MA: Addison Wesley Longman, 1999, p. 91.
Note 1: The diagrams in this chapter are based on the LUCKY insurance problem statement described in Appendix A.
Note 2: A summarized checklist for MOPS appears in Appendix C.

---

*Verification and Validation for Quality of UML 2.0 Models*, by Bhuvan Unhelkar
Copyright © 2005 John Wiley & Sons, Inc.

## 4.1  UML DIAGRAMS IN MOPS

UML in the problem space is used to communicate events in the business arena. Therefore, in creating MOPS, we consider only those elements and diagrams of UML that are helpful in understanding the business and functional requirements of the project. As shown in Table 1.2, the importance of the UML diagrams changes, depending on their purpose in the modeling space. In the problem space, the purpose of UML is to enable understanding and documentation of requirements. Thus UML in the problem space becomes a tool that is used by the business analyst and the user. The UML diagrams that are valuable to these persons are summarized in Figure 4.1. They are as follows:

- Use case diagrams—used as a primary means of interacting with users and understanding the problem. However, of greater importance is the specification of the use cases themselves, which describes the interactions between the user and the system.
- Activity diagrams—used primarily to understand, in further detail, the flow in the use case. They can also be drawn to visualize the overall flow of the system.
- Package diagrams—in MOPS, used as a "grouping mechanism" for the entire project, resulting in a well-organized project (project management).
- Class diagrams—in MOPS, used to model key business entities and their relationships (classes and associations). These class diagrams may also be called "business object models" or "business domain models."
- Sequence diagrams—in MOPS, used to document complex and/or important scenarios that represent interactions within a use case, interactions among business objects or interactions described directly by business users (messages that become methods in a class).
- Interaction overview diagrams—used to model the flow between sequences and/or use cases, with those sequences or use cases appearing as an element (reference) on the diagram. They can also show us how busy an object is (i.e., sending and receiving a lot of messages); this allows us to distribute the workload to other, less busy objects.
- State chart diagrams—may optionally be used in MOPS to model the complex and/or important transitions undergone by a business object. These transitions are the life cycle of an object, as described by the business users. State chart diagrams are useful to model the life cycle of the busy object mentioned above in the interaction overview diagrams.

It is important to note that the aforementioned diagrams are independent of implementation considerations. All technological issues dealing with how to implement a solution are deferred until the solution space is modeled. Thus the modeling effort in the problem space corresponds to the platform independent model (PIM) of the MDA (see Mellor et al., 2004) and is focused on understanding the problem rather than solving it. For example, we identify potential classes as entities

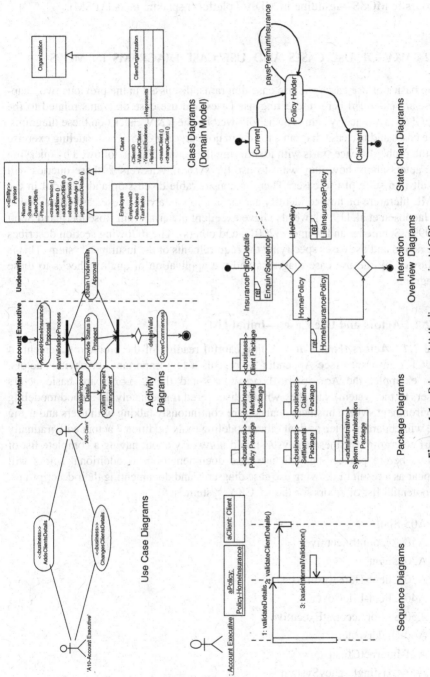

**Figure 4.1** Primary UML diagrams in MOPS.

in MOPS, whereas these classes are converted to language-specific implementation classes in MOSS—resulting in MDA's platform specific model (PSM).

## 4.2 V&V OF USE CASES AND USE CASE DIAGRAMS IN MOPS

The basics of use cases and use case diagrams, discussed in the previous two chapters, are extended here in creating use cases and use case diagrams related to the LUCKY insurance system. This is followed by the V&V checks on these diagrams. Use cases and use case diagrams form a major part of MOPS. The modeling exercise in the problem space starts with identifying the actors. This is followed by querying the actors about how they want to use the system. Answers to these queries will result in a suite of use cases. There is considerable discussion and material in the UML literature on how to identify actors and how to arrive at use cases (in addition to Jacobson et al. [1999], we also have excellent material from Rosenberg and Scott [1999], Schnieder and Winters [2001], and others). The following section describes the actors and use cases specifying the requirements of the insurance system. This is followed by the use case diagrams and the application of quality checks to these diagrams.

### 4.2.1 Actors and Use Cases—Initial List

***4.2.1.1 Actors (First Cut)*** A first careful reading of the problem statement of LUCKY insurance (see Appendix A) reveals a few important yet obvious actors. For example, the `Account Executive` and the `Client` are basic actors (users of the system), and they will be discovered immediately. In a good modeling environment, where business analysts are continuously talking with users and using the whiteboard as often as their other modeling tools, additional actors will gradually start emerging. Business analysts should *not* worry about having a complete list of actors before proceeding with use case documentation, as additional actors will appear as a result of drawing use case diagrams and documenting their descriptions. A potential list of actors for the LUCKY system is:

A05-Staff
A10-AccountExecutive
A20-Client
A30-Client-HomeInsurance
A40-Client-LifeCover
A50-SeniorAccountExecutive
A60-Underwriter
A21-InternetClient
A98-ExistingLegacySystem
A99-Govt.InsuranceRegulatorySystem

The numbered prefixes to the actors' names are optional, but they help in organizing the actors. Furthermore, it is always helpful to create an Actor hierarchy, as shown in Figure 4.2, as that also helps in organizing and relating the actors together. Keeping the actors' relationships in perspective results in better understanding of the use cases and their relationships on the use case diagrams. Consider, for example, the Account Executive shown in Figure 4.2. This actor is derived from staff. This is because an Account Executive will have to do all functions that a staff member does, and more. Senior Account Executive is similarly derived from an Account Executive as the Senior Account Executive does everything that an Account Executive does, and more. This hierarchy immediately starts providing clues to the business analyst; there are commonalities in the behavior of these three actors (such as logging on to the system) that can be factored out as common use cases later on. A similar argument applies to the actor Client. Note how this client actor is further specialized in two actors: Client-HomeInsurance and Client-Lifecover. Later, as the system becomes Internet-enabled, all clients will be able to access most functionalities on the Internet; therefore, an InternetClient is also shown as derived from a client in Figure 4.2.

Another actor of interest, a nonhuman actor, is an external system called the Govt.InsuranceRegulatorySystem, as shown in Figure 4.2. This system is modeled as an actor because our insurance system has to *interface* with this system. As discussed in Chapter 2 (Nature of Use Case Diagrams), interfaces are

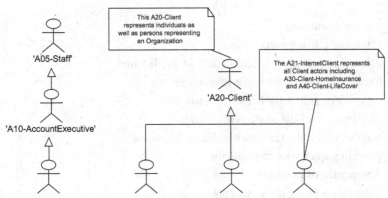

**Figure 4.2**  Insurance requirements—list of actors.

modeled as actors. This is so because an actor is something the system interfaces with; therefore, an actor is something that does not involve any "building" of software—it is not a part of the insurance system. This Govt.InsuranceRegulatorySystem is modeled as an actor because it only provides information to the insurance system, without any modifications to the internals of that regulatory system.

Syntactically, the diagram shows the Internet client at the same level as the HomeInsurance and LifeCover clients. However, the business wants the InternetClient to be both HomeInsurance and LifeCover. This is because the business would expect both clients—for home insurance and for home cover—to be able to access the insurance system over the Internet. An attempt to adhere to this correct process means that the InternetClient is derived from both HomeInsurance and LifeCover clients. This "multiple inheritance" of the InternetClient can lead to unnecessary confusion and should be avoided. Actors at this high level need not be modeled with the language-level precision that is required in the solution space. This difference in the role of the InternetClient as a representative of both HomeInsurance and LifeCover clients, however, should be explained in a good model by means of notes rather than being left to interpretation by the reader.

Once an initial list of actors has been identified, each actor is queried as to how he or she will use the system. Notable exceptions to this list of actors are the nonhuman actors, as they represent the interfaces rather than the roles played by users of the system. This querying will start providing a list of potential use cases. In our example, an initial list of use cases is as follows:

Adding client details
Changing client details
Adding and changing client details on the Internet
Creation of policy for home insurance
Creation of policy for life cover insurance
Maintenance of the respective policies
Valuation of risks for which policies are issued
Providing quotes for the policies
Acceptance of premiums for the policies
Submission of claims for events
Settlement of claims

### 4.2.2  List of Use Case Diagrams

Once we have an initial list of actors and use cases, we can start putting these provisional elements together in use case diagrams. While this is the recommended approach to creating use case diagrams, an alternative approach would be to start drawing the use case diagrams first and extracting the list of actors and use cases from them. In either of the two approaches, iteration is inevitable. The resultant use case diagrams will now be subject to our V&V checklists. The following four use case diagrams are created from the actors and use cases listed above to demonstrate the syntax, semantics and aesthetic checks.

- Client maintenance use case diagram—in addition to describing this diagram, an actor template is filled out while describing this diagram and the quality of the corresponding actors is discussed here.
- Policy creation use case diagram—during the discussion of this diagram, a use case template is filled out to provide basis for V&V of use cases.
- Claims processing use case diagram—the full quality checks as applicable to the entire diagram are shown here.
- Sales campaigning use case diagram—described for the sake of completeness of the requirements model. However, this diagram is further explored in the next chapter, where the checks for the solution space are discussed.

### 4.2.3 Describing Client Maintenance Use Case Diagrams

Figure 4.3 shows a basic use case diagram for client maintenance-a. This diagram is arrived at by querying the actor Account Executive. The Account Executive reveals her need to add details of a client or a potential client to the system. Obviously, input from the client is needed in order to complete this use case. Therefore, the Account Executive actor will need to interact with the Client actor. The use case named 'AddsClientDetails' is shown in Figure 4.3. The fact that input from both the Account Executive and the Client is needed to complete this use case will be reflected in the documentation of the use case. This documentation, which lies underneath the bubble representing AddsClientDetails, will provide complete details of the interactions between the actors and the system that are required in recording the client's details. Note that this use case documentation is not shown in Figure 4.3 but will be mostly linked to the use case in a CASE tool.

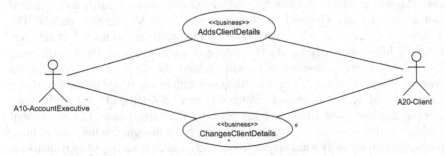

**Figure 4.3** Client maintenance (a) use case diagram.

The use case diagram in Figure 4.3 also shows another use case that deals with changing the details of the client. This is the maintenance of an insurance client and is called 'ChangesClientDetails'. Like the previous use case, this one also deals with the two actors: the Account Executive and the Client. These two actors get together to interact with the system in order to change client details. Figure 4.3 is helpful in discussions with the users, as well as in understanding the scope of the requirements related to maintenance of the client's details.

However, as will become obvious when we consider the description of the actors and use cases for this use case diagram, the visual model is not sufficient to explain all details related to client maintenance. For example, the diagram itself is unable to show that changing the details of a client can happen only if a client is already in the system. This inability of use case diagrams to show detailed behavior of the system and their inability to show dependencies between use cases (AddsClient Details and ChangesClientDetails in this case) of the system was discussed during the SWOT analysis of use case diagrams in Chapter 3.

Another example of the weakness of the use case diagram, as seen in Figure 4.3, is that it is not clear whether the Account Executive is adding the client's details or the Client herself is involved in this addition. Although the Client is shown directly related to both use cases, this does not mean that the Client is interacting directly with the system. Actors can be categorized as direct and indirect; an indirect actor still needs to be shown related to the use case because this actor *initiates the interaction.* If it were not for the Client, the use case would not have happened at all. Despite this explanation, technical modelers tend to interpret this diagram as indicating a direct interaction by the Client with the system. That interpretation is not incorrect when Internet-based access is considered. If an insurance Client is allowed to access the system using the Internet, then obviously she will be able to interact *directly* with the system. In that case, the stereotype can be direct. These are some of the arguments showing why the diagram in Figure 4.3 needs to be improved. There is a need to model both the addition of client details and changes to client details on the Internet.

One way of doing that is shown in Figure 4.4. Here the A21-Internet Client (also referred to as InternetClient to facilitate readability of this text) is shown as inheriting from, or specializing, the normal Client. The use case diagram in Figure 4.4 can be read as follows: An Account Executive and a Client are involved in addition and change to Client details. The InternetClient is able to perform the same functions that normal clients perform (by inheritance, described next)—those of addition and changes to Client Details (although business rules will prohibit the InternetClient from creating all details of the Client as compared with those created by the Account Executive). However, changes to the Client's details, like the Address, Phone Number, and so on, are managed by the InternetClient without the intervention of the Account Executive. Note, though, that this kind of functional requirement, which has preconditions and requires modeling of an if-then-else type of situation, cannot be shown easily on a use case diagram. This lack of

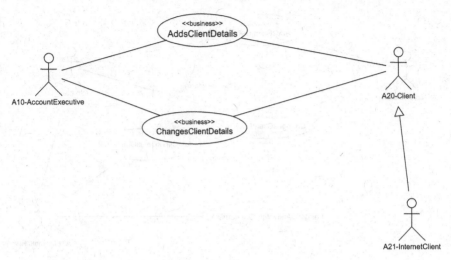

**Figure 4.4**   Client maintenance (b) use case diagram.

dynamicity and dependency in use case diagrams is also in accordance with the discussion of the SWOT of the use case diagram in Chapter 3.

Further, note that the association connecting the actor to the use cases, as shown in Figures 4.3 and Figure 4.4, has been purposefully left without the open arrowhead, as permitted by UML. The reason for not showing the arrowhead is to avoid the potential confusion it creates at this problem space level of modeling. An arrowhead gives an impression of a flow that is not there. So, the only sensible interpretation of an arrowhead going from the actor to the use case is that the actor initiates a particular use case. Only if this information is imperative should it be shown on the use case diagram. Otherwise, it is best to simply draw a line of association (communication) between the actor and the use case.

Figure 4.4 also shows that the `InternetClient` inherits from the `Client`. Using actor-to-actor inheritance has a positive effect on the aesthetic quality of a use case diagram by reducing its visual complexity. Note, however, that this inheritance, shown by the inheritance arrow going from the `InternetClient` to the `Client`, does not carry the same precise inheritance semantics that class-to-class inheritance carries.

As discussed above, with the additional `InternetClient` shown in Figure 4.4, it is still not clear how the usage of the system will differ when a client is added by the `Account Executive` compared with when the client details are added directly by the `Client`. Although some steps are likely to be the same, others will differ. Certainly, the `InternetClient` will not have the same freedom to access and change her details that the `Account Executive` has. This variation is shown in Figure 4.5, which further improves on Figure 4.4. This use case diagram shows how the `InternetClient` would add or change the client details on the Internet as a variation, or *extension*, of the normal

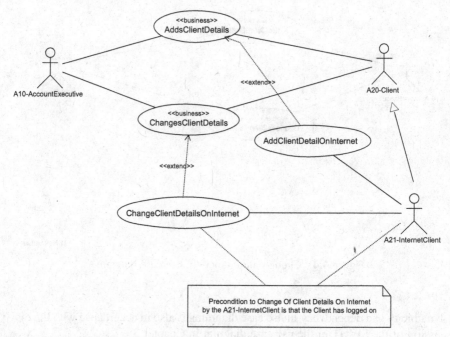

**Figure 4.5** Client maintenance (c) use case diagram.

addition or changing of the client details. Therefore, we not only have Internet Client derived from Client, but we also have this InternetClient associating with the use cases AddClientDetailsOnInternet and Change ClientDetailsOnInternet, both of which are *extending* the respective use cases. AddClientDetailsOnInternet is thus specializing the normal use case AddsClientDetails. The use case to use case relationship of extends is used here.

Figure 4.5 will be read by a UML-literate modeler as: The InternetClient adds client details on the Internet by following most steps of normally adding client details, followed by some variations and constraints to it. For example, there can be a precondition which requires that a client must be registered for Internet usage before being able to add details like Phone Number and Mailing Address on the Internet. Note again how this kind of information is also not easily visible on a use case diagram. Detailed notes can and should be added in order to clarify the diagram, as shown in Figure 4.5. Business analysts should also be mindful of the fact that the use case diagram itself has limited descriptive value and that there is a significant amount of specification and documentation detail underneath each of the use cases.

In Figure 4.5, a note is added that clarifies the fact that changing of client details by an InternetClient will have additional preconditions that the client (A20-Client) is valid and that A20-Client is able to log on to the system. Details of how to log on and what constitutes a successful log on are not available on this diagram. This can be handled by completing the associated use case documentation using a predetermined template or, alternatively, another use case dealing specifically with log in. It is only when all actors and use cases are completely documented that one can say that the use case diagrams are complete. This completion of the documentation is also an iterative and incremental process.

### 4.2.4 Actor–Class Confusion

Before proceeding further with the documentation of the actors and use cases described above, it is worthwhile to note a common confusion that occurs in practice, especially in early attempts at use case modeling. That is the confusion between (in this example shown in Figure 4.6) the `Client` who is accessing or using the system and the details of the client that are stored inside the system. This is a practical semantic issue with actors. While the actors represent external entities, there is invariably a need to store their details *inside* the system. In Figure 4.6, there is an actor `Client`, whose details, such as `Name`, `Address` and `Phone Number`, will have to be stored inside the system. Since these details are physically stored in a persistent class, there will eventually be a need for an entity class called `Client` that will have persistence capability. This business-level class stores the characteristics of the client and is different from the actor client (business user) of the system.

This difference between an actor `Client` applying for a loan and the details of the same client being stored in the system as `Client` leads to an interesting practical problem when entered in a CASE tool. For example, if we have an actor `Client` modeled in a use case diagram within a CASE tool, and we want to also create an <<entity>> class `Client` with the same name, most CASE tools require the modeler to decipher this difference before entering it. Semantically, it

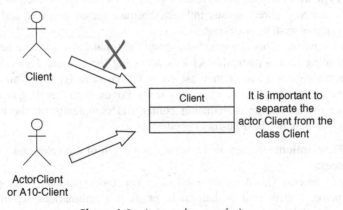

**Figure 4.6** Actor–class confusion.

is important to name the actors with a differentiator, such as prefixing them with an A for actor and, possibly, a simple numbering scheme, such as shown in Figure 4.6. In Figure 4.6, the actor client is named 'ActorClient' or, even better, 'A20-Client'. That is the name of the actor who is going to use the system, as shown in Figure 4.6 with an arrow extended to a class. The class will store the details of the client, such as her Name, Address and Phone Number, as simply Client. This prefixing of Client with a suitable numbering scheme, or just Actor, is very helpful in improving the quality of use case diagrams and their entry in a CASE tool.

### 4.2.5 Actor Documentation and Quality Checks

Actor documentation can be an important part of the requirements model in the problem space. Consistency of actor documentation is achieved by creating and following a template that is predefined by the project team members and that is outside the CASE tool. A template defined externally to the CASE tool can be linked to the actor icon within the CASE tool. An example actor template follows, with the relevant comments inside the < > symbol.

#### 4.2.5.1 Actor Documentation Template

**Actor Thumbnail:** <The name and, optionally, a prefixed number, of the actor> *Quality Comment:* Naming the actor is an important aspect of quality. Potentially confusing issues such as actor versus real person (where an actor represents a role rather than a person) should be carefully handled in naming the actors. A singular common noun should be used to represent human actors. External systems represented by their interface are given the name of the system.

**Actor Type and Stereotype:** <Actors can be of various types, such as primary versus secondary, direct versus indirect, abstract versus concrete and person versus external system or device> *Quality Comment:* This classification, though not mandatory, can be helpful in understanding how a particular actor is accessing the system. This actor type may be loosely described or may assume a formal stereotype. Not all classifications of an actor are based on business needs. For example, creating an abstract actor has the advantage of reducing clutter and complexity on the use case diagram but may not be a business need.

**Actor Description:** <A one- or two-line description of the actor and what he/she/it does> *Quality Comment:* This description provides a succinct summary of the purpose of the actor. It may also be helpful in printing a summarized report of the requirements model.

**Actor Relationships:** <Thumbnails of relevant use cases and/or other actors with whom this actor is interacting. If there is an inheritance hierarchy, thumbnails of generalized/specialized actors will be documented here>
*Quality Comment:* Documenting an actor–use case relationship should be straightforward. What is listed here is the name of the actor or actors that deal with the use case. However, a use case to use case relationship needs more thought. Since the "refactoring" of use cases happens in later iterations (certainly in the later part of an iteration), documentation showing use case to use case relationships will also be completed later. However, if domain experts are able to ascertain reusable aspects of requirements earlier in the life cycle, then those reusable functionalities will be factored out, and shown using the «include» relationship. The other two use case to use case relationships can also be used here, namely, <<extend>> and <<inherit>>.

**Interface Specifications:** <Since, by definition, the actor has to interact with the system, we note here the details of the interface through which the actor performs this interaction>
*Quality Comment:* Interface specifications should not be confused with GUI design. This is only a placeholder for initial thoughts on how the actor will interface with the use case. Typically, this will be a list of the numbers and names of GUI specifications related to this actor—including specifications of Web interfaces. For external systems and devices, it may be a description of the interface or protocol, and not of a GUI.

**Author:** <Original author and modifiers of this actor description>
*Quality Comment:* The author and/or owner of the use case is mentioned here as part of documenting the administrative details of the actor. It is recommended that the owner and the author be the same as far as possible. However, a domain expert or a busy end user may not have the necessary time to document her thoughts. In such cases, the owner should be mentioned separately from the author here.

**Reference Material:** <Relevant references, as well as sources>
*Quality Comment:* Actors may have relevant documentation that may not fit in with this relatively compact template. For example, some actors, like a teller in a bank, may be governed by detailed operational rules that may be documented elsewhere in a bulky folder. Providing a reference to such material keeps the specifications readable. For nonhuman actors, such as interfaces to legacy systems, it is helpful to refer to the interface templates here.

*4.2.5.2 Documenting Actor A10-AccountExecutive* Following are two examples of actor documentation based on actors for the LUCKY insurance system shown in Figure 4.2 and use case diagrams in Figures 4.3 to 4.5.

**Actor Thumbnail**
Actor: A10-AccountExecutive

**Actor Type and Stereotype**
Direct, Human

**Actor Description**
This actor, A10-AccountExecutive, is a part of the insurance organization's staff that deals with providing quotes and selling insurance. A10-AccountExecutive also receives claims for compensation and deals with administrative details of clients and policies.

**Actor Relationships**
Derived from abstract actor A05-Staff
Further specialized into A50-SeniorAccountExecutive
Deals with use cases AddsClientDetails and ChangesClient Details

**Interface Specifications**
This actor will be dealing with most of the functions of the insurance business. Therefore, starting with the login interface (which will eventually become a form or a screen), this actor will have levels of access to other interfaces such as:

Login Screen
Inquiries and Quotes
Client Details
Claims

**Author and History**
Prince Sounderarajan

**Reference Material**
Various levels of staff, their responsibilities and authorities must be considered. These are available for INSYS documentation on the company's intranet (www.insys.com/staff)* or www.lucky.com/insys.

### 4.2.5.3   Documenting Actor A20-Client

**Actor Thumbnail**
Actor: A20-Client

**Actor Type and Stereotype**
Indirect, human

---

*These are hypothetical websites shown here to demonstrate material included in the reference section within actor documentation.

**Actor Description**

The actor A20-Client is the primary actor who initiates business with LUCKY. This actor makes inquiries, asks for quotes, provides her own details as well as details of the risk, and pays the premium. While she is an indirect actor for the most part, for an Internet-enabled system, this actor will perform some functions (particularly inquiries) that will be direct.

**Actor Relationships**

This actor is specialized into two functional actors, A30-Client-HomeInsurance and A40-Client-LifeCover. Its specialization into A21-InternetClient is not at the same level as the previous two specializations (see note in Figure 4.2), as the Internet client can also be the two specialized actors, albeit performing the functions of the two specialized actors on the Internet.

This actor also deals with use cases AddsClientDetails, Changes ClientDetails, CreateInsurancePolicy (and its specialized versions) and MaintainInsurancePolicy, as shown in Figures 4.7 and 4.8, discussed in the corresponding later section.

**Interface Specifications**

The client actor will need a special login screen and other associated screens when the client is accessing the LUCKY system through the Internet. These screens can be as follows:

```
Login Screen
Inquiries and Quotes
Client Details
Claims
```

However, if no Internet access is provided, then the Client actor will remain as an indirect actor. An indirect actor has no access to any of the screens of the system, and all interaction with the system is through nonsoftware means such as across-the-counter interaction with the account executive or on the phone with a call center.

**Author and History**

Roy S'duk.

**Reference Material**

Various actions of the clients must be considered for their access, permission to change their details, types of inquiries and quotes, and payment of simple premiums. These details of various types of client actions are available on INSYS documentation on the company's intranet (www.insys.com/staff).[†]

---

[†]A hypothetical Web site shown here to demonstrate how to write the reference section within actor documentation.

### 4.2.6 Describing Policy Creation and Policy Maintenance Use Case Diagrams

#### 4.2.6.1 *Policy Creation Use Case Diagram*   Figure 4.7 shows the policy creation use case diagram, which describes in detail how an insurance policy is created. First, consider the actors in this use case diagram. There is the `A10-Account Executive` who deals with all aspects of creating an insurance policy. The `A20-Client`, with all its variations, is also involved in the creation of an insurance policy. The use case that shows how the system will be used in creating an insurance policy is shown in Figure 4.7, where it is also shown as associating with both the `AccountExecutive` and the `Client`. (Note: The numbered prefixes are not mandatory, but they assist in organization of the actors. Also, prefixes may be used in descriptions if they do not hinder readability.)

The SWOT analysis of the use case diagrams in Chapter 3 highlighted the challenge of using the inheritance relationship between an abstract and a concrete use case. It was also mentioned there that in terms of use cases, this inheritance relationship should be avoided as far as possible. Nevertheless, Figure 4.7 shows an infrequent but practical situation where an abstract use case may make sense. The figure shows a use case, `CreateInsurancePolicy`, that is abstract. The specification of `CreateInsurancePolicy` will also be abstract and will describe only the

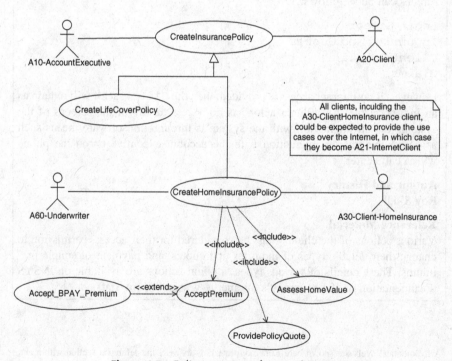

**Figure 4.7**   Policy creation use case diagram.

basic or generic steps in the creation of an insurance policy. Examples of these generic steps are as follows:

1. Assessing the risks
2. Evaluating the risks
3. Providing a quote
4. Accepting the premium

None of these steps are implementable. These steps may also not provide good business domain classes, because they are generic and give a rough indication of what happens during policy creation.

In Figure 4.7, `CreateHomeInsurancePolicy` and `CreateLifeCover Policy` are shown as two use cases derived from `CreateInsurancePolicy`. This means that the flow that was generic in the `CreateInsurancePolicy` use case now becomes concrete in the `CreateHomeInsurancePolicy` use case. The client that is involved in the creation of the home insurance policy is `A30-Client-HomeInsurance`. `A60-Underwriter` is also involved in creating a home insurance policy.

The SWOT analysis of use case diagrams had highlighted the importance of these diagrams as a good organizational and scoping mechanism. This can be seen here in the diagrams in Figures 4.7 through Figure 4.9. Studying the diagrams provides valuable understanding of the scope and extent of the requirements. However, note that these use case diagrams are not precise enough to enable coding from them. For example, in Figure 4.7, not much can be ascertained from the actor generic client (any client) involved in the creation of an insurance policy. It is only when a specific client becomes known, such as a home insurance type of client, that the use case `CreateHomeInsurancePolicy` becomes the focus of discussion.

Furthermore, the use case `CreateHomeInsurancePolicy` includes `assessing the home value`, `providing policy quote` and `accepting premium` use cases. While these three use cases are shown as <<included>> by the `CreateHomeInsurancePolicy` use case, it is not mandatory to have these three use cases separated. In many models they will be put together in the main use case `CreateHomeInsurancePolicy`. Use cases are factored out only when a potential set of interactions are reusable and can be potentially included in more than one use case.

Another situation where we may refactor use cases is if they require a specific set of inputs from (or attention of) a particular specialized user. For example, in Figure 4.7 'AssessHomeValue' is factored out as a separate use case because this might require a substantial amount of work by—potentially—a separate role played by the account executive—that of an `Assessor`. An `account executive` in the role of an assessor might be involved in identifying the value of a home loan, relating it to current home prices in a particular street or suburb, the type of home (a town house, unit, villa, house, terrace, etc.) and so on. Each of these investigations, which might involve access to the LUCKY database, as well as occasional physical verification of the property, calls for a separate use case.

Similarly, providing a policy quote or a quote for a premium amount based on the value of the property may involve considering the type of client, such as a pensioner, a former member of the military or a single parent. A policy quote may also change, depending on whether the client has other types of insurance with LUCKY or whether the client had made any previous claims. In such cases, there will be a substantial amount of business logic that is kept separate from the plain vanilla Create HomeInsurancePolicy use case. That is why I have factored out the use case ProvidePolicyQuote and included it in CreateHomeInsurancePolicy.

While not shown in Figure 4.7, there is a strong possibility that the use case ProvidePolicyQuote may also be included in the CreateLifeCover Policy use case. That will happen if ProvidePolicyQuote is going through the same steps for HomeInsurance as for LifeCover.

Once a policy is created, acceptance of the premium of the policy would include many aspects of financial transactions, including accepting the premium by check, credit card or cash and so on. The premium may also be payable in various periodic forms such as weekly, monthly, fortnightly, quarterly, yearly and so on. All of this calls for a separate use case called 'AcceptPremium'. Once again, the possibility of AcceptPremium being reused by CreateLifeCoverPolicy is high. Should that happen, a separate use case diagram will have to be drawn to deal with assessment providing quotes for and accepting premiums related to the life cover policy. This new use case diagram will reuse or re-present the use cases and the actors that are shown in the policy creation use case diagram.

An example of the third relationship between two use cases is <<extends>>, also shown in Figure 4.7. This relationship is shown by a use case representing the additional requirement of being able to accept insurance premiums through Biller Payment (BPAY). In practice, the chances are good that this new requirement appeared after the original iteration of the use case modeling was complete. Therefore, the original use case was extended by the one with BPAY. Alternatively, paying the premium by BPAY is an example of a use case that specializes or extends an otherwise complete use case called 'AcceptPremium'. Thus the major difference between a use case—here AcceptPremium—being included in CreateHomeInsurancePolicy and being extended by accept BPAY premium is that in the former case, the CreateHomeInsurancePolicy use case is not complete unless AcceptPremium is executed. However, the functionality of AcceptPremium on its own would be complete whether it gets extended by accept BPAY premium or not.

### 4.3.6.2  Policy Maintenance Use Case Diagram
In this subsection we consider Figure 4.8, a policy maintenance use case diagram. If you compare this diagram with Figure 4.7, you will see that this diagram represents a far more simplistic visual view of the requirement of maintaining the details of an insurance policy.

The A10-AccountExecutive and A20-Client are the same as those shown in Figure 4.7. However, instead of creating a suite of use cases, each with

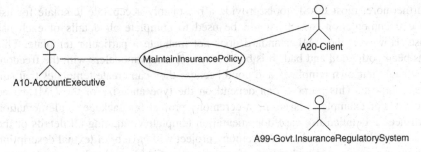

**Figure 4.8** Policy maintenance use case diagram.

a separate set of interactions or responsibilities, this diagram shows only one use case, `MaintainInsurancePolicy`. This use case documents the interactions between the `Account Executive` and the `Client` and how these actors use the system. Maintenance of an insurance policy may not require the same detailed investigations and assessments related to provisions of a quote and acceptance of premiums that are needed when a new policy is created. Thus, this use case diagram gives the right impression that `MaintainInsurancePolicy` is a relatively straightforward interaction. The kinds of interactions taking place inside `MaintainInsurancePolicy` could include changing the frequency of payments, clients changing some of their own details and so on. If the clients are upgrading the value of their policy (that is, of their risks) or if a client status has changed (e.g., the client has become a pensioner or a single parent), then, in that case, the `MaintainInsurancePolicy` use case will document how these details have changed. Other examples of changes to the policy could be administrative in nature, such as a client requesting an extra copy of the printed policy.

After the policy has been created, its status changes to maintenance. In maintenance, the policy can be influenced by a business rule that may state that the government regulatory system should be informed of certain details of the policy. This may happen for work cover or life cover policies that are covered by state or federal legislation. This information is provided to the government system through `A99-Govt.InsuranceRegulatorySystem`, as shown in Figure 4.8. Note that this interface to `A99-Govt.InsuranceRegulatorySystem` is not mandatory for all types of policies, like home content or home insurance policies. This option cannot be shown on a use case diagram easily. Readers are encouraged to document such optional conditions in the requirements using notes.

### 4.2.7 Use Case Documentation and Quality Checks

Similar to the actor description provided earlier, here we discuss the template for use case documentation. This documentation is even more important than the actor documentation and should not be ignored in any serious modeling exercise.

Furthermore, most CASE tools provide a reasonably acceptable template for use case documentation, which should be used to complete all details of each use case. However, the UML standard does not mandate a particular template. This has been both good and bad. It is bad because it leaves modelers with the freedom to create their own templates and good because they can create templates that suit their purpose. This purpose can depend on the type and size of the UML-based project. For example, a large, high-ceremony project for package implementation will need a detailed use case documentation template containing all details of the use case, whereas a small, low-ceremony project will have brief textual description for its use cases. As in the case of actors, most CASE tools allow modelers to attach their external descriptions/specifications of a use case to the use case icon within the tool.

Here is a suggested template on documenting a use case, followed by documentation of two actual use cases: `CreateHomeInsurancePolicy` from the policy creation use case diagram and `AddsClientDetails` from the client maintenance use case diagram. Practical projects using the following template are encouraged to customize it before use to suit their purpose. The minimal headings needed to create satisfactory documentation of a use case are the use case thumbnail (to identify the use case) and the use case text (flow), which describes what happens within the use case. The rest of the information can be helpful (e.g., describing many alternative conditions separately in an alternative flow), but it is not mandatory. Therefore proponents of short use cases working in small projects can decide not to use all of the headings described next. Many authors (Armour and Miller, 2001; Henderson-Sellers and Unhelkar, 2000; Jacobson et al., 1999; Rosenberg and Scott, 1999) have discussed use case documentation. These can be combined by practitioners to create a template of their own.

### 4.2.7.1 Template for Documenting Use Cases

**Use Case Thumbnail:** <Number and name of the use case and, optionally, a version number.>

*Quality Comment:* Naming the use case has an important bearing on the way the use case diagrams are read and interpreted. Good names should be verb-like and should describe the behavior represented by the use case from the point of view of the primary actor. Ideally, use case names should not be nouns. Numbering of use cases can also be done, and that number would form part of the use case name. Numbering use cases can also improve their grouping and organization.

**Use Case Description:** <A one-line description of the use case>

*Quality Comment:* Describing the use case in one line is important not only from an administrative viewpoint (such as printing a list of all use cases together with their description) but also to enable the modelers to focus on the main purpose of the use case. That one-line description is effectively the goal of the use case.

**Stereotype and Package:** <Description of the stereotype and the package to which this use case belongs>
*Quality Comment:* Both stereotypes and packages are grouping mechanisms but at different levels. Since creation of packages is important organizational work, it is important to note to which package the use case belongs. Use cases should belong to logically cohesive packages. Stereotyping of use cases can also play an important role in understanding their purpose and assigning them to modelers. For example, a use case that deals with the administrative job of printing a set of end-of-day reports for a bank branch can be stereotyped as <<admin>> to provide a better understanding of its purpose. While some use cases can be stereotyped as <<system>>, most of them will be stereotyped as <<business>> because of their relevance in the problem space.

**Preconditions:** <Preconditions are the conditions that need to be satisfied before the execution described by the use case can commence>
*Quality Comment:* Use case diagrams are unable to show the flow. Therefore, they cannot show the sequence of execution of the use cases. Preconditions are used to indicate if other condition or use cases need to be completed before this use case can begin. For example, ChangingClientDetails can have the precondition ClientExists. Preconditions are not mandatory.

**Postconditions:** <Postconditions are conditions that must be met at the end of this use case>
*Quality Comment:* Like other sections of the use case documentation, this postcondition section is not mandatory. However, occasionally, there may be a need to document an action or event that should happen on exiting the use case. If this is a distinct event that needs separate attention, rather than being placed within the flow of the use case itself, then it should be described here in the postcondition. For example, PrintReceipt can be a postcondition to WithdrawsCashFromATM in a banking example.

**Actor-Goal Table:** <A list of the actors involved in this use case and the corresponding goals that the actors aim to achieve in interacting with the system in the context of this particular use case>
*Quality Comment:* Each use case has one or more actors. These actors interact with the system in order to achieve their own specific goals. It is very helpful to have an actor-goal table within the use case that can help focus on the goal of each actor. Usually, this will be a one-liner showing the actor-goal relationship in the context of this use case.

**Use Case Relationships:** <Thumbnails of other use cases that are included, extended or inherited>
*Quality Comment:* Use case modeling provides an excellent opportunity to reuse requirements. This reuse can occur when repeatable chunks of requirements are "included" in other use cases. Furthermore, use cases can also be "extended" by other use cases, resulting in extension of an already existing

functionality within the use case being extended. Occasionally, use cases are "inherited." These three relationships provide the options for relating a use case to another use case. The names of other use cases that are included, extended or inherited are shown here.

**Use Case Text** (Main flow within the use case)

>   1.0 <description of step>
>   2.0 <description of step> (A1, E1, E2)
>   3.0 <description of step> (A2, E3)
>   INCLUDES <Thumbnail of Use case/s Included>
>   EXTENDS <Thumbnail of Use case/s Extended>

Another format for documenting the flow within the use cases is:

>   **User Intentions    System Response**
>   1.
>   2.
>   3.

*Quality Comment:* The text description that documents the flow within the use case is a vital part of the use case documentation. In fact, this may be the only mandatory part of the use case documentation. There are a number of ways in which this text can be written, and authors mentioned earlier have all put forward arguments for their own formats. An example format, where numbered statements represent steps in the interaction between the actor and the system, is shown above. Regardless of which format is chosen, this documentation is crucial because from it we derive the list of business domain objects (classes), as well as their attributes and responsibilities. Note that an activity diagram can be drawn pictorially to represent this flow within a use case. Also note that detailed descriptions of the data items being accessed or stored in databases or technical specifications should be avoided here. A common mistake is to put detailed database descriptions and complex business rules underneath any of the steps within the flow.

**Alternative Flow:** A1. <description of alternative steps to the step 2.0 in use case text or main flow>
*Quality Comment:* The alternative flow documents the steps within a use case that are abnormal. Well-constructed use cases will have one or more alternative flows that are not a part of the main flow. However, note that alternative flows, if substantial, can themselves be use cases—in which case they are separated as independent use cases and <<included>>. Alternative courses also provide a general indication of the complexity of the use case. A use case with more than one alternative course will certainly not be simple.

**Exceptions:** E1. <description of exceptions to the normal step 2.0 in use case text or main flow>
*Quality Comment:* When use cases are technical (rather than business), they record technical exception conditions in their flow. Those exceptions are marked in the normal flow and documented here. However, in most business-level use cases, exceptions may not be documented.

**Constraints:** <These are special constraints and/or limitations that are relevant to the use case>
*Quality Comment:* This is a nonfunctional aspect of use case documentation. Although I prefer to have a separate document that records all nonfunctional (or operational) requirements together, it is sometimes helpful to document the constraints here in the use case as well. For example, a use case dealing with creation of a policy may have a constraint that the minimum insurance value for a home content insurance policy must be $5000. These nonfunctional requirements are not easy to record in the text flow and need separate documentation.

**User Interface Specifications:** <number and name of user specifications related to the use case, including Web screen specifications>
*Quality Comment:* As with actor documentation, it may be helpful at times to give the name of the user interface through which the use case will become accessible to the respective actors. No detailed design of the user interface is envisaged at this stage, but naming the user interfaces in the use cases is very helpful in understanding the requirements. This naming of user interfaces will usually happen during the second or third iteration of the use case documentation, as the first iteration may be too early to even identify interfaces.

**Metrics:** <Anything that needs to be measured in relation to the use cases will be put here>
*Quality Comment:* Putting a metrics program together is the first step in moving up the process maturity levels (capability maturity model [CMM] levels). A section in the use case that deals with this administrative aspect of the use case can be used to record how long it took for the use case to be documented or how complex the use case is. A simple/medium/complex rating is commonly used for complexity rating. The criteria for this complexity rating, however, can vary and may depend on the experience of the organization in applying use cases. A use case flow with more than one alternative or exception flow is most likely to be of medium or complex complexity.

**Priority:** <The importance of the functionality described by this use case (high, medium low)>
*Quality Comment:* Priority is a ranking of the use case provided by the user of the system. Users, working with business analysts, are in an excellent position to describe the priority or importance of the use case. This prioritization

can be valuable to both business analysts and project managers in identifying the high-risk and/or more important use cases and undertaking their analysis first.

**Status:** <The completeness of the documentation of this use case (Initial, major final)>
*Quality Comment:* The status of a use case derives from iterative and incremental development and as such falls under the process discussion. It is worth noting here, though, that a use case should not be developed in one attempt. Instead, it should be iteratively developed along with other use cases and their corresponding use case diagrams and, more important, along with their activity diagrams. Furthermore, iterating between use cases and class diagrams representing initial business domain models is also quite common. This gradual completion of use cases is facilitated by the status.

**Author and History:** <Original author and modifiers of this use case>
*Quality Comment:* This is an administrative detail of the use case, and it documents the author and the owner of the use case. While it is preferable to have one person playing both roles, sometimes that may not be possible. In such circumstances, both the owner and author should be documented here. Furthermore, a history of major changes may also be documented here.

**Reference Material:** <Relevant references and sources>
*Quality Comment:* Detailed business rules, lists of data items and tables, complex mathematical formulas, lists of other relevant reference material such as old user manuals, support manuals, training material and so on that is relevant to the use case are referred here. It is not prudent to place all of the reference material here, as this may make the use case unnecessarily bulky. However, it is essential to consider it here.

---

**4.2.7.2  Documenting the Use Case CreateHomeInsurancePolicy**  Based on the above template, the use case `CreateHomeInsurancePolicy` is described here. This use case was shown in the use case diagram in Figure 4.7.

---

**Use Case Thumbnail**
`CreateHomeInsurancePolicy`

**Use Case Description**
This use case deals with the creation of a new home insurance policy by providing a quote and accepting a premium for a new or existing client.

**Stereotype and Package**
<<business>> policy
*Comment: this stereotype and package are not yet shown on the diagram.*

**Preconditions**
Client has a valid risk—a home—to be insured.

*Comment: this precondition ensures that when this use case is executed, the client knows that it is a home risk that is to be insured.*

Client is `A30-Client-HomeInsurance`
*Comment: Because of the actor-to-actor inheritance shown in Figure 4.7, this use case deals exclusively with a client who is undertaking home insurance.*

**Postconditions**
Printing a letter accepting (or rejecting) the policy cover. If the cover has been accepted, then this letter will contain all substantial details of the policy.

**Actor-Goal Table**
`A30-Client-HomeInsurance`—provides all details related to the home risk; get a home insurance policy
`A60-Underwriter`—underwrites the insurance being taken out by the client
`A10-AccountExecutive`—facilitates creation of home insurance
*Comment: Because* `A10-AccountExecutive` *is shown communicating with the abstract use case* `CreateInsurancePolicy`, *from which this use case* `CreateHomeInsurancePolicy` *is derived, this actor* `A10-Account Executive` *will appear in this use case. But documenting it separately is not essential, as the inheritance takes care of that.*

**Use Case Relationships**
Derived from (or inherited from) the `CreateInsurancePolicy` abstract use case.
Includes three use cases: `AssessHomeValue`, `ProvidePolicyQuote` and `AcceptPremium`.

**Use Case Text**
*Comment: This use case is concrete (as against the one it is derived from). Therefore, the text for this use case is written in a more detailed format. This format is also a variation on the one suggested previously and may be used in the first attempt to write the use case.*

| User Actions | System Response |
|---|---|
| `A10-AccountExecutive` identifies the client | System validates the client (A1) |
| `A30-Client-Home Insurance` specifies details of the home to be insured | System accepts the details and performs some basic checks on the details (for a complete list of details, see `HomeInsuranceDetailsGuide`). |
| `<<include>>` `AssessHome Value` | System provides supporting information on home values based on the included use case. |
| `<<include>>` `ProvidePolicyQuote` | System will check with `A60-Underwriter` for underwriting details for the quote, through the included use case. |
| `<<include>>` `Accept Premium` | Acceptance of the premium is performed through this included use case. |

## Alternative Courses
<A1> If the client does not exist, then the account executive will be prompted to create the client details which are documented separately (see Client Details.Doc*).

## Exceptions
None

## Constraints
A30-Client-HomeInsurance is not an Internet client in the description of this use case. However, as specified in the notes on the policy creation use case diagram, if the Home Insurance Client was indeed an InternetClient, then steps within this use case will change to indicate a direct access by the client to Lucky's Web pages to create the insurance policy. In that case, the A10-AccountExecutive will be replaced by the A21-InternetClient.

## User Interface Specifications
Three actors will access the system in this use case. They are, first, A10-AccountExecutive. Coming from the abstract use case Create InsurancePolicy, this actor will access the system by searching details of the client and entering policy details. Other interfaces, dealing with detailed assessment of home values, provision of quotes, and so on, will be described in their respective use cases.

A30-Client-HomeInsurance is the initiator of this use case. She may not directly access any of the screens or interfaces of the system. However, if there is a business need to complete a paper-based form in order to apply for Home InsurancePolicy, then this actor will do so. Alternatively, if the actor is the A21-InternetClient, then a suite of user interfaces will be needed to complete the transaction.

The A60-Underwriter may also be required to check the risks before underwriting them. This can be provided by an interface to the underwriter's system.

## Metrics
Complex use case

## Priority
High

## Status
Initial

*Comment: This is the initial iteration of this complex use case. Good-quality modeling will not attempt to complete this use case in one attempt. Rather, it will iterate this use case with other use cases as well as other diagrams.*

---

*Another hypothetical document, demonstrating references to documents external to the use case.

**Author and History**
Chris Payne

**Reference Material**
Home Insurance Details.Doc.[†]

### 4.2.7.3 Documenting Use Case AddsClientDetails

**Use Case Thumbnail**
`AddsClientDetails`

**Use Case Description**
This use case deals with adding new clients to the insurance system. (Note: creation of an insurance policy is different from creation of a client in this system.)

**Stereotype and Package**
<<business>> Client

*Comment: if this use case is specialized/inherited and becomes* `AddClient DetailsOnInternet`, *then the package may change to* `Internet`. *That will probably happen during the second iteration of the modeling exercise.*

**Actor-Goal Table**
`A10-AccountExecutive`—adds a client correctly to the system
`A20-Client`—provides all relevant details for successful addition

**Use Case Text** (flow within the use case)
*Comment: Note the variation in style here compared with the previous use case* (`CreateHomeInsurancePolicy`). *Both styles are acceptable.*

1. The `Client` provides all basic details to the `Account Executive`. (These can include name and address. For details see reference)
2. The `Account Executive` enters all basic details of the `Client` in the system.
3. The system validates these basic details (format of name, etc., for rules on validation; see reference A1).
4. Once all basic details are validated, the `Client` provides additional details to the `Account Executive`.
5. The `Account Executive` enters all additional details of the `Client` in the system.
6. System validates these additional details (whether the `Client` is a pensioner, etc.; see reference A2).
7. Once all additional details are validated, `Client` details are stored by the system and the use case ends.

[†]Another example of referencing external documents.

**Alternative Flows**

A1 (Invalid or Insufficient Basic Details)

1. Insufficient or inaccurate basic details are referred back to the `Client` for correction.
2. `Client` makes corrections and/or provides additional information on the basic details to the `Account Executive`.

A2 (Invalid or Insufficient Additional Details)

1. Insufficient or inaccurate additional details were provided by the `Client`, so they are referred back to the `Client` for correction.
2. `Client` makes the corrections and provides additional information as required on the additional details to the `Account Executive`.

A3

A complete alternative to this use case is that the main flow (steps 1 through 7), which are currently divided into two major parts—entering of basic details and additional details—is executed as one single entry of client details.

**Exceptions**
None

**Constraints**
In face-to-face addition of `Client` details (i.e., not through the Internet), the information gleaned in this use case from the `Client` may have to be collected on a physical form and entered in the system by the `Account Executive`.

**User Interface Specifications**
UI_ClientBasicDetailsForm
UI_ClientAdditionalDetailsForm

*Comment: For a list of details to be collected, see* Client Details.Doc.

**Metrics**
Medium use case

**Priority**
Medium

**Status**
Initial

**Author and History**
Prince Sounderarajan. Further modifications by Samir El-Masri.

**Reference Material**
Client's details are stored in Client Details.Doc. Some of them are shown below:

Client basic details include: First Name, Surname, Address, Date of Birth (Age is essential for vehicle insurance)
Client additional details include Past Insurance History (claims made), Pensioner Status

### 4.2.8   Describing the Claims Processing Use Case Diagram

In addition to the use case diagrams related to the creation and maintenance of client and policy details, there are additional and important requirements that demand more use case diagrams and use cases. Two additional diagrams are described here to cover these additional requirements. Note, though, that in practice, these diagrams will appear during later iteration of the requirements modeling work. The use case diagrams described here will not be drawn in the sequence in which they appear here.

Figure 4.9 is the claims processing use case diagram. The actors shown here are A20-Client and A10-AccountExecutive. While these are the primary actors interacting with the system whenever claims are submitted and processed, derivatives of these actors are shown in the list of actors in Figure 4.2. These derived actors (e.g., A40-Client-LifeCover and A30-Client-HomeInsurance from A20-Client and A50-SeniorAccountExecutive from A10-AccountExecutive) will also be able to perform the use cases shown in Figure 4.9.

In the claims processing use case diagram, we again see the nonhuman actor A99-Govt.InsuranceRegulatorySystem. This actor is an interface to the Govt.InsuranceRegulatorySystem, which receives some information—which may be legally binding—from the use case NegotiatesClaim, as shown in Figure 4.9.

Figure 4.9 also shows the four use cases that deal with claims processing. They were discovered after the actors were quizzed as to how they will use the system to

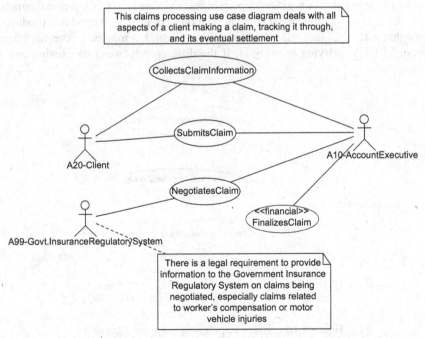

This claims processing use case diagram deals with all aspects of a client making a claim, tracking it through, and its eventual settlement

CollectsClaimInformation

SubmitsClaim

A20-Client

A10-AccountExecutive

NegotiatesClaim

<<financial>>
FinalizesClaim

A99-Govt.InsuranceRegulatorySystem

There is a legal requirement to provide information to the Government Insurance Regulatory System on claims being negotiated, especially claims related to worker's compensation or motor vehicle injuries

**Figure 4.9**  Claims processing use case diagram.

process claims. These use cases are:

- Collects claim information (`CollectsClaimInformation`)
- Submits a claim (`SubmitsClaim`)
- Negotiates a claim (`NegotiatesClaim`)
- Finalizes a claim (`FinalizesClaim`)

As discussed in the previous section, each of these actors and their corresponding use cases will have detailed specifications and documentation associated with them. Additionally, notes are shown on this diagram—describing how `Govt.InsuranceRegulatorySystem` is part of the negotiation process, especially in cases of insurance claims related to worker's compensation. Stereotypes can also appear on this diagram later (not shown here).

### 4.2.9 Describing the Sales Campaigning Use Case Diagram

While all previous use case diagrams dealt with the main and existing business of LUCKY, the sales campaigning use case diagram shown in Figure 4.10 describes an additional and important aspect of the business—the ability to *grow* the business by means such as cross-selling and up-selling. Thus Figure 4.10 shows a separate aspect of the requirements that deals with analyzing the data previously recorded and making marketing estimates based on them. This can be an important aspect of a CRMS implementation or a data warehousing project that plans to analyze the data to help improve business opportunities. Eventually in this use case diagram, `A20-Client` is approached with additional types of insurance or related products. Note that `A20-Client` may not always be a client, but may be a potential client whom LUCKY is trying to bring in. If the difference between an existing and a

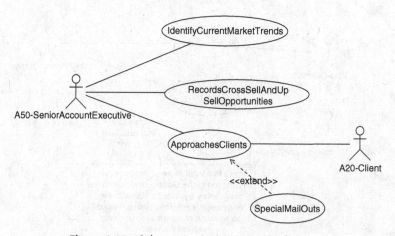

**Figure 4.10**  Sales campaigning use case diagram.

potential client is important, a separate actor for the potential client may be warranted (not shown here).

This diagram, and the previous ones, have been created keeping the quality criteria in mind. We now move to the next level of verifying and validating these use case diagrams and the corresponding use cases (of which only two were documented earlier) by applying the syntax corrections, semantics completeness and aesthetic checks of symmetry and consistency.

### 4.2.10    Syntax Checks for Use Case Diagrams

We are now ready to apply quality checks to the use case diagrams described thus far. We apply the syntax check first, looking only at the UML accuracy of the diagrams. The syntactic correctness of the diagrams will be judged against the artifacts (things, elements) that constitute the use case diagram—the use cases, actors, relationships and additional annotations on the diagrams. Let us see how the syntax checks are applied to the respective use case diagrams (unless specifically mentioned, these checks apply to all use case diagrams, including those in Figures 4.5 and 4.7 through 4.10).

- Check that all elements on this use case diagram are *permissible* as per UML syntax. These elements are the actors, the use cases, their relationships and the notes. This check ensures that no other element (such as a class or a package) are shown on this diagram. For example, the client maintenance use case diagram (Figure 4.5) satisfies this check, as only permissible elements of the diagram appear here.
- Check the notation for each of the elements represented on the diagram. This includes checking to see if an actor uses the correct stickman notation or if it is a circle representing an actor. The stickman icon of the actor must represent all actors. Similarly, check that the use case is represented by the bubble or ellipse. Notational checking is an important part of syntactic correctness of the diagram. It is worth mentioning that many CASE tools enable modelers to create and attach their own icons to represent the modeling elements. Some of these variations are permissible under OMG's guidelines, so long as the notations do not violate the UML meta-model. This means that while a variation on the icon shown in Figure 4.5 for the actor may be permissible, one certainly should not use a zigzag line, for example, to show relationships between use cases.
- The boundary of the system, as discussed originally, by Jacobson (1999) and later, in practice by Rosenberg and Scott (1999) is a notational element that may appear on use case diagrams. This happens particularly if the use case diagram is drawn, at the highest level in MOPS, as a *context diagram*. A boundary is usually drawn as a rectangle on the use case diagram, with all the use cases placed inside it and all the actors outside. A use case diagram drawn with a boundary indicates clearly the responsibility of what needs to be built and what needs to be interfaced. The use cases inside the boundary need to be built, and the

actors outside the boundary only need to be interfaced. If a boundary is indeed present, check that all the use cases are inside it and all the actors are outside.

- In the claims processing use case diagram of Figure 4.9, all actors are correctly represented by their notations. A20-Client and A10-Account Executive are straightforward. The A99-Govt.InsuranceRegula torySystem is the external system with which the new insurance system will interface. If needed, other external systems or existing legacy systems can also be shown here.

- A variation on the actor syntax check is checking the actors that represent external nonhuman entities. While the modelers can still use the stickman notation, it is important that these nonhuman actors are stereotyped as such. Stereotypes of <<device>> and <<external system>> are commonly applied to nonhuman actors. While the actors in the client maintenance use case diagram are all human, the one shown in Figure 4.9, the claims processing use case diagram, is A99-Govt.InsuranceRegulatorySystem, which is the nonhuman <<external system>> and is stereotyped as such.

- Are all actors correctly named (singular, noun, representing a role)? While the naming of actors is not dictated by UML syntax, it is still considered an important syntactic check. For example, the name of the actor representing the client can be Client or A20-Client for the reasons discussed earlier (refer to the actor–class confusion discussion). However, check that the client actor is not given a name such as 'c' or '1', which will have no meaning and will lead to problems in documenting other diagrams.

- Optionally, have the actors been numbered? This check should depend on the local project standard if such a standard has been established.

- Are all use cases correctly named? Use cases are usually named in a verb-like fashion, indicating the use of the system from the primary actor's viewpoint. For example, in Figure 4.9, all use cases have verb-like names and all are named from the point of view of the client: client CollectsClaimInfor mation, SubmitsClaim, NegotiatesClaim, and the Account Executive is shown associated with the use case FinalizesClaim. The style used here can be changed to accommodate your own preferences in naming use cases and making them more readable. For example, instead of 'SubmitsClaim', you may name it 'SubmitClaim' without the 's' at the end Submit. What should be strictly avoided is naming your use case as a noun; for example, Claim is a bad name for a use case.

- Optionally, have the use cases been numbered? This check should depend on the local project standard if such a standard has been established.

- Check the relationships between actors and use cases. The association line drawn between an actor and a use case will invariably cut across the boundary of the system. While the system boundary is not implicit in the use case diagrams drawn here, it is still essential to check that the line showing the communication between the actor and the use case is correctly shown as a thin continuous line.

- The arrowhead on the communication (or association) line drawn between the actor and the use case must also follow the UML syntax and should be an open arrowhead. As discussed in the SWOT of the use case diagrams and earlier in this chapter, it is recommended that this arrowhead be used extremely sparingly, and if possible avoided. The actor–use case relationship should be drawn with an arrowhead only if it is important to show whether the actor is initiating the action or is the final recipient of the action. In Figure 4.9, which shows the claims processing use case diagram, an arrowhead is shown for the relationship between the use case `NegotiatesClaim` and the actor `A99-Govt.InsuranceRegulatorySystem`. This is meant to indicate that LUCKY's insurance system is only sending the information to the government as per legal requirements. If there is an interaction both ways, between the government system and LUCKY's insurance system, the arrowhead showing this interaction should be dropped. Another common example (not shown in our diagrams) is the printer actor (an external device interacting with the system) receiving a message from a print receipt use case. This may be shown with an arrow going out of the use case and into the printer actor. Ensure that the arrowhead is an allowable one and not, for example, the inheritance arrowhead (closed hollow arrowhead). As you can imagine, an inheritance relationship between the actor and the use case will make no sense. In Figure 4.9, the association line that has an arrowhead is the one that goes into the `A99-Govt.InsuranceRegulatorySystem` use case, correctly indicating that the information going out to the external system is the primary purpose of that association.

A very important syntax check occurs in relationships shown *between* two use cases. It is necessary to check the three possible relationships between two use cases, as discussed in detail in Chapter 3, in the SWOT of the use case diagram. Note that syntactically only one of the three relationships is permitted between two use cases. Furthermore, the three allowable relationships between two use cases that need to be checked for syntactic correctness are as follows:

- When use case A is meant to include use case B, the arrowhead on the relationship should point from A to B. This is shown with a dotted arrow and the stereotype <<include>> written on it. This syntax check is a "pass" when applied to Figure 4.7 dealing with the policy creation use case diagram. The `CreateHomeInsurancePolicy` use case <<includes>> `Assess HomeValue`, `ProvidePolicyQuote` and `AcceptPremium` use cases.
- When use case C extends use case B, the arrow should point from C to B. The stereotype <<extends>> is written on the relationship. This syntax check, when applied to Figure 4.7, shows how the use case `Accept-BPAY-Premium` <<extends>> the use case `AcceptPremium`. Furthermore, this check is also a pass when applied to Figure 4.5, where the use case `AddsClientDetails OnInternet` <<extends>> the use case `AddsClientDetails`, and so on.

- When use case D represents a concrete form of use case B, the arrow should point from D to B. However, the type of arrow is a thick line with a closed arrowhead. The word <<inherits>> may or may not be written on the relationship, as the notation for this relationship is unique and self-explanatory. This example is also shown in Figure 4.7, where two use cases, CreateLife CoverPolicy and CreateHomeInsurancePolicy, are shown as inheriting from CreateInsurancePolicy.

- Check the abstract notation for use cases and actors. If the use case is abstract (i.e., unimplementable or uninstantiable), then the name of the use case should be written in italics. Figure 4.7 shows such an abstract use case called *CreateInsurancePolicy*, and it is correctly shown in italics. It is worth noting, however, that a use case *can* inherit from another use case, and both can be concrete—in which both use cases can be instantiated.

- If there are notes on the diagram, they should follow the UML standard for notes, that of a dog-eared rectangle. Notes should be connected to the relevant elements on the diagram by a dotted line. This has been done in all three use case diagrams shown in Figures 4.5, 4.6 and 4.7. Notes can be attached to more than one element on the diagram, and they can also have stereotypes.

- As far as the actual use case specifications are concerned, UML dose not specify much in terms of syntactic correctness. Therefore, we only make a cursory syntax check if such specifications exist. Otherwise, the specification for a use case can be ignored in the syntax check, but it will be subjected to more robust semantic checks.

### 4.2.11   Semantic Checks for Use Case Diagrams

At the semantic level, the intensity of checks focuses on understanding the purpose behind the actors, the use cases and the use case diagrams. Readers can revisit Figure 1.3 to understand the skills needed in conducting successful semantic checks. As shown in Figure 1.3, these semantic checks will need more business knowledge, and experience in the insurance domain, than are needed for the syntax checks in the previous section. The semantic checks will also focus on the completeness of the use case diagrams drawn in the problem space.

- First and foremost, check what each actor represents in the problem space. Does each actor shown in, say, Figure 4.5, the client maintenance use case diagram, have a real semantic meaning behind it in the problem space? For example, does A10-AccountExecutive represent a real potential user who will play the role of an Account Executive? This primary semantic check will, in practice, create a lot of debate and discussion. These discussions should be treated as a sign of a good modeling exercise. Lack of such discussions is a sign of everything being perfect (unlikely scenario) or a lack of good, serious modeling. In fact, getting a set of semantically correct actors is a major step in building a good-quality MOPS. Checking the documentation of the actor and cross-referencing it against the name of the actor is also very helpful in ascertaining the semantic meaning behind the actor and its semantic correctness.

- Check if the actor represents a human user, a device, an external system, an interface, and so on. In Figure 4.9, the claims processing use case diagram depicts A99-Govt.InsuranceRegulatorySystem as an actor. Is that a human actor? The answer is no. In that case, is that actor correctly stereotyped to represent its semantic meaning? This actor should not be representing a person if it is named as a system and vice versa.

- What does each of the use cases represent? This question will be well answered when an attempt is made to document, in addition to the names of the use cases, the one-line description of those use cases. This description will clarify the semantic meaning behind the use case and should be the first important semantic check of the use case.

- Follow the above check by going through the flow or text description of how the use case will be executed. This will provide even more detailed semantic validity of the use case. When these flows within the use cases are checked, the chances that a use case is further refactored (i.e., merged or split) are high. This is also expected and should be welcome. Further, ensure that after each such refactorization of use cases, the new use cases are subject to the same semantic checks that caused the refactoring in the first place.

- Does the use case have pre- and postconditions? If it does, have those conditions been documented? As discussed in the SWOT, use case diagrams do not have a flow. Therefore, if there is a dependency of one use case on another, it can be shown as preconditions. Other preconditions (e.g., status for an account executive) are also possible. Check if they have been documented in the associated use case specification. Alternatively, check if these conditions appear as constraints.

- Check for the alternative and exception flows within the use case specification. If there are no such flows, the use case can be treated as a simple use case. However, more than five alternative and exception flows will require rethinking of the structure of the use case and the possibility of creating additional use cases.

- Check if the use cases have been ranked. Prioritizing or ranking the use cases is based on their semantic meaning, which indicates their importance to the user. While our example use case diagrams have not shown the ranking of the use cases, that ranking can be equivalent to priority, as shown in the use case specification.

- Checking the semantic meanings behind the actor–use case relationship should be straightforward. If an actor initiates a use case or is the prime beneficiary of the use case, then that actor must have a relationship with the use case. A notable exception is when inheritance exists between actors. Semantically, an inheritance of one actor by another inherits all relationships of the higher-level actor. In such a case, the lower-level actor may not relate to any use case on the diagram, but perhaps may relate to other use cases on another use case diagram.

- What does a use case to use case relationship indicate? If a use case <<includes>> another use case, then from the business viewpoint, the meaning of such inclusion should be clarified. In Figure 4.7, the `CreateHomeInsur-ancePolicy` use case <<includes>> the three use cases `AssessHomeValue`, `ProvidePolicyQuote` and `AcceptPremium`. Has the business analyst done a semantically correct job of including `AssessHomeValue` in `CreateHomeInsurancePolicy` or should the reverse be done? This is important semantically, as a syntactically correct <<include>> does not imply that it is semantically correct as well. Check the semantic correctness of all <<include>> relationships.

- What is the meaning of the entire use case diagram? Does it represent a logically cohesive set of requirements or is it just a collection of incoherent use cases and actors? This semantic check will be undertaken during detailed reviews of the MOPS, as the meaning behind the diagram must be clearly expressed and must be clear to all parties involved. Naming of the use case diagram is just as crucial, if not more so, than the use cases themselves. As you can see, all four use case diagrams shown in this example (`Client Maintenance`, `Policy Creation`, `Claims Processing` and `Sales Campaigning`) have a clear focus and represent a logically cohesive area of the insurance business.

## 4.2.12   Aesthetic Checks for Use Case Diagrams

Having checked the use case diagrams drawn in Figures 4.5 through 4.7 for their syntactic correctness and semantic meanings, we now focus our quality effort on checking their symmetry and consistency, resulting in a suite of the aesthetic checks of the diagram. Despite the discussion of aesthetic checks presented here, note that a certain amount of subjective judgment on the aesthetics of a diagram is inevitable.

- Consider Figure 4.5. How many use cases and actors appear in that one diagram? Coming from the classic span of control principle of management (which revolves around the fact that humans can comprehend five to nine elements at one time), one can state that a use case diagram with more than nine actors and/or use cases will be aesthetically inelegant. In the client maintenance use case diagram, three actors and four use cases are shown together. That is a pass for aesthetic checks. Figure 4.7, the policy creation use case diagram, with seven use cases and four actors does not look as good aesthetically as the client maintenance use case diagram. However all these elements are shown here because they represent a logically cohesive set of use cases. Consider, however, the use case `CreateLifeCoverPolicy` in Figure 4.7. While the use case itself is shown here for the sake of completeness, it would be impossible to show all associated use cases that `CreateLife CoverPolicy` includes and gets extended by in this diagram. If all relationships of `CreatLifeCoverPolicy` including its actors are shown in this diagram, the end result would be an unaesthetic use case diagram. Good-quality business analysis will keep in mind that although an actor is likely to use the system in many ways rather than one, it is permissible to show the same actor (and the same use case) in more than one use case diagram—depending on the subject area of the diagram. This ensures that the use case diagrams are aesthetically elegant as well.

- An actor is likely to use the system in more than one way. That is, as one actor may play several roles, the actor is likely to be associated with more than one use case. On average, the actor to use case ratio should be 1:3.

- Consider the use case documentation itself. Is it too long and unwieldy? A use case requiring many pages will defeat the visual purpose of UML. Conversely, if the use case is too short, the use case diagram will be cluttered with too many use cases. The size of the use case is important in enhancing the aesthetic quality of the use case diagram as well. The template for use cases, discussed earlier, and the example documentation should provide sufficient detail for practical modeling.

- In applying aesthetic checks to the entire model, one should consider the number of use case diagrams. It is difficult to state precisely how many diagrams and use cases are enough to document a system completely. However, if discussions and workshops stop providing additional use cases, the model can be considered as moving toward completeness and correctness.

### 4.2.13 Acceptance Testing and Use Case Documentation

The importance of good use case documentation should not be underestimated in a good-quality test plan. The creation of test plans, test designs and relevant test cases benefits greatly from well-documented use cases and quality use case diagrams. Here we highlight the importance of use case documentation in acceptance testing. Thus, even before we reach the acceptance testing stage, documentation of the use cases and its potential in testing should be checked.

- Check that a use case is documented either in the step format or in an "action-response" format in such a way that it can be used as a starting point for test cases. Since, in a quality environment, users are regularly encouraged to participate in use case documentation, the possibility that this documentation provides substantial material for writing test cases is very high. This should be kept in mind as use cases are documented.

- Check the format of the use case documentation. Does it consist of a formal set of steps? Essential use cases are at abstract level and may not be as valuable as concrete use cases in the context of testing.

- While the flow within the use case provides the basis for test cases, the pre- and postconditions, as well as the constraints documented within a use case, can provide rich source for the creation of operational test cases.

- In addition to what is documented in the use case, two extra pieces of information—inputs and expected results—can provide substantial information needed for a suite of test cases. Although it is recommended that use cases not be loaded with testing details, use case documentation including text flow, pre- and postconditions and constraints provides substantial details for acceptance testing.

- For integration projects, the "interface" actors become an important point for testing. All interface actors will have to be tested for the correctness of their interface, as well as their ability to store and retrieve data from the external system.

## 4.3 QUALITY OF ACTIVITY DIAGRAMS IN MOPS

As seen in their SWOT analysis in Chapter 3, activity diagrams model the flow of activities, making them ideal to model business processes. Activity diagrams have their origins in state chart diagrams, but in UML 2.0 they are considered quite independent of their origins (Fowler, 2003). Furthermore, while activity diagrams can be extensively used in modeling MOPS, their use in the other two modeling spaces depends on the modelers' need to show design-level constructs. Within the problem space, they provide the ability to model any flows or processes within the business. Therefore, their V&V should focus on the correctness and completeness of these flows. The activity diagrams in the problem space closely visualize the behavior documented in the use cases. Therefore, during the V&V process, it is necessary to relate the activity diagrams to the corresponding specifications and documentation of the use cases. Let us consider an activity diagram in the problem space to provide a basis for our subsequent quality checks.

### 4.3.1 Describing the AddsClientDetails Activity Diagram

Figure 4.11 shows an activity diagram called `AddsClientDetails`. This diagram is named after the use case `AddsClientDetails` that appears in Figure 4.5. This activity diagram has the same name as the use case because this diagram visually represents the activities happening inside the use case `AddsClientDetails`. Earlier in this chapter, we saw the detailed specification of the use case `AddsClientDetails`. The activity diagram shown in Figure 4.11 depicts two basic actors to start with, namely, the `Account Executive` and the `Client`. These actors are shown in two specific partitions. Further recall that the documentation in the use case `CreatesHomeInsurancePolicy`, particularly the text, had a "user action–system response" format. Those system responses can be documented in an activity diagram by the system partition. Figure 4.11 shows the system partition for the `AddsClientDetails` activity diagram.

This activity diagram starts when the client provides basic `Client Details` or information. Recall that, in describing the corresponding use case, it was mentioned

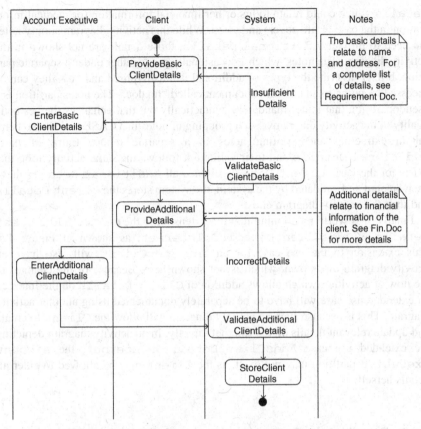

**Figure 4.11** `AddsClientDetails` activity diagram.

that these details might be provided by the `Client` in the form of a paper-based document. There is an explanation, in the form of a note, attached to this first activity in this diagram. This note explains to the reader of the diagram that the basic details provided by the `Client` relate to the `Name` and `Address`. For a complete list of all the basic details, the note tells the reader to go to an additional document, Requirement.Doc.

The `Account Executive` is then shown, in this activity diagram, as entering the `Basic Details` provided by the `Client`. This entry of basic details data will be invariable, via a screen interface provided by the system.

The next activity performed is validation of all the details provided by the `Client` and entered by the `Account Executive`. This is shown in the system partition in Figure 4.11. If the details are insufficient or incorrect, then the flow of activities goes back to the first activity, `ProvideBasicClient Details`.

If the basic `Client Details` entered by the `Account Executive` are accepted and validated by the system, then the `Client` provides `Additional`

`Details` which could relate to his or her financial information (or medical information in the case of life cover) and so on. While this activity diagram simply notes the need to provide `Additional Details`, those details are not shown in the activity diagram. The notes, which I occasionally put together under a separate partition, briefly describe the types of additional details required and how they can be accessed by going to an external document called "fin.doc." The notes partition is a pseudopartition that is not mandatory syntactically but that enhances the aesthetic quality of the activity diagrams. Such grouping of notes in a CASE tool is also helpful in extracting and printing notes in a separate report. Entry of these `Additional Details` and their validation follows the same activity loop that exists for the basic `Client Details`. Once all `Additional Details` have been entered and validated by the system, the system stores the `Client Details` and then the activity diagram ends.

Finally, it is worth mentioning that the extension to the use case `AddsClient Details` is `AddsClientDetailsOnInternet`, as shown in Figure 4.5. This extension to the use case for an `InternetClient` will also have an activity diagram of its own, which is not shown here. Because of the changes to the flow of activities, which allows addition of `Client Details` on the Internet, an extended use case will have to be separately documented using another activity diagram. This is because such an activity diagram will allow the `Client` to create and update relevant details on the Internet directly. In an activity diagram depicting the extended use case `AddsClientDetailsOnInternet`, the `Account Executive` partition may not exist, as the `Client` may be allowed to enter all details herself.

### 4.3.2 Describing the CreatesHomeInsurancePolicy Activity Diagram

Figure 4.12 shows another example of a good-quality activity diagram, `Creates HomeInsurancePolicy`, based on the use case `CreatesHomeInsurance Policy` shown in Figure 4.7 (hence given the same name as the use case). Note that occasionally, more than one activity diagram may be associated with a use case. In such cases, instead of giving the activity diagrams the same name as the use case, an additional numbering scheme that prefixes or suffixes the activity diagrams may be considered. Alternatively, activity diagrams can be named after the use case and the additional flow of activities they represent. This is most likely to happen if the alternative flow in a use case is substantial enough to warrant an activity diagram of its own.

The activity diagram shown in Figure 4.12, `CreatesHomeInsurance Policy`, has four partitions representing the four actors:

`Accountant`
`Account Executive`
`Underwriter`
`Client` (prospect)

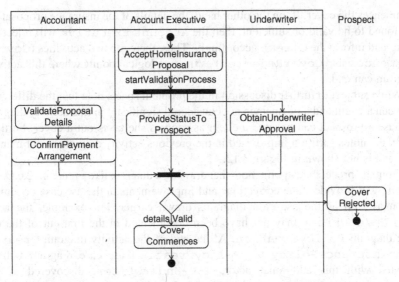

**Figure 4.12** `CreatesHomeInsurancePolicy` activity diagram.

This activity diagram begins when the `Account Executive` accepts a home insurance proposal. However, mere acceptance of the proposal document (a variation of this would be acceptance of the proposal document on the Internet, which has not been considered here) does not constitute acceptance of the risk. When the acceptance of the proposal is completed, the validation process commences. The activity diagram at this point splits into multiple threads—three in this case. Each of these threads is a set of activities performed by different actors at the same time. The start of this multithread process is shown by a horizontal bar in Figure 4.12, which is also called a "fork." The three threads of activities are independent of each other, and they continue in parallel as follows:

- The `Accountant` starts validating the proposal details and may also be able to confirm the payment arrangement (e.g., by credit card, check, etc.).
- The `Account Executive`, meanwhile, is shown as providing the `Status to Prospect` (or the potential client) regarding the progress of the policy application.
- In some insurance proposals, there might be a need to `Obtain Underwriter Approval`.

Since these three threads do not depend on each other, they can continue in parallel until they all meet at another sync point or join. This is shown by the second horizontal bar in Figure 4.12.

This meeting of three different threads at the sync point is followed by a decision point for the `Account Executive`, who, having found that all details are valid commences the cover. If, on the other hand, the details of the insurance proposal are not found to be valid or sufficient, then the Account Executive will reject the cover and inform the Client accordingly. Thus, there are two activities (Cover-Commences and CoverRejected) as the two logical points where this activity diagram can end.

While subject to further discussion in the problem space, note that the difference between a client and a prospect is not considered significant in this activity diagram because a prospect can become a client as soon as she takes out a cover. Furthermore, the notes partition improvised in the previous activity diagram is not mandatory and is not shown in Figure 4.12.

From the process viewpoint, note that drawing a diagram like Figure 4.12 can and usually will provide some corrections and improvements in the use case documentation as well as the use case diagrams drawn earlier. For example, the actor A60-Underwriter may not have been documented in the first cut of the use case diagram PolicyCreation. At the end of the activity diagram Creates HomeInsurancePolicy the PolicyCreation use case diagram will be updated with this additional actor, A60-Underwriter, discovered as the business analyst went through the details of creating this activity diagram. By going through the activity diagrams along with the users in a workshop format, we can identify missing actors as well as missing activities and alternate flows.

Having described the two activity diagrams in detail, let us see how we can apply the syntax, semantic and aesthetic checks to them.

### 4.3.3   Syntax Checks for Activity Diagrams

- Check for all the *permissible* elements on the activity diagram. These are all the basic ingredients described for an activity diagram in Chapter 2, including the actors, start and stop states, forks and joins, activities, decision points, flows, notes and partitions. Nonpermissible UML elements include a use case or a component on an activity diagram.
- Check that there is a start activity—but only one. This activity provides information on where to start reading an activity diagram. This can be verified as correct in the two activity diagrams drawn earlier.
- There may be one or more stop activities to indicate where the suite of activities will finish. As Figure 4.12 shows, the activities end in two places. However, there can be situations where the activity diagram may not end—typically in models of embedded systems. In practical MOPS, though, that may not happen, and we will usually have an end activity.
- Check that the notation for activity is correctly used. Due to the earlier legacy of state machine diagrams, it is common to confuse the activity notation with the notation of a state.
- Make sure that the notation for transition is correctly used. This is an open arrow pointing to the transition from one activity to another. Ensure that the correct arrow is used and that it is pointing in the right direction.

- Check that the notation for sync points (forks and joins) is correctly used to represent the forking of multithreads and then their joins.
- Check that for a fork there is a join. If there is no join, then the possibility of one thread ending prematurely or dangling without a logical conclusion is high. Syntactically, a fork without a join or the reverse should be immediately investigated.
- Check that the notation for the decision points, a hollow diamond, is correctly used.
- Make sure that whenever partitions are introduced, the partition notation, as well as the corresponding actor notation for that partition, is correctly used.
- Check for object notation if objects are used on activity diagrams. The use of objects, and to a certain extent multithreads with forks and joins, may be an advanced use of the activity diagramming technique. Some of these features of activity diagrams may not be relevant in the problem space.

### 4.3.4  Semantic Checks for Activity Diagrams

- Check to ascertain the correctness of the names of the activities and their corresponding meaning within the business domain. For example, the activity diagram shown in Figure 4.12 contains the activities AcceptHome InsuranceProposal, ProvideStatustOfProspect and so on. Do the names of these activities represent the actual work carried out by an actor?
- Check the implications of the partitions (provided that they exist). In MOPS, the partitions will usually represent the swimlanes in which respective actors are performing their activities ("swimming") as they perform the activities. Ensure that the actors in the use case diagram correspond to the partitions' actors in the activity diagram.
- Check for semantically correct dependencies between activities. For example, in Figure 4.11, you cannot have ValidateBasicClientDetails without ProvideBasicClientDetails. This checking of the dependencies between activities in a large, complicated activity diagram requires business knowledge. Such checks are also best performed in a workshop environment.
- Is forking semantically correct? Is joining correct? Check that the activities that are supposed to be in parallel are indeed so. For example, in Figure 4.12, three sets of activities are going on in parallel. While the validation of the proposal takes place, the underwriter approval is also sought. If there is a dependency on the underwriter, which states that unless a proposal is valid the underwriter will not approve it, then the forking shown in Figure 4.12 will not be valid and will have to be modified. In the current scenario, the underwriter's approval is provided only for a given amount against a given risk and is conditional upon the proposal's being valid.

### 4.3.5   Aesthetic Checks for Activity Diagrams

From the bird's-eye view of this diagram, along with other activity diagrams, we will need to check the following:

- How many activities are there on a diagram? Sometimes it may be necessary to have a complex set of activities all represented on a single diagram. This may be necessary to provide one logically cohesive flow on the activity diagram. In most cases, though, activity diagrams should not have more than 14 activities on one diagram. I am doubling the span of control (seven) number here, because activities depict dependencies rather than a static structural view. Furthermore, activity diagrams are at a lower level of granularity than use case diagrams. Therefore, it may be aesthetically acceptable to have more activity elements on an activity diagram than, say, use case elements on the use case diagrams. Figure 4.11 contains seven activities, as does Figure 4.12. If more activity details have to be shown, there is still space on these two diagrams to show them.

- The use of decision points, as well as forks and joins, must be considered from the aesthetic viewpoint. Are the decision points confusing? This becomes important especially when the decision points show the control of flow going back to a previous activity. It is not uncommon for more than two decisions to come out of a decision point. However, more than four decisions (flows) coming out of a decision point will become inelegant and confusing.

- Having partitions in an activity diagram is not mandatory. However, if partitions are shown, they should be limited to approximately four. More than four partitions will reduce the comprehensibility of the diagram. If more partitions are needed, an additional activity diagram should be considered.

- How many activity diagrams are associated with a use case? Usually just one activity diagram will represent pictorially what is happening in the use case. For a complex use case depicting a complex flow, two or three activity diagrams may be associated with the use case. If more than three activity diagrams are needed to represent what is happening within a use case, one should seriously consider factorizing the use case itself.

- Activity diagrams are not restricted to representing the flow within use cases. They could also represent an overall flow within a business process. Check to see if there are activity diagrams in MOPS that represent the business context. There should not be more than two such "context" activity diagrams. These context activity diagrams are at the highest level of the model, and they represent what happens overall in the system. More than two such diagrams, and the purpose of having them at the highest level, representing the business context, will be lost.

- Check if sufficient notes have been added, and that these notes are all placed in a readable format in the activity diagram. Consider our earlier discussion on placing the notes in a partition of their own when describing business activities in MOPS.

- Objects should not be represented in the activity diagrams in the problem space by business analysts. We do not discuss activity diagrams in the solution space in this book, although they can be used there. It is only in such usage of the activity diagrams in the solution space that objects should be used. Using objects in activity diagrams in MOPS is aesthetically inappropriate.

## 4.4   QUALITY OF PACKAGE DIAGRAMS IN MOPS

As mentioned during its SWOT analysis in Chapter 3, the package diagram is mainly an organizational diagram that helps, to divide a large system into smaller, more manageable chunks called "subsystems." While packages themselves are easy to show in a CASE tool, usually the dependencies between packages, the meanings of their stereotypes, and so on are limited by the ability of the corresponding CASE tool to draw the package diagram. Therefore, like the business domain model (which may be a class diagram showing business entities or classes at a very high level), the package diagram may end up showing the highest elements within the system through the packages. Here we look at a package diagram for the LUCKY insurance system and then apply the three levels of quality checks to this diagram.

### 4.4.1   Describing the LUCKY Package Diagram

Figure 4.13 is an organizational package diagram that shows how the LUCKY system has been divided into five major packages at the business level. These packages are:

```
Policy Package
Marketing Package
Client Package
Settlements Package
Claims Package
```

These packages represent subsystems (in an organizational sense, not in a strictly technical sense) that contain all the relevant diagrams and associated specifications and documentations. However, this same package diagram may also be considered in detail by the person playing the role of an architect in MOBS, where all detailed technical issues like components, dependencies, distribution of executables on the network, and a detailed database, as well as interface elements and security frameworks, will appear as additional technical packages. These additional packages will enable implementation of whatever is considered here in the problem space. These additional packages are described in Chapter 6, where we discuss the quality of MOBS.

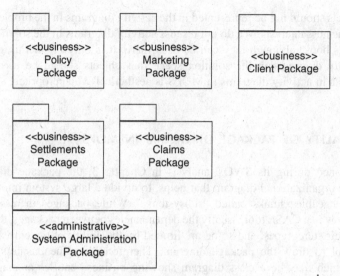

**Figure 4.13**   The LUCKY package diagram.

In addition to the packages stereotyped as <<business>>, there is a System AdministrationPackage. This has been stereotyped as <<administrative>>, because it deals with the administration of LUCKY's new insurance system. Examples of issues considered in administration of the system include maintaining the list of users (e.g., the Account Executives, the Senior Account Executive and their levels of logins; backup of the data and, more important, backup of software; etc.).

### 4.4.2   Syntax Checks for the LUCKY Package Diagram

- Check the package diagram, similarly to other diagrams, to ensure that only the permissible elements appear. These valid elements include the tabbed rectangle and the name of the package inside it.

- Package names should represent the major areas or subsystems of the system. These packages names should conform to the internal standards of the project and the organization. Package names are usually nouns representing different areas of business. For example, the LUCKY insurance system package diagram has clear, crisp names representing the areas of business, such as management of all Client Details (Client Package), and managing the Claims (Claims Package).

- Package diagrams can also show the relationship between packages. While these relationships are not shown in Figure 4.13, if used these relationships show the dependency between packages. Check the dependency relationship arrow if it is used. It should be an open dotted arrow showing the dependency between packages that depends on another package for its services.

• If packages are shown with a stereotype, then check that the stereotype conforms to the UML notation for stereotypes.

• If present, check for notes explaining the packages.

• Check if the packages are more than just subsystems. They can be technical packages, as in the Java programming language. In that case, packages specify a directory structure—telling the compiler where to find the class files. For most of the work in MOPS, this will not be an issue, but it should be kept in mind in naming and dealing with packages.

### 4.4.3 Semantic Checks for the LUCKY Package Diagram

• What does a package represent? This is the first and major semantic check of the package diagram. Does the Client Package represent all the details of client maintenance or does it also include details of employees? In our example, if the Client Package deals with maintenance of names and addresses of all persons, then it may be necessary to place employee classes in Client. Alternatively, the semantic check may result in creation of a new level within the package that deals with employee maintenance. Domain experts must be involved in conducting this semantic check, as they are in the best position to indicate the cohesiveness and meaning of each package.

• Are packages leveled? Leveling of packages is allowed in UML but should be attempted only when it is semantically necessary. For example, the Client Package can be repackaged into three packages: Person, Employee and Client. In that case, the packages Employee and Client will appear within the Person package, and will be named Person::Employee and Person::Client. (We have not shown this in our examples.)

• Are the dependencies necessary? Dependencies between packages should be shown only if necessary. However, being pedantic about dependencies will result in a package diagram showing dependencies from all packages to all other packages. Packages on a package diagram may usually be left, as shown in Figure 4.13, without any lines. Notes may be added to explain a particular dependency.

• Check the manner of package creation. There are two ways to develop packages—bottom up, after the use cases and a few business classes have been drawn, or top down, with the use cases drawn later, underneath a package. If it is a bottom-up creation, a package will appear later in the life cycle, but it is likely to be relatively stable. A top-down approach to package creation will usually have to handle redrawing of packages. This is because drawing use case and activity diagrams is likely to reveal flaws in the creation and naming of packages. Therefore, checking the manner of package creation is crucial from the semantic viewpoint.

• Do the packages belong to the right team of modelers and developers? This check also relates to the CASE tool being used in the modeling exercise.

For example, each of the packages shown in Figure 4.13 will belong to a team of modelers and developers—with the insurance expert looking at the requirements of the `Policy Package` and `Claims Package`, the accountant providing specialized input into the `Settlements Package`, and the marketing director involved in the `Marketing Package`. This division can be carried right through to implementation, where respective programmers will handle the coding of each of these packages based on the related UML diagrams (e.g., class diagrams).

- Ensure that nonbusiness packages, such as GUI, `Admin` and `Database` are not given undue importance at this MOPS level of modeling. While these packages will eventually be required, it is advisable to focus attention on the business packages at this MOPS creation stage.

- Packages can be used as architectural constructs in addition to their organizational usage. While they have been discussed here almost exclusively as organizational constructs, if they are used as architectural constructs their semantic meaning will change. For example, each of the business-level packages shown in Figure 4.13 will have to be supported by corresponding technical packages like graphics, charting and printing packages. These types of packages are further described in Chapter 6.

### 4.4.4   Aesthetic Checks for the LUCKY Package Diagram

- Check the size of the package. Theoretically, each business class can be a package. However, that will be too fine granular a model to make good use of the package concept. Alternatively, the entire system with all of its diagrams can be placed within a package. This will be a very coarse package diagram and will not be aesthetically elegant. Furthermore, in a medium-sized to large project, a single package will not be able to accommodate parallel development. Therefore, there should be a reasonable balance of the number of packages in a good model. A medium-sized project may have 10 to 15 business-level packages.

- Leveling of packages is also an aesthetic issue. Even if a multilevel suite of packages is syntactically permitted and semantically needed, creating more than three levels of packages will reduce comprehensibility. Three levels are recommended, and as seen in Figure 4.13, it may not be necessary to create any levels at all—at least in problem space modeling.

## 4.5   QUALITY OF CLASSES AND CLASS DIAGRAMS IN MOPS

In this section, we discuss the quality of classes and class diagrams in the problem space. Because of the extreme importance of classes, they must be treated separately from the class diagrams in which they reside—in terms of their creation and the quality assurance activities performed on them. As a result, the following discussion is divided into two parts—the V&V of classes and then the class diagrams.

Identification of classes from use case descriptions, or from any other source, is a subject of intense study. There are techniques like "noun analysis" (Booch et al., 1999) and CRC carding, which have been discussed sufficiently in the object-oriented (OO) literature. Therefore, we assume that readers are familiar with identification of classes and proceed with two classes, Policy and Client, their documentation and quality checks. This will be followed by discussions on the quality of the class diagrams.

### 4.5.1 Documenting a Class

Figure 4.14 shows two classes—Client and Policy. In MOPS, however, these are business entities. These business entities have associated specifications. The specifications of a class can be documented either directly in a CASE tool or in separate external documentation. In the very early stages of MOPS creation, modelers may not necessarily have access to CASE tools. A class can then be documented by business analysts using a template. In this example too, the detailed specification of the class is documented outside of a CASE tool. The template described here can help ensure that a class is satisfactorily discussed before being placed in MOPS. If techniques such as CRC carding (Beck and Cunningham, 1989) are used, the following template can be directly helpful in documenting the details of the business classes and their responsibilities initially discovered. This template, like most other templates discussed in this book, is not fixed in form. Readers are advised to modify the given template to suit their purposes of problem space modeling. Name, attribute and responsibilities are the only things that are close to being mandatory in this class description.

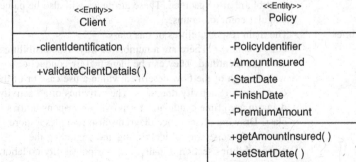

**Figure 4.14** Classes Client and Policy.

### 4.5.1.1  *Suggested Class Template*

---

| | |
|---|---|
| <<Stereotype>><br>Class Name | <A one-word singular common noun name for the class; The name is prefixed by the optional stereotype. The stereotype indicates, for example, whether this is an interface, persistence or control class><br><br>*Quality Comment:* Naming the class correctly is extremely helpful in enabling the modelers to focus on the purpose of the class and the programmers to understand that purpose. A singular common noun is suggested. If more than one word is needed for a class name, the words should be combined into a compact, readable entity. In MOPS, the first cut of these class names will be the most prominent words in the business domain. For example, `Client`, `Claim`, `Policy` and `Settlement` are obvious business classes for an insurance domain. |
| Description | <A one-line description of the class><br><br>*Quality Comment:* The best way to focus on the purpose of the class is to describe it in one line. A class should not contain many different areas of responsibility, as that will result in an unnecessarily complex class. By requiring a succinct description, the purpose of the class becomes clear. If more than one line is needed for its description, then one should consider creating more than one class and then relating them to each other. |
| Relationship | <A list of other classes and the type of relationship they have with this class ><br><br>*Quality Comment:* Class-to-class relationship shows how classes will collaborate with each other in order to achieve a given functionality. Two of the basic relationships between classes at this stage are <<inheritance>> and <<association>>. Occasionally, the association between two classes is close enough to warrant the <<aggregation>> relationship. |
| Attributes | <A list of all attributes of the class><br><br>*Quality Comment:* The attributes here are merely listed at the analysis stage. During detailed design, their types, initial values and access control are also specified. These attributes will also be named as singular common nouns. |
| Responsibilities | <The main responsibilities of this class><br><br>*Quality Comment:* There are a number of ways responsibilities of a class are identified. They can be identified by conducting a walkthrough of the flow described within a use case or of the corresponding activity diagrams. The activities of an activity diagram are prime candidates for providing responsibilities of the class. Drawing of sequence diagrams also provides a more concrete/precise way of identifying and upgrading the responsibilities section. Finally, class-responsibility-collaboration cards and workshops can also be used. During system modeling in MOSS, these responsibilities may translate into one or more operations/methods. |

---

| Business Rules | <Special business rules and constraints that are not easily listed under responsibilities> |
| | *Quality Comment:* In specifying a class, it is important to describe the business rules separately, as these rules will eventually affect the algorithms within the operations of the class. Certain nonfunctional requirements can also be documented here. Examples of such rules include "calculating premiums based on the amount being insured" and "the number of insurance policies a single client can hold." |
| Complexity | <Simple/medium/complex> |
| | *Quality Comment:* The complexity level can be used to ascertain class-related metrics like the number of relationships the class has with other classes or the depth of inheritance if the class is part of an inheritance hierarchy. Once again, there are no formal criteria to classify a class into one of these three degrees of complexity, so experience plays a role in making this classification. |

### 4.5.1.2 Documentation of the Class Client

| <<Stereotype>> Name | <<entity>> Client |
| --- | --- |
| Description | This class maintains all administrative details of a client who does business with LUCKY. |
| Relationship | Associated with Policy; also has two specialized classes: PersonalClient and OrganizationalClient. (*Note: in order to see how* Client *evolves into a higher-level class, with the individual and organizational clients derived from it, you should jump ahead and look at Figure 4.17, where the client relationships are shown. Alternatively, you can carry on with an implied understanding that the* Client *class is specialized.*) |
| Attributes | Client ID: An alphanumeric identification generated by the insurance system to identify client. |
| | Value-of-Client: This information is added by the account executive to indicate the importance of the client to LUCKY's insurance business. A high-value client will have to be treated differently from an average client. |
| | Years-in-Business: This is the number of years this client has done business with LUCKY. This not only adds to the value of the client, but also has an impact on the rebate or concessions given to a "safer" client, who has a low history of claims against his cover. |
| | Retiree: This may be additional information indicating that there may be a government requirement to provide low-priced life cover or home cover to retirees. |

(*continued*)

| <<Stereotype>><br>Name | <<entity>><br>Client |
|---|---|
| Responsibilities | Create basic details of the client<br>Add additional details of the client<br>Change details of the client<br>Flag a client as "deleted" if there is no more business with the client |
| Business Rules | A client can only add and change basic details<br>If the client has a worker's compensation policy, he cannot change personal details<br>A client cannot view details of another client |
| Complexity | Medium<br>*Note: This is the complexity of the class, and is an important piece of information that the modelers provide to the developers. This is not a business characteristic of the class but rather its administrative detail.* |

## 4.5.1.3   Documentation of the Class Policy

| <<Stereotype>><br>Name | <<entity>><br>Policy |
|---|---|
| Description | Most details of all types of Policy are maintained here. |
| Relationship | Associated with Client.<br>*(Note: Policy, in a real insurance system, will be associated with numerous classes such as Claims, Settlements, and Marketing, in addition to the Client association described here. In the first iteration of modeling, you may want to skip documentation of any relationship at all.)* |
| Attributes | PolicyIdentifier: Used in identifying the insurance policy.<br>RiskCategory: Provides details of the type of risk being insured, such as vehicle, home or life.<br>RiskDescription: The description of the risk being insured. During solution space modeling, this description is most likely to be moved to another "reference" entity.<br>AmountInsured: The amount for which the risk is insured. While this will depend on the value of the risk itself, it is common to apply business rules here to indicate the allowable amount insured.<br>StartDate: The date from which the risk is covered by LUCKY.<br>FinishDate: The date on which the cover ends unless it is renewed.<br>PremiumAmount: The amount the client will pay for the policy.<br>SpecialConcessions: Depends on business rules and government rules. |

(*continued*)

| <<Stereotype>> Name | <<entity>> Policy |
|---|---|
| Responsibilities | Create and maintain details of the policy<br>Maintain details of the risk<br>Calculate the allowable insurance amount<br>Calculate premiums<br>Validate policy dates |
| Business Rules | AmountInsured cannot be greater than the value of the risk. The value of the risk will be available for home and vehicle risk categories, but not for life and hospital cover. |
| Complexity | High—as the class will have many variations to comply with, and will probably be specialized into respective risk categories. |

## 4.5.2 Syntax Checks for Classes

While the Syntax checks for a class are described here separately, they will make more sense when the classes are represented on a class diagram. Furthermore, in the descriptive specifications of a class, the UML checks are not as intense as they are on a class shown in a diagram.

- The class name is a noun. While this will not cause the system to crash, it will usually be part of the internal project standard. Hence, it is important to check the name of the class for its correct representation. In Figure 4.14, both Policy and Client are nouns that correctly represent the business entities in the problem space. This check is not more of a project standard than of a UML standard.

- The class name starts with a capital letter. Like the previous check, this will be a part of the project standard.

- Class names are singular. A class, representing a collection of objects, is still a singular noun. For example, the class Client represents many clients in the system. But when named, it is called Client, not Clients. Similarly, the Policy class is a singular noun representing a class of policies.

- If a stereotype is used to classify the class further, then check that it is correctly represented using the stereotype notations. The three basic stereotypes are entity, boundary and controller. The entity stereotype is the only one appearing in MOPS.

- If the class description has attributes, they are also singular common nouns describing the characteristics of the class.

- Responsibilities of a class should be clearly described, based on the requirements appearing in the use case and activity diagrams.

- Is this an abstract class? If so, is it represented by its name shown in italics?

- If the class description has operations, check that they are derived from behaviors associated with the class.

### 4.5.3   Semantic Checks for Classes

- Check that a class represents one and only one logical concept. Both Policy and Client represent a singular concept. Variations of the concept of policy and client will eventually appear, and will result in factorization of these classes into more classes.
- Check that a class is given a cohesive set of responsibilities. For example, the class Policy will only manage details related to insurance policies, and will not be responsible for managing details of a client.
- Check that a class represents the intended meaning of the class in the problem space. The class Policy should not be representing details of clients, and the class Client should not be managing policy details.
- Are there opportunities for generalization and/or specialization of classes? At the MOPS level, it will not be necessary to consider inheritance in as much detail as in modeling in the solution space. However, if there is an opportunity to create an abstraction that represents a business abstraction, then that should be attempted here. (For example, Policy itself might be a higher-level abstraction, and could be shown as an abstract entity even by a business analyst. The specialized classes from Policy would be specific policies such as home cover, car cover or health cover.)
- The semantic check for each class should go through the additional documentation, comments and business rules for the class. This would include the documentation, as well as the additional information that goes with each of the classes.

### 4.5.4   Aesthetic Checks for the Client Class

- A class should be well balanced. This means that a class should be comprehensible as a single entity. If a class represents multiple concepts from the business domain, its comprehensibility will be reduced. Thus, the size of a class is important from an aesthetic viewpoint.
- A class should have the right number of attributes. While this will change, depending on the language of implementation, it can still be stated that a class at the business level (in the problem space) should have approximately $15 \pm 5$ attributes.
- Similarly, a class should not have too many or too few operations or methods. While operations may be further stereotyped in the solution space in MOPS, they represent responsibilities. Business responsibilities of a class should total about five to seven. These responsibilities will then translate into a number of operations and, subsequently, into methods in the solution space.

### 4.5.5  Describing the ClientDetails Class Diagram

Figure 4.15 shows the first attempt to create the domain model. Some basic or first cuts of classes, also called "business entities", have been discovered and are shown on this diagram. Analysis of the use cases AddsClientDetails and Changes ClientDetails provides some basic business entities. One such entity, described and documented in the previous section, is the Client.

As modeling in the problem space progresses, it will be possible to derive the class Client from another invented class, Person. This may happen in the second iteration of modeling. Such classes as Person will also be obvious for people with domain modeling expertise. The class Person is shown as an abstraction on Figure 4.15. It will store and manage all attributes and behavior related to any person in the system.

The Client, shown on this diagram, has evolved further from the simple description of a client provided in the previous section. In Figure 4.15, the Client is actually the representative of an organization that is taking out insurance cover with LUCKY. Thus, the Client is a person who is representing the client organization. Thus, all the institutional or organizational clients that might come out of analyzing a use case will have a representative who will deal with the insurance system, and it is this representative that is shown as the Client derived from the class Person.

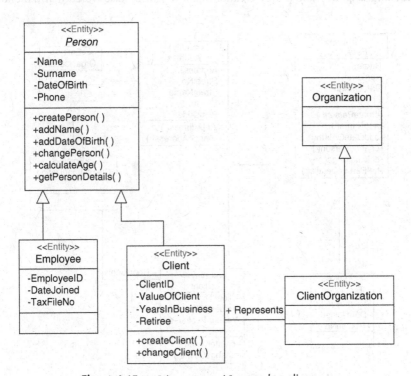

**Figure 4.15**  ClientDetails–a class diagram.

In addition to the above discussion on Client, as a representative of an organization, we also create a Client Organization as derived from an organization. This leaves the opportunity open to derive other types of organizations that might deal with the insurance system, an example being LUCKY as an organization itself. The Name, Trading Name and Business Identification Number of all types of organizations can be managed by the class Organization, facilitating reuse.

All organizations also have an address that is common to the Client Organization or any other type of organization. Therefore, the address details should be kept up in the class Organization. However, all persons represented by Person also have addresses. Thus we find that the address, which has typically a street number, name, suburb and postal code, is applicable to both Person and Organization. Therefore, this has been factored out, and shown as aggregated with Person and Address. This is shown in Figure 4.16.

While the debate between black and white (or filled and unfilled diamonds) continues to rage, we simply use the aggregation notation here to indicate a much closer or tighter relationship between the person and the address, and that the same class Address is shared by an Organization which also needs an address. The rest of the diagram remains the same.

However, once again, if further study is carried out on addition of client, as well as looking at policy and policy creation, then it will be discovered that the client

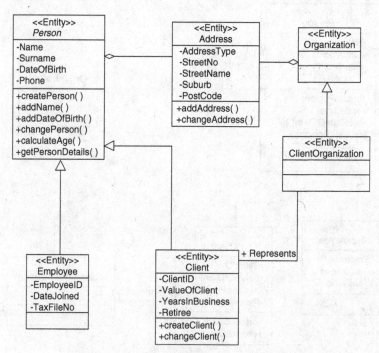

**Figure 4.16**  ClientDetails-b class diagram.

is either the person or the organization that does business with LUCKY. This information is gleaned from further study of the use cases. For example, study of Figure 4.12, as well as the `AddsClientDetails` use case, provides this helpful information on the commonality of client attributes, enabling the modeler to create a separate business entity called `Client`.

This client is not the person originally discovered, but has evolved into an entity that does insurance business with LUCKY and that can be both an organization and a person (shown as `personal`, although you may want to use individual). Therefore, two more business classes, `OrganizationalClient` and `PersonalClient`, are shown as inheriting from `Client` in Figure 4.17. In that diagram, `Organization` associates with a client representative who is the actual person during business with LUCKY on behalf of the organization.

Individual `Client` (or `PersonalClient`) is not only a client of LUCKY, but is also a person. Therefore, in Figure 4.17, the class `Individual` is shown as inheriting not only from `Client`, but also from `Person`. This part of the model shown in Figure 4.17 brings in the issue of multiple inheritance. While most experts advise avoiding this situation, it has been shown here on purpose with the caveat that multiple inheritance, as shown here for the personal client, need not be implemented as such in the solution space. In fact, some implementation languages expressly prohibit the implementation of this model. However, implementation concerns the

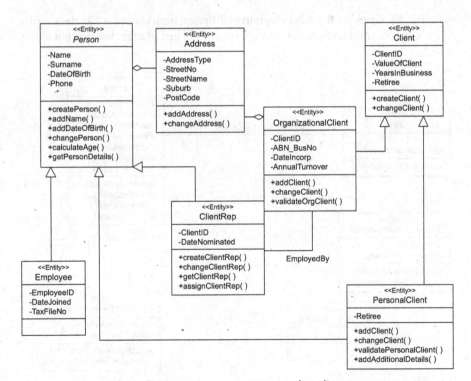

**Figure 4.17** `ClientDetails-c` class diagram.

solution space and should be discussed separately. Here, Figure 4.17, with its `PersonalClient` inheriting from `Client` and `Person`, makes sense and hence is retained.

### 4.5.6   Describing the PolicyDetails Class Diagram

Figure 4.18 shows a class diagram called `PolicyDetails`. This diagram shows the major classes that deal with insurance policy–related details. Like Figure 4.17, this class diagram is arrived at by analyzing the use cases, their descriptions and the corresponding activity diagrams. While identifying and describing the `Policy` class was straightforward in the previous section, in this policy details class diagram, we also see the class `Policy` being specialized into `Policy-HomeInsurance` and `Policy-LifeCover`. Note that although `Policy` may be abstract, this is not mandatory and is not shown as abstract in Figure 4.18. Every `Policy` has `UndewriterDetails`. `Policy` is also associated with `Client`, but the `Client` is in the role of a `PolicyHolder`. This differentiates the `Client` playing some other role in the system (e.g., being used for marketing purposes).

### 4.5.7   Syntax Checks for Class Diagrams

Syntactically checking the class diagram is different from checking the class itself. At the class diagram level, the checks are related not just to a single class, but to the

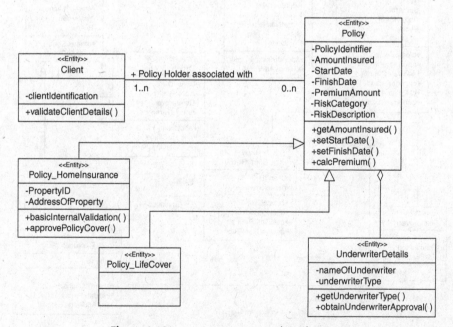

**Figure 4.18**  `PolicyDetails` class diagram.

entire diagram. Here are the syntax checks that we would apply to Figures 4.17 and 4.18, as well as to any other class diagram that we draw in creating MOPS.

- Check the allowable elements on a class diagram. The most important of these notations are the class, relationships, multiplicities and stereotypes. Therefore, we cannot have a use case or an activity on a class diagram. Both of the class diagrams under inspection have only allowable elements.
- Check the notation for a class. It is a rectangle, as described in putting together a class diagram in Chapter 2.
- Check the relationship notations—the association, aggregation and inheritance relationships. All three relationship notations are acceptable in the class diagrams we are inspecting.
- Check all the association relationships. When a straight line is drawn between two classes, it implies an association. Is association represented by a straight line? `OrganizationalClient` and `ClientRep` are associated in Figure 4.17, and `Policy` and `Client` are associated in Figure 4.18.
- Does the association relationship line have an arrowhead? If so, is it an open arrowhead? This represents a directional association. There is no directional association on `Client` details or `Policy` details class diagrams.
- Does the inheritance relationship line have an arrow, with a closed unfilled arrowhead, representing one class inheriting from another class? There are many inheritances on `Client` details and in `Policy` details class diagrams, and all pass this quality syntax check.
- Does aggregation appear on the class diagram? If so, does it have the aggregation line, with a diamond on the side of the "senior" class? `Organization` (`OrganizationalClient`) and `Person` both have an address in Figure 4.17, and `Policy` has `Underwriter` details in Figure 4.18.
- Does the aggregation line show an arrowhead? If so, is it an open arrowhead? These directional aggregations do not appear at this stage in either of the two figures under inspection. However, directional aggregation (and directional association) will usually appear during the second iteration of modeling these class diagrams.
- Check if multiplicity is shown on the class diagram. If so, is it shown for the association relationship only? (It cannot be shown for inheritance.) The multiplicity between `Policy` and `Client` is correctly shown in Figure 4.18.
- Check if constraints are shown on the class diagram.
- Check if tagged values are shown on the class diagram.
- Are stereotypes shown for classes? Are stereotypes shown on relationships? Check for the notational correctness of these stereotypes.
- Are notes added to the diagram using the notation of a bent dog-eared box (rectangle)?

### 4.5.8    Semantic Checks for Class Diagrams

- Check the meaning of each class on the class diagram. This check would have been completed for the semantics of each class, but it should be repeated when checking a class diagram.

- Check the attributes and operations for each of the classes, if already defined. These appear on the class diagram based on the use case descriptions and activity diagrams.

- Check the meaning of each relationship. Does the association mean that one class "uses" another class? It is common to come across a "has" relationship in common parlance, but in practice it becomes an association only, and not an aggregation (e.g., although a Client has a Policy, the semantic modeling of this relationship will be an association, not an aggregation).

- Check the semantics of inheritance. When one class inherits from another class, that inheritance should be justifiable from a business viewpoint. For example, Policy-HomeInsurance inherits from Policy in Figure 4.18, and that is a semantically acceptable inheritance. In the solution space, though, this semantic meaning may not always hold true.

- Does the aggregation represent a genuine "has a" relationship? Semantically, an aggregation can be an "aggregate aggregation," as in a Policy that has Underwriter details, or it can be a "composite aggregation" or simply composition. Composition is not shown on our diagrams. If it must be shown, my suggestion is to continue to use the simply unfilled (white) diamond supplemented with notes.

- Check for the semantic meanings of multiplicities. Multiplicities contain business rules. For example, Figure 4.18 shows that a Policy must have at least one Client but can have as many clients as needed. However, a Client may not have any Policy, or can have as many policies as needed. Check for these semantic meanings behind multiplicities.

- Check the meanings behind constraints and tagged values.

- Check the reasoning behind stereotypes. In most cases, the stereotype in MOPS will be <<entity>>.

- Is any multiple inheritance appearing on the diagram? If so, provide additional information on how it can be converted eventually into a simpler model.

- Are roles shown on association relationships? If so, are the roles correctly representing the role played by the class in a particular relationship? In Figure 4.18, the role shown is PolicyHolder when the Client interacts with Policy. Is that the meaning behind the relationship?

### 4.5.9    Aesthetic Checks for Class Diagrams

- An aesthetically elegant class diagram will have a comprehensible set of classes. Once again seven plus or minus two is the ideal number of classes for a class diagram.

- Check the relationships on the class diagram. If there appears to be more than one association between a given pair of classes, this should be reduced by providing roles between the two classes.
- Since classes can be shown on more than one class diagram, depending on the context, check that classes are *repeated* sufficiently, in as many class diagrams as required, ensuring that their relationships and the roles they play are clear.
- How many diagrams are there? While there is no limit on the number of class diagrams in a given model, a large number of class diagrams should be placed in separate packages to make them elegant.
- In addition to its semantic importance, inheritance has an aesthetic angle. In the problem space, it is recommended that the depth of inheritance be not more than three. Once technical classes in the solution space are added to this hierarchy, the total depth can easily become incomprehensible. Therefore, it is essential to keep the inheritance depth under control in MOPS.

## 4.6 QUALITY OF SEQUENCE DIAGRAMS IN MOPS

### 4.6.1 Describing the CreateClient Sequence Diagram

Figure 4.19 shows a very brief sequence of how a `Client`, in this case `Personal Client`, is created in the system. `A10-AccountExecutive` is shown as sending the message `'createPerson'` to the object `aClient` belonging to class `PersonalClient`.

After a certain amount of validation, as shown by the message `'validatePerson'`, the `Account Executive` sends another message, `'addClient'`.

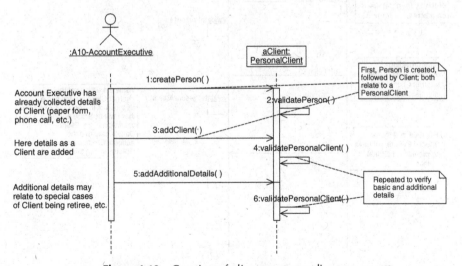

**Figure 4.19** Creation of client sequence diagram.

Once the `Personal Client` receives the message 'addClient', additional validation related to the details of the `Personal Client` takes place. This is followed by additional details sent by the `Account Executive` and further validation of the `Personal Client`. The notes explain the focus of the two messages being repeated on the diagram. There is some text description on the left corresponding to the three messages that the `Account Executive` sends to the `Client Object`.

There are some additional notes on this diagram that explain how a `Person` is created first, followed by a `Client`.

### 4.6.2   Describing the CreateClientOnInternet Sequence Diagram

This creation of client sequence described above would change if the entire system is moved to the Internet or if it provides for an Internet interface that allows clients or potential clients to carry out some functions—in this case, that of creating their own details. Figure 4.20 shows the creation of client on the Internet sequence. The actual sending of messages, as you would have noticed, remains the same. These are the creation of `Person` and validation of `Person` followed by adding `Client`, its validation and addition of `Client Details`. Once again, this diagram has text description on the left and some notes. The most interesting and most important aspect of this diagram is the fact that all the actions or messages that the `Client` object was receiving in Figure 4.19 from the `Account Executive` are now all received from the `InternetClient`. This is important for

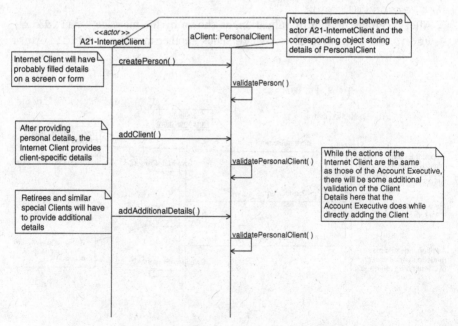

**Figure 4.20**   `CreateClientOnInternet` sequence diagram.

e-commerce applications—and even for the modern day CRMS implementation—where `InternetClient` assumes an importance of its own and is likely to carry out many tasks, especially inquiries that would otherwise be carried out by the `Account Executive` only.

Needless to say, because this is a MOPS diagram, it is merely recording the problem definition. This diagram can be further extended in the solution space, where it will need a few more implementation objects such as screens, forms, and databases or database tables.

### 4.6.3 Describing the ApprovePolicy Sequence Diagram

The sequence diagram on approval of policy shown in Figure 4.21 starts with the `:AccountExecutive`, sending the message 'validateDetails' to `aPolicy` object that belongs to `Policy-HomeInsurance` class. The text description on the left ensures that there is a sufficient explanation of what the messages are doing. The object `aPolicy` sends a message to the object `aClient` asking the `Client` object to validate the details of the `Client` (validate `ClientDetails`). Some internal validations of the policy are conducted by the

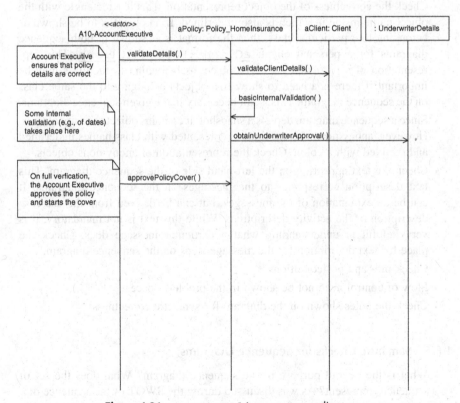

**Figure 4.21** `Approvepolicy` sequence diagram.

`aPolicy` object, followed by a message sent to the `UnderwriterDetails` object for obtaining `Underwriter` approval. Once these sequences of events are completed, the `Account Executive` is able to `approvePolicyCover`.

There are a number of alternatives to this sequence which are not shown here. For example, what happens if the `Underwriter's` approval is not obtained? This will necessitate another sequence diagram, not a variation of this diagram.

### 4.6.4   Syntax Checks for Sequence Diagrams

- Check for the basic syntax of the diagram, ensuring that only allowable elements of sequence diagrams appear. The most important of these elements are the objects, their time lines and the messages shown between objects.
- Check for the syntactic correctness of an actor (represented as a stickman). For example, in Figure 4.19, `A10-AccountExecutive` is shown correctly as an actor, but this is a specific actor and therefore it is underlined. This `:A10-AccountExecutive` may read as `John:A10-AccountExecutive` if a specific actor needs to be shown in the sequence diagram.
- Check for message lines with arrowheads.
- Check the correctness of the object representation. This is a rectangle with the object name inside it, which is also underlined. If an object is to be shown as belonging to a particular class, then the format is as shown in both sequence diagrams for a personal client: `aClient:PersonalClient`. This representation of a particular `Client` object as belonging to the class may be important if there is a need to show two objects belonging to the same class on the sequence diagram. This is not necessary in the given sequence diagrams.
- Since a sequence diagram depicts a snapshot, it contains objects and not classes. However, anonymous objects can be represented with class names underlined and prefixed with a colon. Check the representation of anonymous objects.
- Check the text appearing on the left-hand side of the sequence diagram. This text description corresponds to the messages on the sequence diagrams. It can be an explanation of the messages, but can be derived from the use case description or the activity descriptions. While this text is not mandatory, it is very helpful in understanding what a particular message does. Check the place for text description for the message steps on the sequence diagram.
- Check pre- and postconditions.
- Flow of control need not be shown in the problem space.
- Check the notes shown on the diagram for syntactic correctness.

### 4.6.5   Semantic Checks for Sequence Diagrams

- What is the overall purpose of the sequence diagram? What does the set of sequences represent? As was discussed during the SWOT of the sequence diagrams, they can be drawn for a scenario within a use case or for a thread within an activity diagram. They need not have a one-to-one mapping with the use cases.

- Objects on the sequence diagram correspond to classes in the model.
- In modeling the problem space, there is no need to show the message signatures and the return values. While showing this information is not syntactically wrong, it will be going into more depth than is necessary in the problem space.
- Sequences (messages) also correspond to operations in the class. While this might be a technical requirement, it is advisable to map messages to operations even in the problem space.
- A message sent from one actor to another, although outside of the actual software system, may still be important in MOPS. For example, business users of the insurance system may need to show the interaction between the Account Executive and the Client on a person-to-person level. Semantically, it makes sense to create and document such interaction, especially if part of it deals with the system itself.
- For example, if the Account Executive creates details of a Client based on a manual process of receiving a form filled out by the Client, then that handing over of a filled form by the Client to the Account Executive *may* be shown as an actor-to-actor message. (This actor-to-actor messages for a Passenger to Check-in Clerk for an airline check-in sequence diagram has been shown in an interesting way in Hudson, 2001.)
- In the problem space, it is extremely important to check the semantic meaning of the entire sequence diagram. Thus CreateClient is meant to show what is actually happening in the corresponding use case and activity diagrams.
- The objects shown here should belong to the corresponding classes and should be checked to ensure that they make sense in the particular sequence.
- Some semantic checks will include ensuring that each method and each message shown are in the right sequence. For example, validatePerson cannot take place before Person is created. Similarly, all sequences must be checked to ensure that they correspond to a semantically correct flow.
- In performing semantic checks, we also focus on the completeness of whatever has been represented. As seen during the SWOT of the diagram, the sequence diagram is incomplete because it shows a snapshot. Therefore, the semantic check must ensure that whatever comes before this sequence starts and whatever happens after the sequence is complete is noted somewhere in the model.
- Description of this step shows that the Account Executive has collected a certain amount of information of the PersonalClient that is not shown on this diagram. It is also interesting to note that a PersonalClient is a person. Therefore, some messages that the PersonalClient receives (createPerson and validatePerson) are actually responsibilities of the abstract class Person from which PersonalClient has been derived. In performing semantic checks, it is essential to trace these messages to their respective classes.

- Check that this is indeed a business system diagram. There is a different type of sequence diagram that only shows the set of interactions between the actors and the system. This system sequence diagram may be important, but it is not drawn here. If it is a system sequence diagram, then instead of objects shown on the right, it will be just "system." Such a diagram will not be implementable, but it will be helpful in understanding the problem space.

### 4.6.6  Aesthetic Checks for Sequence Diagrams

- Sequence diagrams, if written in great and pedantic detail, can become very unwieldy. Check that the sequence diagram does not try to show every conceivable sequence.
- Ensure that the diagram contains a sensible sequence or a sensible snapshot of some steps in the system.
- Figure 4.19 provides an opportunity to add many more messages before the first message is shown or if there is a need to describe what happens before createPerson occurs. If that description has to be shown in terms of sequences or messages in the sequence diagram, this diagram will grow into an unnecessarily long and complex sequence. Text descriptions and notes should be judiciously added to maintain the aesthetic quality of this diagram.
- Since a sequence diagram is made up of objects, in UML there is no syntactic objection to representing multiple objects belonging to the same class in this diagram. However, this can lead to confusion. For example, an Account Executive could be creating aClient, which would then depend on bClient for some information. For instance, a husband and wife could be two objects belonging to PersonalClient object, one of which might be an existing client and the other one being newly created. In this case, messages can be shown between two objects belonging to the same class. Also, one actor might be dealing with another actor. It is possible that an Account Executive might interact with an actual Client; aesthetically, even that interaction is not necessary. Splitting a diagram into two or showing two separate creations of clients, as done here in Figures 4.19 and 4.20, is part of aesthetic quality. While both sequences could be shown syntactically correctly on one diagram, aesthetically this is not correct. The number of objects, number of messages and number of notes are all part of aesthetic checks. That is why we created creation of client A and creation of a client on the Internet as two sequence diagrams.

## 4.7  QUALITY OF STATE MACHINE DIAGRAMS IN MOPS

### 4.7.1  Describing the Client State Machine Diagram

In putting together a state machine diagram and in discussing its SWOT in Chapter 3, we mentioned that this is the only truly dynamic diagram in UML. While other

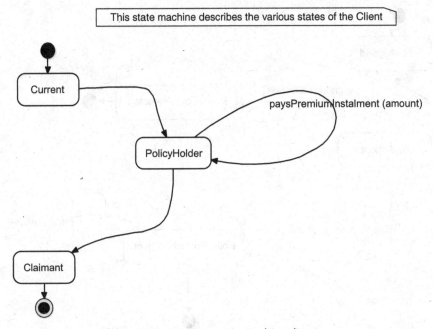

**Figure 4.22** `Client` state machine diagram.

diagrams show time, this is the only diagram that shows the changes to the states of a particular object as it progresses through a life cycle. The state machine diagram drawn in Figure 4.22 shows the changes to the life cycle of an object `Client` that belongs to the class `Client`.

The state machine diagram starts with the state of a Client as `Current`. Once the client pays the premium, the status of the client changes to `PolicyHolder`. This part of the model tells us that a Client may be `Current`, but still may not be a `PolicyHolder` unless the client pays for the policy. Once the `PolicyHolder` makes a claim, the status changes to that of a `Claimant`. If this state machine diagram is extended further, then it will show what happens to the `Claimant` once the claim has been paid by the insurance company.

### 4.7.2 Describing the Policy State Machine Diagram

The state machine diagram shown in Figure 4.23 describes the various states of the `Policy` object. It starts with the state of the policy as `PolicyApplied`. If the details of the policy that are provided are insufficient or incorrect, the policy is rejected and the status changes to `PolicyCoverRejected`. If that is not the case, then the policy is accepted, with its status changing to `PolicyAccepted`. Once accepted, the policy continues to provide cover and the status changes to

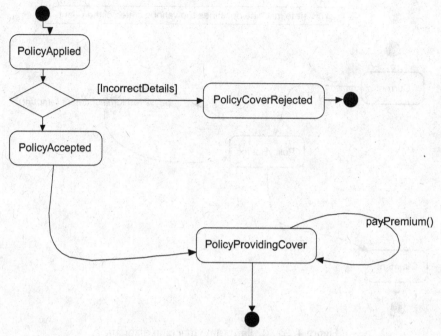

**Figure 4.23**   Policy state machine diagram.

PolicyProvidingCover. This status continues as long as the premium continues to be paid.

### 4.7.3   Syntax Checks for the ClientStates State Machine Diagram

- The elements on the state machine diagram indicate the various states of the object only (rather than activities or use cases). Are these states clearly shown on the diagram? Is the object for which these states are shown clearly marked?
- At this problem space modeling stage, there is no need to show detailed, complex nesting of the states. However, if it is necessary to show nesting, it should follow the UML syntax of states within states.
- As in the previous check, there is no need to show historical states at this level of modeling. If these states are shown, though, they should be syntactically correct and shown by an H in a circle.
- Are the states correctly represented by the rounded rectangle notation on the state machine diagram?
- Is a start state shown on the diagram? (Only one start state is allowed.) Note that if nesting is used, the substate can also have a start state of its own.

- Are end states shown on the diagram? They are not mandatory, and a state machine can have multiple end states. They should be correctly represented by the bull's-eye notation for end of state.
- While state machines are similar to activity diagrams, they are not the same. Check to ensure that there is no confusion between them.
- Are events correctly shown on the diagram? Events will cause changes in states.
- Further syntax checks for state machine diagrams include transitions, events and guard conditions. Ensure that these elements are correctly represented on the state machine diagram.

### 4.7.4  Semantic Checks for the ClientStates State Machine Diagram

- Is the state machine diagram drawn for an important object? In our case, `Client` appears to be one of the most important objects, and it is worthwhile drawing the state machine for this object.
- The semantic check deals with the meaning of each of these states. This implies checking whether the states are well defined or unclear. If the steps are not clearly defined and understood (i.e., if they are fuzzy), then investigate the meanings behind the states and redo the diagram to ensure that the states are clearly defined.
- Each state has a specific business meaning—as in the case of `Client` in its state of being a prospect or being current. Transitions and self-transitions also have semantic meaning. When a transition occurs from one state to another, it is worth investigating if that transition is driven by a business need, and whether it is a business transition (as in a claim changing its state) or a technical transition (as in a message being sent to the database that changes its state). Further, consider if it is just the value of a flag that is changing or whether a state transition is occurring because of a combination of changes in the values of attributes.

### 4.7.5  Aesthetic Checks for the ClientStates State Machine Diagram

- State machine diagrams tend to evolve rapidly into a highly complex diagram, especially if messages going to and from another object are also shown. It is important to keep in mind that state machine diagrams are used to show the life cycles of a complex and/or important objects only. Therefore, the complexity of the diagram itself can be managed by restricting the diagram to a single object.
- Even within an object, it is possible to show various life cycle flows. For example, two policy objects are likely to follow two separate paths. If situations arise where multiple paths need to be shown and the diagram is becoming complex, consider the possibility of showing two separate state machines for the same object. This will enhance the aesthetic quality of the state machine diagrams.

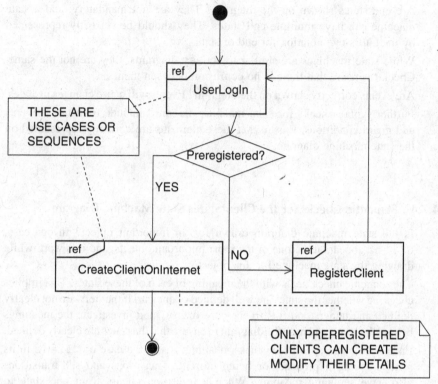

**Figure 4.24** Interaction overview diagram for CreateClient.

## 4.8 QUALITY OF INTERACTION OVERVIEW DIAGRAMS IN MOPS

### 4.8.1 Describing the CreateClient Interaction Overview Diagram

During the SWOT analysis of the interaction overview diagrams in Chapter 3, it was noted that these recently added diagrams in UML 2.0 show the flow or overview of interactions, not merely between two activities but also between two or more diagrams. For example, in Figure 4.24, we see that a flowchart is depicting the conditions in which three separate sequences will be executed. These sequences, easily represented by their respective sequence diagrams, are User LogIn, RegisterClient and CreateClientOnInternet. As noted in the figure, they may also be use cases describing the interaction of the actor with the system to accomplish these three behaviors. This behavioral diagram shows that initially the user logs in to the system. Then there is a check on whether the user is preregistered with the system to perform certain tasks. If so, the next sequence that is executed is CreateClientOnInternet. This sequence can be interpreted as the ability of a preregistered client to create her own details on the Internet.[2] If, however, the user is not registered at all, then this diagram directs the user to the registration process—which is shown as a `Register Client` sequence. The Interaction overview diagram is suitably adorned with notes.

### 4.8.2 Syntax Checks for Interaction Overview Diagrams

The syntax checks for the interaction overview diagram are based on the activity diagrams and are as follows:

- Check the start and stop pseudoactivities, as they increase readability of the diagrams.
- Check the references to the other sequences/use cases. These are the rectangular boxes within the interaction overview diagram.
- Check the accuracy of the arrows indicating the flow of the diagrams. Arrows should indicate direction and dependencies.
- Check for the "conditional checks." This is the check for satisfaction of a condition under which the flow will branch off. In Figure 4.24, it is the check for `'Preregistered?'` client.

### 4.8.3 Semantic Check for Interaction Overview Diagrams

The only significant check for interaction overview diagrams concerns the meanings of the references. In the interaction overview diagram under study, `UserLogIn`, `CreateClientOnInternet` and `RegisterClient` should all correctly represent the underlying sequences or use cases. This check is similar to the check of meaningful names behind activities and use cases. The meaning of the entire interaction overview diagram is reflected in its name. Therefore, the diagram should be named based on the suite of interactions whose overview it is representing. In this case, the diagram is called "Creation of Client" to indicate that it deals with sequences involved in creation of a client (although it may also be called "Creation of Client Details," depending on the vocabulary in the problem domain).

### 4.8.4 Aesthetic Check for Interaction Overview Diagrams

Aesthetically elegant interaction overview diagrams contain approximately five to nine references to sequences or use cases. With more than nine references, the diagram will become confusing. Therefore, for large numbers of sequences, additional interaction overview diagrams should be drawn. These diagrams are usually drawn within the packages where the corresponding sequences have been modeled. However, for sequences that belong to different packages, the interaction overview diagram should ensure that the external packages are also included in the referencing.

---

[2]However, variations on this sequence may occur, depending on the business rules of the organization. In some cases, creation of client details may include registration for login and password. In such cases, the interaction overview described here may not apply.

## 4.9 VALIDATING THE ENTIRE MOPS

The discussion thus far in this chapter has focused on applying the three levels of checks: syntax, semantics and aesthetics, to UML diagrams. These checks should enhance the quality of the diagrams in MOPS and increase the comfort of the business analysts involved in modeling in this space. In addition to V&V of the diagrams themselves, there are other important considerations in enhancing the quality of the model in the problem space. These considerations are primarily those of aesthetics at the highest level of the model, as well as the semantic meanings of various cross-diagram dependencies (the skill levels of these model level checks were discussed in Chapter 1 and shown in Figure 1.4). These considerations include the following:

- Dependencies of the various diagrams on each other. For example, a sequence diagram can (and does) update the class diagram. Have these dependencies among diagrams been considered? One of the best ways to do these dependency checks is to perform walkthroughs of the business processes (documented in a use case) and check to see if the UML diagrams are working in unison to satisfy these business processes.
- Documentation outside the diagrams that deals with the problem description but cannot be easily and visibly placed in the diagram (e.g., mathematical formulas) should also be checked to ensure that it is complete.
- Consideration of legal, contractual, third-party documentations that would comprise material in the problem space, and would influence the UML-based work, but may be in plain English documentation form rather than the elaborate diagrams of UML. This should also be considered in modeling of the problem space to ensure that there are no nonmodeling surprises at the end of the project.
- Completeness, correctness and consistency among the diagrams and documentation of MOPS, as well as their iterative dependency on other models in the solution and background spaces, should be considered.

Some of these interdiagram dependencies are briefly discussed here. Other dependencies will be discovered as the project progresses and should be actively sought by the quality analyst together with the modelers.

### 4.9.1 Use Case to Activity Diagram Dependency and Quality

Have you considered an activity diagram for every use case? This is not mandatory, but it is highly advisable, as activity diagrams show pictorially what is happening within a use case.

If an activity diagram is drawn for a use case, for every step within the text or flow of the use case, is there a corresponding activity within the activity diagram? This check will influence (and update) both the activity diagram and the use case documentation.

Some of these checks will happen as suggested by the process for software development. Other checks will have to be carried out outside of the process. However, the quality techniques discussed in Chapter 6 can be applied to these checks.

### 4.9.2 Use Case to Class Diagram Dependency and Quality

It is normal and acceptable for multiple use cases to influence class diagrams, as well as the attributes and operations of the classes within these diagrams.

Software development processes will recommend the approach to identification of classes from use case descriptions and related issues. However, after the classes have been identified and the class diagrams drawn, it is important to consider additional classes that may not have appeared by simply analyzing the use cases. Once these classes are discovered, it may be necessary to go back and update the use case descriptions.

Going back and forth between use case descriptions and classes on a class diagram is not only acceptable but should be encouraged. While use case diagrams and their descriptions provide the starting point for class identification, the reverse should also be carefully considered. Many business analysts, especially those with good domain knowledge and experience, start identifying classes even before they have drawn and documented the use cases. In such instances, it is important to correlate the classes identified with the corresponding use cases. It is worthwhile ensuring that every class can be traced to the descriptions of use cases and that, if there is no trace, there is a good reason for this lack of correlation between a class and at least one use case.

### 4.9.3 Class to Sequence Diagram Dependency and Quality

One of the important cross-diagram dependencies in UML diagrams is that between class and sequence diagrams. A sequence diagram provides a pictorial representation of an example of a use case. Therefore, by going through the sequence diagram, it is possible to prepare a list of potential classes (just as, by stepping through the use cases, one can obtain a list of good classes). However, sequence diagrams are more precise than use case descriptions, and they are also related closely to the class diagrams by the UML CASE tools. Thus, creating a new object on a sequence diagram will result in the creation of a new class in a class diagram if that class does not exist. Creation of a new message on a sequence diagram will also relate to a new method in a class on a class diagram if that method does not exist. The message signatures on sequence diagrams are also cross-checked against the method parameters on a class in a class diagram—mostly automatically by good CASE tools.

### 4.9.4 Interaction Overview Diagram to Sequence Diagram and Use Case Dependencies

As mentioned during the quality checks for interaction overview diagrams, these diagrams provide an overview of the flow between sequences and use cases. Therefore, they reference the sequence diagrams and use cases in the use case diagrams.

Ensure that the elements shown on the interaction overview diagrams have corresponding elements and/or diagrams in MOPS.

### 4.9.5   Quality of Documentation Associated with MOPS

As mentioned at the beginning of this section, some documentation may not fit within the UML specifications and documentation in the problem space. Examples of such documentation are business policies and procedures, mathematical formulas and government regulations. Business rules that may not fall within the purview of a single use case or class will also remain outside UML documentation. These additional types of documentation should be tied together and verified for correctness and completeness.

### 4.9.6   Aesthetics of MOPS

After completing all the checks on the UML elements and diagrams and cross-checking the dependencies among the diagrams, it is worthwhile to consider the entire MOPS from a bird's-eye viewpoint. It is important to perform this check at the highest level, because it is not the check of a specific element or diagram in the model and, therefore, is not likely to be as obvious as the other checks. Therefore, it is essential to take a step back, after a reasonable amount of modeling is done, to consider the aesthetic quality of the entire MOPS. This reasonable level of modeling is perhaps the final step of each of the iterations within the development process. Thus, the aesthetics of the MOPS should be checked at the end of initial, major and final iterations.

## 4.10   SUMMARY OF QUALITY CHECKS FOR MOPS

A summary list of all checks that need to be performed on each of the UML diagrams used to express MOPS is available in Appendix C in table form. This table can be used as a reminder of what needs to be checked. Readers are encouraged to add to this list their own specific checks, which may arise out of internal project standards, preproject discussions or their specific needs to use the UML. For example, a data warehousing project will need additional checks for the class diagrams that deal specifically with data tables, primary and foreign keys, and so on, but that project may not need the extensive checks needed for, say, the use case diagrams.

## DISCUSSION TOPICS

1. Which diagram should be used first, upfront, in a requirements modeling exercise?

2. We have drawn the use case diagrams. What happens next?

3. We have heard that activity diagrams are fairly technical. You are suggesting their use to document the flow in use cases. Is it allowed?

4. How are the UML diagrams outlined here related to each other?

5. Discuss the levels of checks applied to the UML diagrams and their importance with respect to UML artifacts, diagrams and MOPS.

6. How is the quality of the syntax of a class diagram different from its semantic quality? Differentiate with examples. Also describe how these checks differ when applied to a class as opposed to a class diagram.

7. How is the semantic quality of a use case diagram different from its aesthetic quality? Differentiate with examples. Also describe how the semantic checks of a use case diagram differ from those of a use case.

8. Discuss how a semantic check of a sequence diagram can change and improve the diagram.

9. Draw a sequence diagram first, without drawing any other diagrams, for a given requirement (e.g., a customer lodges an insurance claim). Try to create a class diagram based on the objects identified while drawing the sequence diagram.

10. What are the two best-known uses of an activity diagram?

11. How does an activity diagram compare with an interaction overview diagram?

12. How does a sequence diagram compare with an interaction overview diagram?

13. Discuss why a state chart diagram is more appropriate for a class than a class diagram? Also discuss why it is more appropriate for a class than a use case.

14. What is the source of common confusion between actor and class?

15. How does a use case help in creating an acceptance test plan?

16. Why is the use case to use case relationship confusing? What will you do to reduce this confusion?

17. Draw the diagrams in MOPS for a problem domain of your choice (airline, hospital, etc.). Apply the syntax, semantics and aesthetics quality checks to the diagrams and associated documentation.

18. What is the type and size of the LUCKY insurance project? Why does MOPS take more time and effort than the other two modeling spaces in these types of projects?

## REFERENCES

Armour, F., and Miller, G. *Advanced Use Case Modelling*. Boston: Addison-Wesley, 2001. (The accompanying CD has some practical templates that are worth considering.)

Booch, G., Rumbaugh, J., and Jacobson, I. *The Unified Modelling Language User Guide*. Reading, MA: Addison Wesley Longman, 1999.

Fowler, M. *UML Distilled*, 3rd Edition, Boston: Addison-Wesley Professional, 2003.

Henderson-Sellers, B., and Unhelkar, B. *OPEN Modelling with the UML*. London: Addison-Wesley, 2000.

Hudson, W. "A User-Cantered UML method," in *Object Modelling and User Interface Design: Designing Interactive Systems*, M. Van Harmelen ed., Addison-Wesley, 2001, Chapter 9.

Jacobson, I., Booch, G., and Rumbaugh, J. *The Unified Software Development Process*. Boston: Addison-Wesley, 1999.

Rosenberg, D., and Scott, K. *Use Case Driven Object Modeling with UML: A Practical Approach*. Reading, MA: Addison-Wesley, 1999.

Schneider, G., and Winters, J. *Applying Use Cases: A Practical Guide*, 2nd Edition. Boston: Addison-Wesley, 2001, Chapters 3 and 4.

Chapter **5**

# V&V of the Quality of MOSS

Every problem comes with a solution. The trick is to find it![1]

## CHAPTER SUMMARY

This chapter focuses on V&V of UML diagrams in the solution space. These diagrams include advanced class diagrams, advanced sequence diagrams, corresponding communication diagrams, object diagrams, advanced state machine diagrams and timing diagrams. The discussion of each of these diagrams is followed by detailed V&V checks of their syntactic correctness, semantic completeness and consistency and aesthetic quality. The chapter ends with a section on the importance of implementation, which is the ultimate purpose of modeling in the solution space.

## 5.1 UML DIAGRAMS IN THE SOLUTION SPACE (MOSS)

The UML diagrams of relevance to the technical work in the solution space, particularly for the system designer, are as follows (Figure 5.1):

[1]Source: Unknown.
Note: The diagrams in this chapter are based on the LUCKY insurance problem statement described in Appendix A.

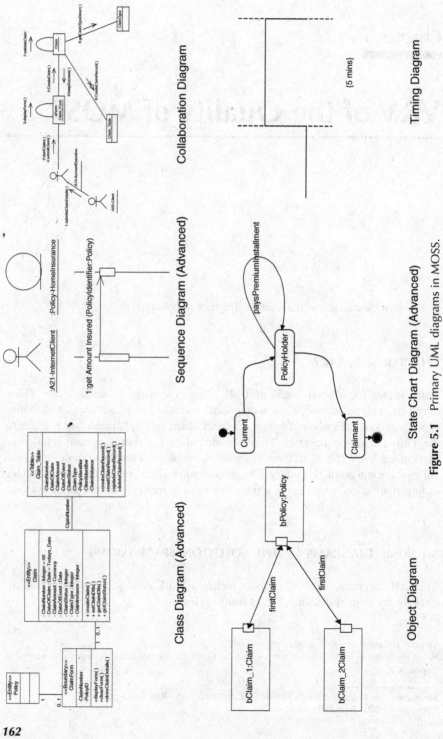

**Figure 5.1** Primary UML diagrams in MOSS.

- Class diagrams (advanced)—the most important diagrams in the solution space. They embellish the business class diagrams to make them implementable. Being closest to the code, they can also be used in code generation, a feature of some CASE tools.
- Sequence diagrams (advanced)—support and augment the classes created in the solution space by adding to and cross-checking operations in a class diagram that are used in implementing messages and their sequences.
- Communication diagrams—provide information similar to that of sequence diagrams. These diagrams are favored by many system designers, especially those who have used the Booch (1991, 1994) to OO modeling. In that original Booch approach communication, diagrams were used particularly to show the sending and receiving of messages between objects.
- Object diagrams—provide a snapshot of how various objects will be linked with each other at run-time and at particular points in time. Object diagrams are also helpful in analyzing multiplicities shown on class diagrams.
- State machine diagrams (advanced)—show the state changes of an object, thereby depicting the object's life cycle. Considered the only genuine dynamic diagrams, state machine diagrams are extremely relevant in modeling real-time systems.
- Timing diagrams—depict the state changes of one or more objects, thereby also facilitating comparison between state changes to different objects.

## 5.2  ANALYZING MOPS FOR MOSS FOR A SOLUTION

The modeling effort in the solution space builds on the models already created in the problem space. Therefore, analysis of MOPS is an ideal starting point for creating and verifying the quality of MOSS.

### 5.2.1  Analysis of Use Cases in the Solution Space

Chapter 4 described the model of the problem space for the LUCKY insurance system through four use case diagrams. Those diagrams and their corresponding documentation were further analyzed to identify business classes in Chapter 4. In the solution space, these use case diagrams, and their corresponding use cases, are revisited (analyzed) to ensure that they are supported by the solution—"Are we building the product right?" The process for this analysis is described as the business analysis process component in detail by Unhelkar (2003). Use case analysis reveals implementation-level information for a class such as attribute types and operation signatures. The focus, in stepping through the use cases in the solution space, is to ensure that the implemented solution is able to handle the functionalities specified in the use cases, an exercise embedded the V&V process.

Consider, for example, Figure 5.2, which repeats the use case diagram shown in Figure 4.9. This diagram, and the specification and documentation of the use cases

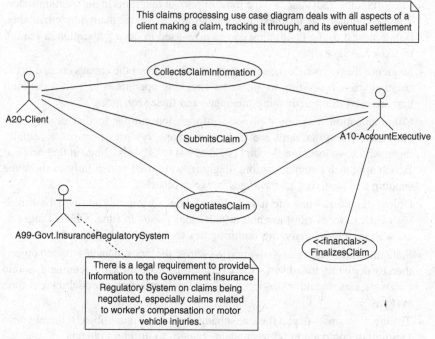

This claims processing use case diagram deals with all aspects of a client making a claim, tracking it through, and its eventual settlement

CollectsClaimInformation

A20-Client

A10-AccountExecutive

SubmitsClaim

NegotiatesClaim

A99-Govt.InsuranceRegulatorySystem

<<financial>> FinalizesClaim

There is a legal requirement to provide information to the Government Insurance Regulatory System on claims being negotiated, especially claims related to worker's compensation or motor vehicle injuries.

**Figure 5.2** Analysis of the claims processing use case diagram in the solution space.

underneath it (not shown in the diagram), will reveal the classes shown in Figure 5.3. Notice how the class Policy may have been discovered elsewhere (e.g., in the policy creation use case diagram shown in Figure 4.7), but the class Claim is discovered while analyzing this claims processing use case diagram. Analysis of the claims processing use case diagram will thus reveal new classes (e.g., Claim), as

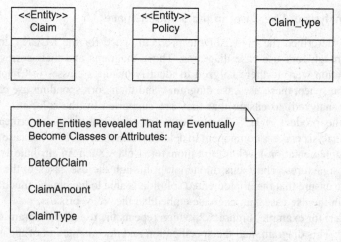

<<Entity>>
Claim

<<Entity>>
Policy

Claim_type

Other Entities Revealed That may Eventually Become Classes or Attributes:

DateOfClaim

ClaimAmount

ClaimType

**Figure 5.3** Some classes revealed by the SubmitsClaim use case.

well as embellish classes already discovered (e.g., `Policy`). Similarly, analysis of each of the use cases in the claims processing use case diagram will reveal further information on the classes already discovered. For example, analysis of the `SubmitsClaim` use case will not only show important attributes like `Date OfClaim` and `ClaimAmount`, but will also indicate to the system designer that the type of the attribute `DateOfClaim` is a DATE. As mentioned before, discovering attribute types and operation signatures is important in solution space modeling.

## 5.2.2 Analysis of Business Class Diagrams in the Solution Space

While MOPS creates class diagrams to document business entities, their attributes and their behaviors, these same class diagrams are further extended in MOSS with the aim of converting them into implementable entities. Thus, business classes discovered in the problem space, such as `Policy` and `Client` (shown in Figure 4.14), will be analyzed and fully defined in the solution space. The actors, use case documentation and even notes attached to the use case diagrams are analyzed to get a complete picture of the classes required and additional information on the classes already discovered to facilitate their implementation. This qualification and definition of classes and class diagrams in the solution space will result in the following:

a. Additional attributes and operations inside the classes enabling implementation and execution of the classes.

b. Additional information about the attributes and operations (such as attribute types, their initial values, and operation signatures) that are necessary for the implementation of a class.

c. Creation of GUI and database classes that will enable display and storage of information.

d. Refinement of classes by capitalizing on the concepts of quality and reuse promulgated by object orientation.

## 5.2.3 Analyzing Activity Diagrams in the Solution Space

The activity diagrams drawn in the problem space are further analyzed by system designers to ensure that the activities documented in MOPS have corresponding implementation-level constructs in the solution classes. Consider, for example, Figure 5.4. This diagram provides information on the behavior of the class `Claim`. By stepping through it and ensuring that there is an operation in the `Claim` class to handle each of the activities described in this diagram, a good-quality `Claim` class is modeled. Forking and joining (as shown in Figure 5.4 for the two activities `StoreDetails` and `InformUser`), as well as the `Claim` object, showing a partially completed claim, are additional pieces of information that will be discovered in the solution space by the system designer and used by her to ensure complete documentation of classes, that is the class `Claim`.

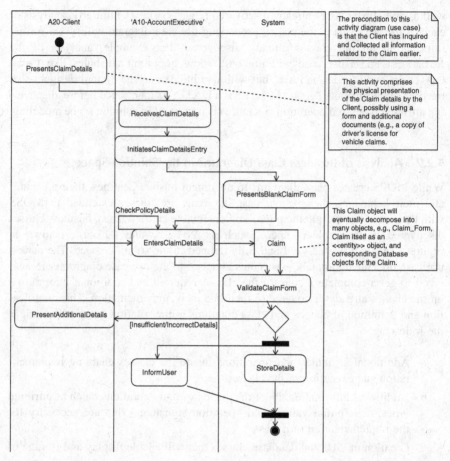

| A20-Client | 'A10-AccountExecutive' | System |
|---|---|---|

The precondition to this activity diagram (use case) is that the Client has Inquired and Collected all information related to the Claim earlier.

PresentsClaimDetails

This activity comprises the physical presentation of the Claim details by the Client, possibly using a form and additional documents (e.g., a copy of driver's license for vehicle claims.

ReceivesClaimDetails

InitiatesClaimDetailsEntry

PresentsBlankClaimForm

CheckPolicyDetails

This Claim object will eventually decompose into many objects, e.g., Claim_Form, Claim itself as an <<entity>> object, and corresponding Database objects for the Claim.

EntersClaimDetails

Claim

ValidateClaimForm

PresentAdditionalDetails

[Insufficient/IncorrectDetails]

InformUser

StoreDetails

**Figure 5.4** Analyzing the `SubmitsClaim` activity diagram (for the corresponding use case).

## 5.3 QUALITY OF CLASSES AND CLASS DIAGRAMS IN MOSS

In this section we discuss the syntax, semantics and aesthetic checks used to verify and validate the quality of classes and class diagrams in the solution space. We also treat classes differently from class diagrams, although in practice the quality checks may be applied to both simultaneously.

### 5.3.1 Syntax Checks for Classes in the Solution Space

Of the many classes that are likely to emerge as a result of use case analysis, we consider two in detail here to demonstrate the application of quality checks in the solution space. The two classes are `Policy` and `Claim`. While their names and basic

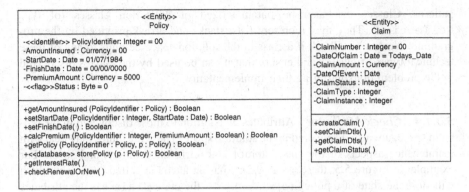

**Figure 5.5** Upgrading class operations (behavior) by the previous analysis.

attributes were discovered in MOPS, far more information is now added to these classes, as shown in Figure 5.5. This is the implementation-level information we focus on in ensuring the quality of the advanced classes and advanced class diagrams. For example, the class Policy in Figure 5.5 has operations that deal with databases and other implementation-level constructs. The following are the syntax checks we apply to classes in MOSS:

### 5.3.1.1 Check Class Names

Verifying the correctness of class names is as important in the solution space as in the problem space, although from a UML viewpoint, this is still a convention rather than a strict syntax. However, this should be the first thing checked when verification begins. As in MOPS, class names should be singular common nouns. Class names should also comply with the implementation language standards and with name spaces in terms of packages. So, if a class is placed in a package, its name becomes Package.Class name. If there are multiple levels of packages, all those packages will appear as prefixes to the class name. Exceptions to this class name check are the technical language-level classes that will be reused in the design, whose class names are provided by the language of implementation.

### 5.3.1.2 Check Class Stereotypes

Stereotypes should represent further classification (grouping) of classes. These classes should be represented by the name of the stereotype enclosed in << >>. Both classes shown in Figure 5.5 have <<entity>> stereotypes, but in MOSS, one would expect additional implementation-level stereotypes for classes such as the <<boundary>> stereotyped classes that act as interfaces between external actors and the system, and for <<database>> stereotyped classes that—as the name implies—deal with persistence and other database issues.

### 5.3.1.3 Check Type of Class

Many solution-level types of classes appear in MOSS. For example, such classes can be created based on templates or design patterns. Classes can also be parameterized or collection classes (of type `Collection`). They may represent lists, stacks and arrays provided by the programming language. Check if a class in the solution space belongs to any of these technical types of classes and ensure that it can be used by the classes discovered in the problem domain during their implementation.

### 5.3.1.4   Check Attributes

Attributes, in addition to those discovered in the problem space, are also discovered in the solution space. These attributes may deal with maintenance aspects of the class, storage and retrieval, counters, and so on. For example, in Figure 5.5, the class `Policy` has an attribute called `Status`, which will store the state of a policy object. Similarly, the class `Claim` has the attributes `ClaimStatus` and `ClaimType`, which may be discovered during analysis of the `SubmitsClaim` use case by the system designer. It is important to subject these attributes to syntax checks that are programming language specific. For example, naming conventions for class and attribute names and related standards must be adhered to in naming the attributes. Consider a specific example in Java, where "identifiers" (attributes in our current discussion) should begin with letters, numbers, underlines or dollar signs, or any Unicode characters with a code above 192. An attribute name outside of these restrictions will be syntactically incorrect. Other programming languages may have different restrictions on the starting character for attribute names. Similar to classes, local project standards should also be considered in naming attributes. For example, a project may decide to use lowercase letter as starting characters for all attribute names but capital letters for all class names. These restrictions should also be verified here. It is also recommended that attribute names be singular common nouns.

### 5.3.1.5   Check Attribute Types

While checking the type of an attribute is informal and optional in the problem space, it is a vital and mandatory check in the solution space. Attributes in MOSS have types such as CHAR, INT, DATE or AMT. Ensuring that each attribute has the right type assigned to it is important syntactically as well as semantically. A syntax check, however, will dictate that only those types are assigned to attributes that are allowed by the language of implementation. For example, it may be acceptable in the problem space for the business analyst to describe the `claimNumber` attribute of type `integer`. In the solution space, though, it must be formally described as INT. Furthermore, implementation language considerations for these attributes (e.g., DATE as a formal attribute type in C++ and Java)[2] must be considered by the system designer in the solution space.

In Figure 5.5, the attribute types assigned to the attributes in the class `Policy` are `Integer` to `PolicyIdentifier`, `Currency` to `AmountInsured` and `PremiumAmount`, `Byte` to `Status` and `Date` to `StartDate` and

---

[2]Most UML CASE tools ensure that only allowable types for attributes are used in describing attributes. However, this will require the modelers to install the UML CASE tools for specific programming languages.

FinishDate. Similarly, the class Claim has a number of attributes whose types are Date, Currency and Integer.

### 5.3.1.6 Check Attribute Initial Values

In addition to specifying the types of attributes, it is important to check their initial values. While not mandatory, it is *highly recommended* to provide an initial value for most attributes in a class. This initialization does the job of "wiping the memory clean" before doing anything with the attribute. Furthermore, once specified, the initial values should make syntactic sense. For example, if the type of attributes is Integer, specifying an initial value of ABC is both syntactically and semantically wrong, and the results of such incorrect initialization remain unpredictable. Ensure that the types of values used in initialization of the attribute and the attribute type assigned to it are compatible.

### 5.3.1.7 Check Attribute Visibility

The UML allows attributes to have visibilities of *public*, *private* and *protected*. These visibilities provide the rules by which other classes in the system are allowed to access the attributes of the class under consideration. Syntactically, attributes should default to *private*, and this should be indicated on the classes by a "–" as a prefix to the attributes. Attributes that can be "seen" by other classes will be *public* and are indicated by a "+" in front of them. Attributes that have partial visibility can be seen only by derived classes. These attributes have protected visibility and have a "#" in front of them. UML CASE tools provide their own variations on these standards. In Figure 5.5, the classes Policy and Claim have all their attributes shown as private (with the "–" sign), which is correct.

### 5.3.1.8 Check Attribute Stereotypes

The additional attributes appearing in MOSS (compared with the MOPS) deal with identification of the class, access keys, counters, state flags and so on. Check if these language-level attributes have been correctly stereotyped. While not mandatory, it is still worth considering stereotyping attributes especially in the solution space, as this facilitates the grouping of attributes, readability of the class and ease of implementation.

### 5.3.1.9 Check Operations

Check operations to ensure that their format complies with the language of implementation. Each operation can have detailed specification, which should be checked against the implementation language. An operation format can be "visibility-stereotype-name of the operation-signature-return" value. This sequence of operation format should be acceptable to and implementable in the programming language.

### 5.3.1.10 Check Operation Signatures

Operation signatures have parameter lists and, optionally, return values. Check for the correctness of the parameter list, number of parameters, parameter types, their declarations and the return values in the operation signature for syntactic correctness.

**5.3.1.11   *Check Operation Visibility***   Like attributes, this feature of an operation in a class must be checked to ensure that it has syntactically correct visibility—namely, *private, public* or *protected.* Usually, operations that represent the facilities provided by the class will be *public,* whereas those that deal with the internal behavior and logic of the class and do not need to be seen by other classes in the system will be `private`. Both classes in Figure 5.5 show operations that are `public`, represented by a "+" prefix.

**5.3.1.12   *Check Operation Stereotypes***   Stereotypes help classify operations. Stereotypes in operations should be checked for their syntactically correct representation. Unlike the checks for visibility and attribute types, stereotype checks do not have a direct language-level requirement. For example, consider the operation +storePolicy() in class `Policy` in Figure 5.5. This operation belongs to a group of operations that deal with storage, calculations and retrieval of attribute values (data). Operations like these should be stereotyped as <<database>> or <<persistence>> operations. (Note: UML does not mandate a particular name for these operation stereotypes. However, they should be represented correctly on the diagrams.) The << >> notation should be used for this representation.

**5.3.1.13   *Check Exception Class***   Check if the class is an exception class. You can create your own exceptions by taking a language-provided exception class and inheriting from it. This creation of exception classes will also have testing connotations, as all possible exceptions need to be tested. In MOSS, check the correct use of the exception class.

**5.3.1.14   *Check Error Handling***   Check how error handling is modeled and implemented in the class. The manner in which error handling is implemented will certainly influence the quality of the class; however, error handling itself will be influenced by the programming language. See, for example, if EXCEPTION-TRY-CATCH is specified correctly and whether it is able to handle exceptions when they occur. For example, exceptions thrown are objects in Java but not in C. Eiffel would throw the exception as a number, and the programmer has to decipher the error by looking at an error table.

## 5.3.2   Semantic Checks for Classes in the Solution Space

**5.3.2.1   *Check Meaning of Class Name***   This is a check similar to the one in MOPS, where the meaning of the class is ascertained. For solution-level classes, especially those that are reused from a third-party class library, class names have already been determined, leaving little control over them. However, the meaning behind class names used at the solution level must be clear to the system designer and the programmer within the project.

**5.3.2.2   *Check Meaning of Attribute Name***   As in the problem space, in MOSS it is important to check that an attribute represents what the designer means. The meaning of an attribute's name play an important quality role in both problem and solution modeling spaces. For example, an attribute that is used as a flag to check whether an account is open or closed should never be named Date. However, that is precisely what many good COBOL programmers did a couple of decades ago.[3]

**5.3.2.3  Check Attribute Types and Initial Values**    Initial values of attributes can be made to represent more semantic meanings than is apparent. Therefore, these initial values should be checked for the correctness of their semantic business meanings. For example, a START-DATE attribute that describes the starting date of an insurance policy may have a business rule associated with it that prevents back-dated insurance. In that case, the initial value of START-DATE can only be equal to or greater than TODAYS-DATE (the actual date the policy starts).

**5.3.2.4  Check Meanings of the Operations**    Each operation that has public visibility (i.e., is prefixed by a "+") should be named from the point of view of the calling classes. This will correctly inform readers of the model that the called class is providing its services to the calling class. For example, class Policy in Figure 5.5 has operations named getAmountInsured() and getPolicy() (as against, say, provideAmountInsured() and providePolicy(), respectively). Similarly, class Claim in the same diagram provides information to any class that calls it with getClaimDtls() and getClaimStatus() operations. Additionally, check the meaning of the operation and whether that meaning is reflected in its name and format. Furthermore, check for the common confusion that occurs when two different classes are asked to provide similar functionality. For example, class Claim is capable of providing the +getClaimDtls() operation, but class Policy may also be required to know about the claim details. In such cases, class Policy should contain an operation named '+getClaimDtlsForPolicy()' indicating the difference between the two operations belonging to two different classes but having the same purpose.

**5.3.2.5  Check Pre- and Postconditions of Operations**    Operations, based on what they mean to the business, can have pre- and postconditions. These contain the semantic meanings of the operation. For example, in Figure 5.5, for class Policy, the getPolicy() operation will be a precursor to the calcPremium() operation—although it cannot be visually shown on the class diagram. Occasionally, an entire sequence (as represented by a sequence diagram) may be a precursor to an operation. These pre- and postconditions should be checked for their semantic correctness, probably against corresponding activity diagrams or use case documentation.

---

[3]This author is guilty of moving 999999 to a Date field to represent a closed account. The move of HIGH-VALUES to a Date field and using that as a flag was syntactically correct but semantically wrong. The Y2K saga proved that this supposedly clever trick was wrong in every way.

**5.3.2.6 Check Signature of the Operation** The signature of an operation will contain a list of parameters. As described in the syntax check for the operation signature, each parameter within the signature will have a type, optionally a value, and also a scope. Each of these parameters, and the overall signature, has a business and a technical meaning. For example, the operation `calcPremium()` in Figure 5.5 would, in fact, be made up of a number of smaller calculations (not shown in Figure 5.5). These calculations would include the need to calculate the value of the risk, the current interest rates that may help in extrapolating the risk during the period for which insurance cover has been provided and so on. Furthermore, each of the internal operations that support the signature of an operation needs to be checked for correctness and completeness.

Finally, check in the signature that the return value of the operation is semantically correct. For example, an operation that is meant only to return a `Boolean` should not try and return any other value, like an `Integer` or a `Char`.

**5.3.2.7 Check Stereotypes of Operations** The meaning of the stereotypes should be correct. For example, created, read, update and delete (CRUD) are the standard database-related operations, which should be stereotyped as such. The <<database>> stereotype itself was discussed in the earlier section on syntax quality. Usually, these database-related operations appear in persistent classes, although they can appear elsewhere in the system, as shown in this case in entity classes. Stereotypes are also assigned to operations that deal with manipulation of data and storage of states. In all cases, it is important to ensure that the stereotypes are assigned correctly to the operations and that they are meaningful.

**5.3.2.8 Check Scope of Operations** Is an operation applicable across a single class or does its scope cut across many classes? Checking the scope of operations is important in MOSS because it decides how long an operation is "active." If a class is based on a pattern, then the pattern should be understood before being used. Basing a class on a pattern (e.g., a singleton pattern for database interface classes) will enhance the quality of classes and should be encouraged. Check whether appropriate patterns have been considered.

**5.3.2.9 Check Overloading of Operations** Overloading occurs when an operation in a class is repeated in the class with a different parameter list. Check if the operations of a class are overloaded and ensure that the overloading is semantically (and syntactically) correct.

**5.3.2.10 Check Overriding Operations** Operations of a class can be overridden by its subclasses. Ensure that the overriding operation has the same name as the operation in the class it is inheriting from. Further, ensure that the overriding operation is fully implemented.

**5.3.2.11 Check Overriding Variables** Some programming languages allow overriding of variables. This check will ensure that the overriding variables are semantically correct.

**5.3.2.12 Check Encapsulation** Each class should be specified and designed with the concept of encapsulation in mind. In designing the implementation details of a class, the system designer should ensure that all responsibilities of a class are satisfied through the list of operations that have been specified. This check of encapsulation ensures that a collection of attributes is encapsulated by an operation, resulting in a semantically cohesive class.

### 5.3.3 Aesthetic Checks for Classes at the Design Level

Although in the solution space one would expect two to three times the number of attributes per class in the problem space, it is still important to maintain a manageable list of attributes within a class. For example, a class with more than 50 attributes will start becoming large and complex. Unless absolutely necessary due to programming language needs, classes with large numbers of attributes should be refactored in order to improve their quality and readability.

**5.3.3.1 Check Number of Operations** Like the number of attributes, the number of operations in a class should be manageable. Since implementation will require addition of new operations that enable the class to, for example, retrieve, store and display objects, the total number of operations will be two to three times those discovered in MOPS.

**5.3.3.2 Check Load on Operations** How much work is an operation or implementation method performing? Theoretically, a single operation can be made to do all the work that a class is assigned to do. However, an aesthetically elegant class will distribute its functional responsibilities over a number of operations, ensuring that a single operation is not doing everything in a class.

**5.3.3.3 Check Load on the Class** A class, in theory, can be an entire system. That, of course, would be an inelegant solution. Therefore, it is necessary to distribute the load of system functionality over a number of well-balanced classes. Classes that are third-party and/or reused classes will not provide much opportunity for improving their designs, but one would hope that the providers of such classes have applied the quality criteria of balance to the classes designed.

### 5.3.4 Describing Class Diagrams in MOSS

Because of the overriding importance of a class in the solution space, we focused on checking the quality of a class in the previous sections. In this section, we check the quality of advanced class diagrams made up of solution-level classes. An example of

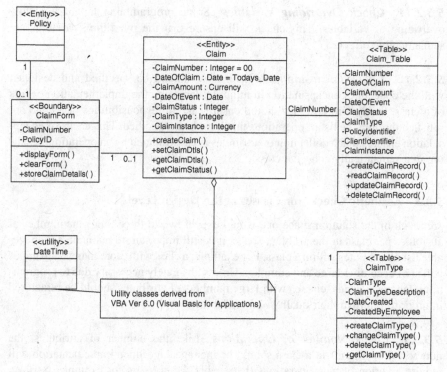

**Figure 5.6** Addition of design-level classes in MOSS (GUI, database, utility, etc.).

a solution-level class diagram is shown in Figure 5.6, where some implementation-level classes that are needed in order to implement the class Claim are shown.

Thus, while the classes Claim and Policy would have been discovered in the documentation and analysis of the problem space, on their own they are unimplementable. Additional classes that facilitate the implementation of "claim" in the solution space are shown in Figure 5.6. For example, the class ClaimForm represents a GUI class that will be essential in implementation, as it is through this boundary class that the details of Claim and Policy will be displayed to the user of the system.

Claim is also shown as associated with Claim_Table, which is a class essential to store the details of the Claim. Detailed thoughts on how data will be stored in a database are, however, of interest to a system architect together with a database manager. The association between Claim and Claim_Table is enabled through the key, ClaimNumber, which is also shown (rectangle) in Figure 5.6. Notice, further, how the shared aggregation between Claim and ClaimType also has a direction, indicating that ClaimType is known by Claim but does not need to know anything about Claim. The <<utility>> DateTime class is shown here from a VBA class library. Needless to say, the classes shown here are still example classes, and additional attributes, operations and language-specific classes will be required to make this entire diagram implementable.

### 5.3.5 Syntax Checks of Class Diagrams in MOSS

***5.3.5.1 Check Class Names and Relationship Names*** A syntactically correct class diagram will have all of its classes and relationships conform to the standards of the language of implementation. This means that the classes and relationships are named (and optionally described) in a way that ensures that they can be implemented in a programming language.

***5.3.5.2 Check Relationships*** At the implementation level, OO languages provide support for inheritance and client-server-type relationships between two classes. While inheritance is syntactically relatively easier to implement and check, other relationships of association, aggregation and its variations, will eventually be implemented in a programming language using references and pointers. For example, in Figure 5.6, the class Claim aggregates the class ClaimType, and it is essential for the programmer to ensure that this tighter relationship between the two classes is coded correctly. This means that when a Claim object is instantiated, so is a ClaimType object. Furthermore, shared aggregation (as shown by the unfilled diamond in Figure 5.6), compared to normal aggregation, also needs to be implemented "by hand" by the coders.

***5.3.5.3 Check Multiplicities*** Check that the multiplicity on an association is correctly represented on the class diagram. Multiplicities in the solution space are represented similarly to the way they are represented in the problem space—with numbers, number range "N" or "*" for unknown multiplicities. Any other characters used to represent multiplicities will be syntactically incorrect.

***5.3.5.4 Check Stereotypes*** Stereotypes, represented by << >>, can be used on classes, attributes, operations and relationships on a class diagram in the solution space. As discussed in Chapter 2, some stereotypes are standard, whereas others are created within a project. Additionally, technical stereotypes will appear in solution class diagrams. Check that all stereotypes in the class diagram are syntactically correct.

***5.3.5.5 Check for Correct Representation of Roles on the Class Diagram*** Roles enable better organization of relationships by showing the role in which one class associates with another class. In the solution space, this will result in a subset of operations of one class using or providing services to another class.

***5.3.5.6 Check Association of Classes with Language Libraries*** For example, inclusions and imports of classes from the programming language libraries will take place in MOSS, and at times, it may not be practical to model every small class of the implementation language on the class diagram. In these situations, classes from the programming languages may be represented by a language package, and only that package will be shown on class diagrams. Examples of language-level libraries include Java.utils and MFC. Check the correctness of association with such language libraries.

***5.3.5.7   Check Package-Level Visibility for Classes in Packages***   If classes are placed within packages, it is essential to check the package-level visibility, which essentially provides two levels of class visibility—one within the package and one outside it. Packages remain an organizational entity, but when logically cohesive classes are put together in a package, the implementation of the classes in the solution space must be considered together with their visibility within a package.

### 5.3.6   Semantic Checks of Class Diagrams in MOSS

***5.3.6.1   Check the Meaning of the Entire Class Diagram from the Implementation Viewpoint***   Does the entire class diagram represent a cohesive business and implementation logic?

***5.3.6.2   Check the Meanings of the Relationships on a Class Diagram***   In addition to the relationship checks in the problem space, in the solution space it is necessary to check the meaning of the association between business and implementation classes. Business classes are also routinely inherited from a language-level class. For example, a class representing a list of claims for a particular policy may inherit from a List class provided by the programming language. This would be implementation inheritance, and although it is syntactically correct, its semantic mismatch should be carefully noted.

***5.3.6.3   Check Directions of Association***   During implementation, the direction of association is very important in improving the design efficiency. For example, if class Client needs to know about class Policy but not the reverse, then the association between Client and Policy will end with an association arrowhead pointing towards Policy.

***5.3.6.4   Check for Collection Classes***   For example, while all claim details are provided by the Claim class, the total number of claims will be provided by an additional collection class. Check for the existence and correctness of these collection classes.

***5.3.6.5   Check Roles for Classes***   Roles for classes should be checked here for semantic correctness. For example, a person in the role of a client versus that of an account executive will have different semantic meanings.

***5.3.6.6   Check Business Rules Behind Multiplicities***   For example, if only four claims are allowed on a policy, then this should be correctly represented on the class diagram using multiplicities. More important, if multiplicities are shown, ensure that they are many-to-many multiplicities. If multiplicity is known, it is advisable to show it on class diagrams.

***5.3.6.7 Check for Association Classes*** Do this especially when many-to-many multiplicities are involved. In such situations, creation of association classes will facilitate easier implementation of the classes, especially in a database where the association classes will translate into "link tables."

***5.3.6.8 Check for Overloading of a Specialized Class*** Check if the operations of a class that has been specialized (inherited from) are overloaded. If so, polymorphism may be implied by the system designer. While polymorphism is a run-time construct, it is still important to check the correctness of operation names and signatures in both super- and subclasses in design to ensure its correct implementation. Languages like Visual Basic facilitate polymorphism resulting from implementation inheritance only. Check the meaning behind all polymorphic designs.

***5.3.6.9 Check for Encapsulation*** Encapsulation indicates that the attributes correctly have private visibility and that they are made available through operations, which are public.

***5.3.6.10 Check for Reuse*** Classes can be reused from class libraries and pattern libraries, as well as from previous projects (internal reuse). Check that all implementation-level classes are meaningfully reused. This is important because, although syntactically an inheritance reuse may be correct, semantically it may not be. For example, syntactically, a `Frame` class can inherit from a `Scroll bar`, but it will not be semantically correct. During semantic checking, it is important to note that inheritance is not the only way to reuse classes. Peer-to-peer reuse by association is also important. Scope of parameter lists become an important check.

***5.3.6.11 Check Language Constructs for Implied Meaning*** Language constructs that are subject to interpretation should be checked for their implied (semantic) meaning. A common example is DATE classes provided by almost all languages and the corresponding behavior provided for them. Is a DATE class able to add dates (e.g., the "next" function)? If a DATE class needs to skip weekends, it will need a semantic check at the MOSS level to ensure that the DATE math is carried out as required by the business. The reason this check is likely to happen here, rather than in MOPS, is that the language-specific interpretation of DATE will happen only in the solution space.

## 5.3.7 Aesthetic Checks of Class Diagrams in MOSS

Aesthetic checks concerning the number of classes on a class diagram (and related issues of granularity) cannot be applied as strictly in this solution space as in the problem space. This is because in the solution space a large number of implementation classes will be inserted in the class diagrams, many of which come directly from the programming language, over which the system designer will have little control. However, it is still advisable to consider how complex a class diagram is in the solution space. For example, readability of the diagram can be improved by ensuring that technical classes are represented only by their names rather than by their entire qualification (of attributes and operations).

The aesthetic quality of class diagrams in the solution space can also be improved by letting the entity classes appear in more than one diagram. In each class diagram, classes could play different roles. These roles should also be shown against the classes on the class diagrams.

Compared to a problem space class diagram, a class diagram in the solution space may have innumerable association lines drawn from every class to every other class. In such situations, the aesthetic quality of the class diagram can be improved by redistributing the classes and their associations across more than one class diagram.

Ensure that sufficient explanatory notes are provided on the class diagrams to make them aesthetically elegant and readable.

The project manager, together with the quality manager, needs to decide the extent and intensity of checking of the UML diagrams in the solution space. The situation in the solution space differs from that in the problem space because the models in the solution space are very close to implementation. It is essential to achieve balance between a model and full implementation. To ensure that the full benefit of the iterative and incremental approach to development is achieved, it is essential to keep the implementation free of too much detail in the first iteration. Therefore, an aesthetically elegant class diagram will continue to hide, or elide, irrelevant things from the view. For example, it may be essential to show a collection class in a solution class diagram, but not all operations and attributes of that collection class.

## 5.4   QUALITY OF SEQUENCE DIAGRAMS IN MOSS

### 5.4.1   Describing the Sequence of Submission of a Claim

Figure 5.7 describes the basic sequence of how claims are submitted in the insurance system. The Account Executive is able to SubmitClaim that is received by aClaim object belonging to the class Claim. This is a very basic diagram depicting the sequence of submitting claims and would probably belong to the problem space. It is shown here with a view to expanding it into the sequence diagram shown in Figure 5.8, where detailed technical objects and messages are shown. The A20-Client and the A10-AccountExecutive are involved here in a sequence that deals with the submission of an insurance claim. The collaborating objects representing the ClaimForm user interface and the Claim object itself, as well as the database table objects Claim_Table and ClaimType, are all shown on this sequence diagram together with the messages.

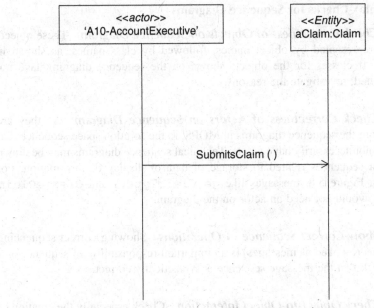

**Figure 5.7** `SubmitsClaim` basic sequence diagram.

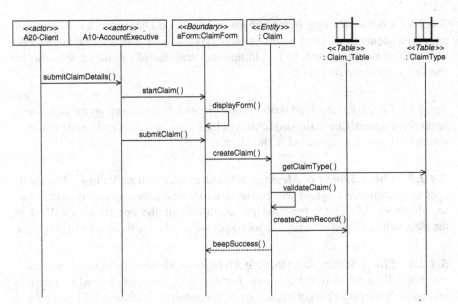

**Figure 5.8** `SubmitsClaim` advanced sequence diagram.

## 5.4.2   Syntax Checks for Sequence Diagrams

### 5.4.2.1   *Check Correctness of Objects on Sequence Diagram*   These objects should be represented by object names, followed by class names, as shown in Figure 5.8. If classes for the objects shown on the sequence diagram have not been identified, investigate the reasons.

### 5.4.2.2   *Check Correctness of Actors on Sequence Diagram*   As they are different from the sequence diagrams in MOPS, in the solution space sequence diagrams may not necessarily have actors. Technical sequence diagrams may be drawn to represent sequences related to storage of data or display of information. For example, in Figure 5.8, messages like getClaimType() and CreateClaim Record() would not need an actor on the diagram.

### 5.4.2.3   *Show Correct Sequence of Operations*   Showing correct sequencing of operations (invoked as messages) is an important responsibility of sequence diagrams. Check that the message sequence is syntactically correct.

### 5.4.2.4   *Check Object-to-Object Interaction*   Check especially the creation of one object by another, as well as its destruction afterward. When an object is created, the creating message should directly hit the object box rather than its lifeline. Destruction of an object is shown by a cross on its lifeline. Note that it is possible for an object belonging to a class to create another object belonging to the same class.

### 5.4.2.5   *Check Message Types Shown in Sequence Diagram*   Types of messages on a sequence diagram include simple, synchronous and asynchronous messages (not shown in Figure 5.8). Addition and removal of list items will also be shown by sequence diagrams.

### 5.4.2.6   *Check Return Protocols*   Return protocols are shown on messages on a sequence diagram. Check the correctness of the return protocols and ensure that they match the operations specified in the classes.

### 5.4.2.7   *Check Syntax of Message Signatures and Return Values*   The messages on a sequence diagram will be based on the operations specified in the class specifications. Therefore, pre- and postconditions of the operations specified in the class will be important when the messages are checked in the sequence diagrams.

### 5.4.2.8   *Check Syntax for Multiple Messages*   Multiple or iterative messages are shown by a * before the message. For example, if there is a need to ascertain all claims belonging to a policy, the getClaimType() message will be prefixed by *getClaimType().

**5.4.2.9  Check for Multiple Objects on Sequence Diagram**  Multiple objects are shown by an object with tiles. For example, if a `Policy` has to get details of all claims on the `Policy`, it is not necessary to show three, four or five `Claim` objects separately on a sequence diagram. These multiple claim objects can be represented by a single notation, which is a tiled object on a sequence diagram.

### 5.4.3  Semantic Checks for Sequence Diagrams

**5.4.3.1  Check Purpose or Meaning Behind Sequence Diagram**  Ensure that the sequence diagram represents a cohesive sequence, which may have been described in a use case. The sequence diagram may also be representing a technical sequence such as storage or retrieval of data in a database.

The semantic meaning behind each message on a sequence diagram will correspond to the meaning of each operation of a class on the class diagram. In Figure 5.9, an interesting aspect of this advanced sequence diagram is the message `submitClaimDetails()` from `A20-Client` to `A10-AccountExecutive`, which has potential for confusion. Technically, this is a redundant message, as it may not have a corresponding software message. If such a message appears on a sequence diagram, its implied meaning must be investigated. For example, what is implied here is that the `Client` is interacting with the system through the `Account Executive`. If, on the other hand, the `Client` accessed the system directly (as would be the case for an Internet-based `SubmitsClaim` sequence), the messages would not be shown as coming through the `Account Executive`.

**5.4.3.2  Check Meaning of Focus of Control**  Check the meaning behind the focus of control shown by the thickened lifeline on a sequence diagram. Ensure that the object that has the focus of control is meant to keep control during the particular sequence.

**5.4.3.3  Check for Creation and Destruction of Objects**  Check if the sequence diagram depicts creation and destruction of objects. If so, ensure that the objects are created at the right time and place, and by the actors or objects that are meant to create them.

**5.4.3.4  Check Use of Patterns**  Is the sequence diagram based on a pattern? Design patterns like the database interface pattern of Gamma (1995) can and should be used to improve the quality of sequences depicting data access and storage. While database access and storage can be shown in sequence diagrams at the MOSS level, the design of the database is the responsibility of the system architect and the database manager operating in the background space.

**5.4.3.5  Check Alternative Flows**  Sequence diagrams are unable to show if-then-else scenarios properly. Check if there are such alternative flows in a sequence and create separate sequence diagrams for them.

### 5.4.4 Aesthetic Checks for Sequence Diagrams

***5.4.4.1 Ensure that Interactions Are Cohesive*** Ensure that the sequence diagram shows a cohesive set of interactions between collaborating objects. If the diagram deals with more than one subject area, it is highly advisable to split it into two or more.

***5.4.4.2 Check for Notes and Annotations*** Ensure that the sequence diagrams have sufficient notes and other annotations to explain the technicality of the diagrams.

***5.4.4.3 Check Number of Objects and Messages*** While five to nine objects are still preferred on one diagram, it may be acceptable to have a slightly larger number of objects on this diagram in the solution space. Similarly, the number of messages on the sequence diagram in the solution space will be greater than in the problem space. Up to 20 messages may be acceptable in a complex sequence diagram, although 12 to 15 are preferred in the solution space. If there are more than 20 messages, consider creating additional sequence diagrams.

## 5.5 QUALITY OF COMMUNICATION DIAGRAMS IN MOSS

### 5.5.1 Describing the SubmitsClaim Communication Diagram

Figure 5.9 shows a communication diagram for submission of claims. This diagram has information similar to that in Figure 5.8, which depicts the sequence in a

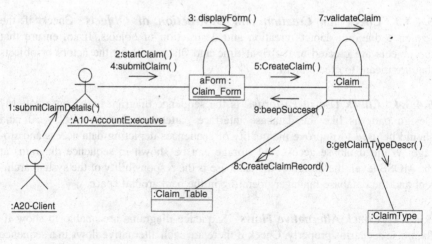

**Figure 5.9** Creating a SubmitsClaim communication diagram.

different view. The actor `A20-Client` sends message `1:submitsClaim Details()` to the actor `A10-AccountExecutive`, who, in turn, starts the process of claim submission by `2:startClaim()`. Message `4:submitClaim()` is another message sent by the `Account Executive`, but only after a form for claim submission is displayed by message `3:displayForm()`. The `aForm` object sends a message to `Claim` object called `5:CreateClaim()`, followed by `6:getClaimTypeDescr()` from the `ClaimType` object (from the database). Validation of the claim details is done by the `Claim` object by sending a message to itself, `7:validateClaim`. Assuming that all details here are correct and the claim has been validated, message `8:CreateClaimRecord()` will create the record in the `Claim_Table`. A message of success is beeped to `aForm`. Notice that an unsuccessful creation of a claim is not shown on this collaboration, as this will require another communication diagram.

### 5.5.2 Syntax Checks for Communication Diagrams

The syntax checks for communication diagrams are similar to those for sequence diagrams. Variations on the checks will arise due to the visual difference between the two diagrams, but the essence of the checks will remain the same. These syntax checks are as follows:

Check the correctness of all objects and messages on the communication diagram. Objects should be represented by object names, followed by class names, as shown in Figure 5.9.

Ensure that all messages are correctly numbered. Without such numbering, it is impossible to figure out the sequence in which the messages will be executed. Note that this is not the case with sequence diagrams, where the sequence flows from the top down and numbering of messages is optional.

If actors are shown on the communication diagram, check their correctness. As with the sequence diagram, the communication diagram may not have actors.

Check that the numbered message sequence is syntactically correct.

Check object-to-object interaction, especially the creation of one object by another, as well as its destruction afterward.

Check the message types appearing on the communication diagram.

Check the correctness of the return protocols and ensure that they match the operations specified in the classes.

Check the syntax of the message signatures and return values.

Check the syntax for multiple messages. Multiple or iterative messages are shown by a * before the message.

Check for representation of multiple objects. It will be a tiled object.

### 5.5.3 Semantic Checks for Communication Diagrams

Check the purpose or meaning behind the communication diagram. If this diagram is drawn independently of the sequence diagram, its purpose is likely to be more technical.

Ensure that the communication diagram represents a cohesive sequence that would, for example, manage the storage or retrieval of data in a database.

The semantic meaning behind each message in a communication diagram corresponds to the meaning of each operation of a class on the class diagram. Check if a return protocol is implied or if it needs to be shown explicitly.

Check if the communication diagram depicts creation and destruction of objects. If so, ensure that the objects are created at the right time and place.

Is the communication diagram based on a pattern? If so, check the pattern on which it is based to ensure that it is used correctly.

Communication diagrams are unable to show if-then-else scenarios properly. Check if there are alternative flows in a sequence and create separate communication diagrams for them.

### 5.5.4 Aesthetic Checks for Communication Diagrams

Fan-in and fan-out metrics can be seen on the communication diagram. If an object is overloaded, its work can be distributed among other objects or a new object (and its corresponding class) can be introduced.

Ensure that the communication diagram shows a cohesive set of interactions between collaborating objects. If the diagram attempts to deal with more than one subject area, it is highly advisable to split it into two or more.

Ensure that the communication diagram has sufficient notes and other annotations to explain its technical aspects.

Ensure that the communication diagram has neither too many nor too few objects. The right number of objects is discussed in terms of the aesthetic checks of the previous (sequence) diagram.

## 5.6 QUALITY OF OBJECT DIAGRAMS IN MOSS

Although object diagrams are an important part of modeling in the solution space, the best place to draw object diagrams is on whiteboards. It is not necessary to have them permanently drawn in CASE tool-based modeling deliverables. If needed, communication diagrams have been used to draw the object diagrams in a CASE tool, although that is also not recommended.

### 5.6.1 Describing the Object Diagram for Policy and Claim

An object diagram related to the insurance domain is shown in Figure 5.10. Figure 5.10A describes the object aPolicy linked with multiple instances (objects) of aClaim belonging to the Claim class. The same link is further expanded and made explicit in Figure 5.10B, where bPolicy is shown linked to bClaim-1 and bClaim-2.

Thus, object diagrams can be used to show multiplicities explicitly. They can also be used for robustness analysis to make sure that objects belonging to GUI and entity

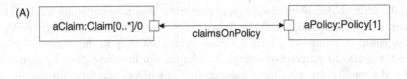

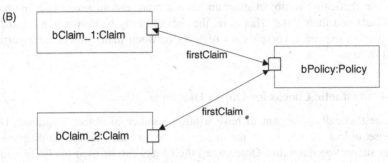

**Figure 5.10** An object diagram for `Policy` and `Claim`.

stereotypes do not talk with and among each other (quality of robustness diagrams is discussed in greater detail in the background space discussion in Chapter 6). Object diagrams, as snapshots of objects and links in memory, are frozen in time. Therefore, they should be used to find out how many objects and how many links between them exist in memory. Object diagrams are also used as a whiteboard discussion technique, especially when multiplicities and robustness are discussed in both the problem and solution spaces.

### 5.6.2 Syntax Checks for Object Diagrams

Check the correctness of representation of objects. Objects are represented by rectangles with the underlined object name inside them.

Object relationships are shown by links, which are straight lines between objects. Links can be stereotyped, but more often than not, a link indicating a direct relationship between two objects is sufficient to express the relationship.

Check that only one object is represented in a rectangle.

Attributes or operations cannot be shown in object diagrams.

Object diagrams do not have multiplicities shown as numbers. This is because multiplicities of class diagrams are converted into actual numbers of objects shown on the object diagram itself.

Check if notes were provided for additional explanation of the diagram.

### 5.6.3 Semantic Checks for Object Diagrams

Ensure that only meaningful and relevant object diagrams are drawn. For example, if a client can have up to four insurance policies and if a policy can be jointly owned by a maximum of two people, then the possible object diagrams can run into $4 \times 2 = 8$!

Avoid creating object diagrams for every possible combination of multiplicities. Only example object diagrams should be drawn, whenever needed, to clarify the links.

Semantic meanings of object diagrams relate not only to the meanings of the objects but also to the corresponding class diagram or the corresponding communication diagram or the robustness diagram that this object diagram is trying to support. Aesthetically an object diagram cannot represent all possible combinations of objects and their links. Therefore, they should only be drawn in a limited way and only to explain a complex set of links between many objects at a particular point in time.

### 5.6.4 Aesthetic Checks for Object Diagrams

It is aesthetically inelegant to have a large number of object diagrams. This is because object diagrams are not meant to be primary modeling diagrams but rather supporting diagrams. Objects and their links can be used to clarify multiplicities and/or business rules, but beyond that, their purpose will not be served and they will not pass this aesthetic check.

Object diagrams are mostly discussion-level diagrams. Once drawn and debated, they should end up upgrading the class diagrams, the relationships within the class diagrams, and, more important, their multiplicities.

## 5.7 QUALITY OF STATE MACHINE DIAGRAMS IN MOSS

### 5.7.1 Describing an Advanced State Machine Diagram for Claim

Figure 5.11 shows a state machine diagram for an object belonging to class Claim. While state machine diagrams drawn in the solution space are detailed and technical, they are helpful for classes that come from the problem space. State machine diagrams for pure implementation classes (like lists and arrays) may not be very helpful even in the solution space. However, states for database tables and rows can add quality to models in the solution space.

### 5.7.2 Syntax Checks for State Machine Diagrams in MOSS

Check for correct representation (notation) of states on the diagram.

Check for the correctness of transitions between states.

Check that the events that start the transitions are correctly specified on the diagram.

Check that the guard conditions that start the transitions are correctly represented within [ ] brackets.

Check if there are entry conditions to the state and, if so, that they are correctly represented.

Check for exit conditions out of the state.

Are there ongoing actions to be performed while the object is in a particular state? If so, it should be represented by a 'Do/' within the specifications of the state.

Are there activity states on the diagram and, if so, are they correctly represented?

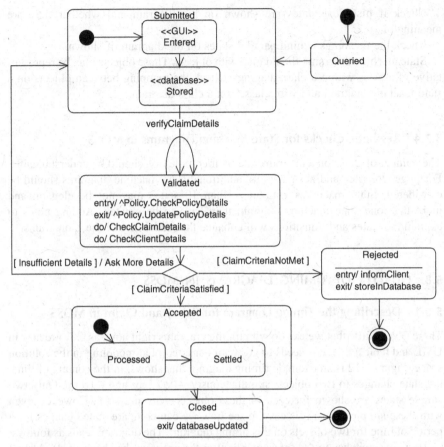

**Figure 5.11**    Advanced state machine diagram for Claim in the solution space.

Are there action states on the diagram and, if so, are they correctly represented?
Check for existence of start and stop states on the diagram.

### 5.7.3   Semantic Checks for State Machine Diagrams in MOSS

Check the meaning behind the state machine diagram. Is it simply the state of an
object, or is it the state of the system that is being shown? State machine diagrams
may also be used to represent what, for example, cookies do to maintain the state of a
client GUI object in a Web application.

Check if there are messages going to other objects in the system. This should be
shown only if absolutely necessary. Otherwise, notes should be used to represent
such messages.

Check if messages are being received from other objects.

Check if the diagram needs to show nested states. In the solution space, it may be
necessary to show nesting between complex states.

Check if historical states are shown on the diagram and whether they are meaningful.

Check the meanings behind parallel states on the diagram, if shown.

State machine diagrams should map with objects. These objects may be representative of a class within a class diagram. Check the mapping between objects on a state machine diagram and with classes on a class diagram.

### 5.7.4 Aesthetic Checks for State Machine Diagrams in MOSS

The number of states on a diagram, and their complexity, should be understandable. For large, complex and nested states, additional state machine diagrams should be considered. State machines with more than 10 states may not be elegant, and more than one state machine diagram may have to be created. Adding notes to explain the states and transitions will enhance the readability of these diagrams.

## 5.8 QUALITY OF TIMING DIAGRAMS IN MOSS

### 5.8.1 Describing the Timing Diagram for Policy and Claim in MOSS

There is very little that we can do with timing diagrams right now, as they are new in UML and their usage still needs to grow. In our attempt at modeling in the solution space, Figure 5.12 is an example timing diagram that shows, in the context of time, the state changes to two objects simultaneously—Policy and Claim. Only two simple states are shown for each of these objects—On and Off. However, even with these simple states, it is easy to see how we can compare state changes for a period of time for two objects on this timing diagram. The diagram reads as follows:

Policy switches to On (presumably after the premium has been paid). After 2 weeks, an event/accident occurs, resulting in a Claim. This changes the state of Claim from Off to On. The diagram indicates that it takes 12 weeks to resolve the claim, whereas the policy itself expires within 5 weeks of making the claim.

### 5.8.2 Syntax Checks for Timing Diagrams in MOSS

Check for the correct representation of the state lines on the diagram. The objects, their states (i.e., On and Off) and the optional constraints should all be shown as in Figure 5.12.

### 5.8.3 Semantic Checks for Timing Diagrams in MOSS

Timing diagrams should be semantically meaningful and should be drawn to compare two or more object states, as in Figure 5.12. Since not much is known in the UML domain about these diagrams, we can only infer the approach to ensuring their semantic quality.

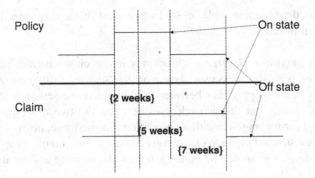

**Figure 5.12** Timing diagram for `Policy` and `Claim` in the solution space.

### 5.8.4 Aesthetic Checks for Timing Diagrams in MOSS

Aesthetically, these diagrams should be used for a limited number of objects and their states to ensure that they remain readable.

## 5.9 CONVERTING MODELS INTO SYSTEMS

One important aspect of quality in UML-based projects is the conversion of the model into its corresponding software. Better still, we can view this aspect as the implementation of the model, while some UML models would be implemented in Java, others in C++ and still others would be satisfied by third-party packages or COTS. While quality control or testing would appear in the final stages of a software life cycle, in any of this implementation it is also important to consider how the models are converted into code. This is a crucial aspect of quality assurance, because a good conversion or a good implementation depends on a good model and a good process. Models, as we have seen in the earlier definition of modeling, are by necessity incomplete. If they comprised the actual implementation, there would be no need for modeling. Because of this necessary incompleteness, a certain amount of skill is needed in converting the models into their implementation. Good quality assurance will ensure that this conversion is process based and has been prototyped properly. Finally, there are checks and balances at the end of each step within the conversion of the models into their corresponding implementation before a full release is produced.

## 5.10 CROSS-DIAGRAM DEPENDENCIES

Finally, it is worthwhile to mention some of the cross-diagram dependencies between the various UML diagrams discussed here in the solution space. These dependencies must be considered when semantic and aesthetic checks are applied to the entire model in the solution space. Therefore, checks related to the cross-diagram dependencies will be used when most of the diagrams in the model have been completed.

*Class and Sequence Diagrams.* Operations in the class diagram have a direct mapping with the messages shown on the sequence diagram. As a result, there is a close dependency between the two diagrams. Semantic and aesthetic checks ensure that the dependencies between the two diagrams have been checked for message-operation correlation. Furthermore, objects of sequence diagrams should belong to classes on class diagrams. An object without a corresponding class should be investigated for its meaning and for its existence, for that matter.

*Activity and Sequence Diagrams.* Typically, a thread running through one suite of activities within an activity diagram can be represented by one sequence diagram. Therefore, it is advantageous to check for relationships between activity diagrams and sequence diagrams. Although this is not a syntactically dictated relationship, the semantic meaning behind a thread through an activity diagram and the corresponding sequence diagram should be established. One activity diagram may relate to many sequence diagrams. This should be checked to ensure that aesthetically they are all properly related and that it is possible to track these diagrams easily.

*Class to State Machine Diagrams.* A class on a class diagram is related to the life cycle of its corresponding object on a state machine. Therefore, it should be possible to establish the link between the class and a corresponding state machine.

*Sequence to Communication Diagrams.* These two diagrams are merely views of each other. Therefore, for an aesthetically elegant solution, both diagrams may *not* be required. The need for the diagrams will depend on the interests and needs of the modelers.

*State Machine to Timing Diagrams.* Although new to UML, timing diagrams appear to have the potential not only to show the states, but also to enable their comparison between multiple objects. These objects may have corresponding state machine diagrams that show the state changes and transitions in great detail. Thus, together, the two diagrams provide a complete and comparative picture of objects, states and transitions. The semantic meanings behind the objects on the two diagrams should be very easy to establish— merely by checking the names of the objects. The aesthetic check can include checking for the number of objects shown on the timing diagram and any additional notes to clarify the cross-diagram dependency.

## DISCUSSION TOPICS

**1.** Why is it necessary to consider modeling separately in the solution space?

**2.** Once MOSS is created, what happens to MOPS?

**3.** Discuss the differences between syntax checks, semantic checks and aesthetic checks as performed on a class. Repeat the same when performed on a class diagram.

**4.** What is the difference between checking the quality of a class in the solution space (MOSS) and checking its quality in the problem space (MOPS)?

**5.** What new stereotypes are likely to appear on a class diagram in the solution space?

**6.** When ascertaining the correctness of a sequence diagram, you would focus primarily on which check?

**7.** In what situations would one use a communication diagram?

**8.** Explain how the discussion on the quality of an object diagram will help in documenting and improving the multiplicities on a class diagram.

**9.** Discuss the syntactic correctness and semantic incorrectness of the figure below. Also, discuss why multiplicity is redundant between the two classes shown in the figure below.

**10.** Draw a class diagram with no more than two business-level classes (e.g., Customer and Account). Show a simple association relationship between the two classes. Now expand this class diagram in the solution space by considering all possible additional classes that will be required in implementing the business model. (Hint: based on your language of choice, like VB or Java, you may want to bring in all classes, such as the boundary classes (Forms) the database classes (Tables) and other implementation-level classes.

**11.** Is it necessary to maintain consistency between MOSS and MOPS as business requirements change in time?

**12.** Which is the most important diagram in MOSS? Give reasons.

## REFERENCES

Booch, G. *Object-Oriented Design with Applications*, Redwood City, CA: Benjamin/Cummings, 1991, 1994.

Gamma, E., Helm, R., Johnson, R., and Vlissides, J. *Design Patterns: Elements of Reusable Object Oriented Software*. Reading, MA: Addison-Wesley, 1995 (known as Gang of Four or GOF).

Unhelkar, B. *Process QA for UML-Based Projects*. Boston: Addison-Wesley, 2003.

## Chapter 6

# V&V of the Quality of MOBS

The design of a large software product is an intellectual adventure. Too much self-confidence can hurt.[1]

## CHAPTER SUMMARY

This chapter discusses the UML 2.0 diagrams for the LUCKY Insurance system and demonstrates the application of V&V checklists to these diagrams in the background modeling space. The UML diagrams in background modeling space include package diagrams that help organize the information architecture; class diagrams that deal with persistence (storage and retrieval of data) and robustness diagrams that introduce control classes to ensure robustness of architecture; component diagrams including architectural diagrams for Web design or Web application servers; composite structure diagrams that show run-time decomposition of components or objects; and finally, the deployment diagram, which represents the deployment of hardware and its mapping with the components.

[1]B. Meyer, *Object Oriented Software Construction*, 2nd Edition. Upper Saddle River, NJ: Prentice Hall, p. 673.
Note: The diagrams in this chapter are based on the LUCKY insurance problem statement described in Appendix A.

*Verification and Validation for Quality of UML 2.0 Models*, by Bhuvan Unhelkar
Copyright © 2005 John Wiley & Sons, Inc.

## 6.1   WORKING IN THE BACKGROUND SPACE

This chapter discusses the application of V&V checklists comprising syntax, semantic and aesthetic checks to the UML diagrams produced as part of MOBS. The primary activities in this modeling space are architectural in nature, although activities related to overall project management can also be considered in the background space. The UML diagrams produced in the background influence both MOPS and MOSS, and at the same time are influenced by both of these models.

## 6.2   UML DIAGRAMS IN THE BACKGROUND SPACE (MOBS)

The UML diagrams of importance from an architectural viewpoint in the creation of MOBS are shown in Figure 6.1. These diagrams are briefly described as follows:

- *Package diagrams* in MOBS are an extension to the package diagram drawn in MOPS. In this architectural space, the package diagrams include packages for implementation including packages representing databases and GUIs.
- *Class persistence diagrams* in MOBS extend and enrich the class diagrams drawn in the other two modeling spaces to ensure database modeling and implementation. Class diagrams in this background space consider database mapping, active classes, granularity and reuse and related issues.
- *Class robustness diagrams* add value to the class diagrams drawn in the background space by separating the entity classes from the boundary classes and from one another, ensuring robustness and flexibility of designs. This robustness is ensured by inserting control classes at the right place within the class diagrams.
- *Component diagrams* are drawn in the background space as a major architectural constituent of the system. These are the physical implementation diagrams in UML, depicting where and how the classes designed thus far are to be implemented. Additional diagrams, which show the thin-client-thick-server or Web application architectures, are frequently drawn in MOBS to support the component diagrams.
- *Composite structure diagrams* model the run-time decomposition of a component or an object.
- *Deployment diagrams*, the only hardware specific diagrams in UML, are drawn in the background space to outline the physical deployment of the system, including its nodes and processors.

Relevant to the aforementioned list of diagrams are architectural concepts of layering, dividing (slicing) and granularity of the system. These are discussed in the next section before the V&V checklists for the UML diagrams are presented.

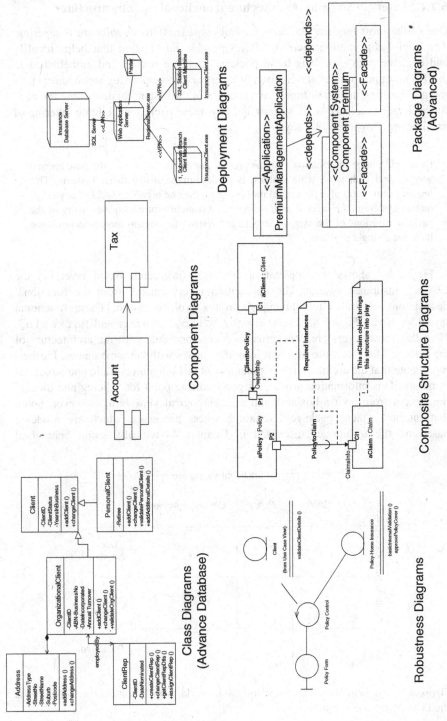

**Figure 6.1** UML diagrams in the background space.

195

### 6.2.1   Layers in Software Architecture (Functional vs. Infrastructure)

One of the most fundamental architectural considerations in software is layering. The brief initial requirements in MOPS provide information that helps identify and evaluate packages. It is these packages that are refined and embellished in this background space by the creation of layers and corresponding architectural prototypes resulting in overall fitness of a package in the system. In describing the need for packages in a large-scale system and how these packages facilitate layering of architecture, Fowler (1997) says:

> Developing large information systems present particular challenges, the fundamental way to deal with large scale systems is to decompose it to smaller systems. This requires some form of architectural modelling ... the first organising tool of any information system is the layered architecture ... this architecture identifies many of the package divisions of the system. In a larger system the domain model becomes too large for a single package.

Figure 6.2 shows the application- versus infrastructure-based layers in the LUCKY insurance system. The application layers emerge from the functional descriptions of the system attempted in the problem space. These functional layers shown in Figure 6.2 are Client, Policy, Claims and Marketing. Note that these layers are conceptual in nature and deal with the architecture of the system. They are quite different from the classes with the same names. Furthermore, note that the architectural information on this diagram is static and structural in nature. This information provides a good starting point for "slicing and dicing" the system from both a business and a technological viewpoint. However, noted that internally these packages contain business processes, which are modeled based on the techniques discussed in Chapter 4—typically using behavioral

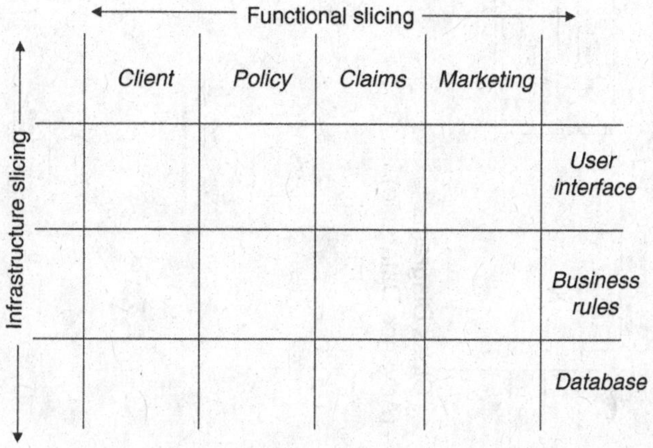

**Figure 6.2**   Application- versus infrastructure-based layering in software architecture for the LUCKY insurance system.

modeling diagrams such as the use case and activity diagrams. When the influence of the problem space on the background space is considered, it is discovered that the business processes do not remain contained within one package. Rather, some business processes transcend many packages. This is understandable, as businesses modeled on processes (rather than departments) are unlikely to be compartmentalized in packages. Keeping this in mind is helpful as we create packages, because although packages represent subsystems, these subsystems will have dependencies on each other. (Note: The discussion on business processes leads to the interesting work on business process reengineering-BPR-but outside the scope of this book.)

In line with the technical discussion on business processes, however, Erickson and Penkar (2000) provide a good architectural description—particularly using UML—of how a process-based organization would span divisions or departments that form the structural part of the organization. Thus, this business process aspect of good-quality architecture must be kept in mind in arriving at the application- versus infrastructure-based divisions of the system, as shown in Figure 6.2. While these functional and infrastructure divisions form the basis of good architecture, they are likely to be influenced by the use cases and activity diagrams drawn in the problem space. MOPS, as discussed in Chapter 4, models the business from a process viewpoint. Hence, provision must be made for its influence on MOBS, as discussed here. The reverse is also true. Modeling in the background space may reveal major organizational constraints (such as limited bandwidth or unavailability of a content management system) which will influence the models representing the problem domain.

In the LUCKY case study, the insurance business does not consist of separate divisions or departments, as might appear if Figure 6.2 is viewed in isolation. Instead, the process of creating a policy or submitting a claim spans all four functional slices shown in the figure. Thus, in dealing with the modeling work in the background space, we add to the work we have done in the problem space (that of creating packages called `Client`, `Policy`, `Claims` and `Marketing`). Each of these functional slices of the application is a candidate for a package to be represented in a package diagram. It should also be mentioned that there are many areas of the business that *may* be fully contained within a package. For example, some activities—like marketing and investigating prospective clients— may be in the area of the `Marketing` package itself. These activities may not interact with activities in the `Policy` or `Claim` packages. Overall, though, these architectural layers stand to benefit greatly when consideration is given to inputs from domain experts, business analysts and users working in the problem space.

In addition to considering the influence of MOPS on the background architecture, it is essential to consider similar influence from MOSS, or solution space models, on the architecture of the system. Thus, from a solution (implementation) perspective, each of the business packages will need at least three slices of technical infrastructure to carry out its responsibilities. These infrastructure slices, as shown in Figure 6.2, are the `User Interface`, `Business Rules` and `Database`. This is the commonly known three-tiered basic architecture applicable to a system or, in the case of large systems, to subsystems or packages.

The architectural work shown in Figure 6.2 also influences iterative and incremental project planning, as briefly discussed in Chapter 7. The development project plan can contain iterations that facilitate creation of software artifacts *inside* these packages, whereas the incremental aspect of the project plan would include development of newer packages.

### 6.2.2 Relating the Functional Slices to the Infrastructure

Getting the overall architecture of the system right is one of the most significant steps toward achieving quality. Therefore, it is essential to discuss the relationships between the application and infrastructure architectures further. This relationship is made clearer in Figure 6.3, which is the top view of the architectural arrangements. Instead of thinking of the architecture as slices of the system related to each other, in Figure 6.3 it is visualized like a set of tiles placed on top of each other. The diagram is a tile diagram based on the Chinese game of mah-jong. In mah-jong, tiles are arranged not only with respect to each other, but also on top of one another. A good software architecture would also have packages that are not only related to each other, but also layered on top of each other appropriately.

To understand this multilayered architecture, consider the four main functional tiles appearing in Figure 6.3—Policy, Claims, Marketing and Client. Additionally, a separate tile called Settlement may appear. This Settlement can either be considered as part of Claims, or it may be treated separately, as in this figure. The top view indicates that the database and user interface remain on a lower supportive layer, whereas all the business functionalities are on top of this layer.

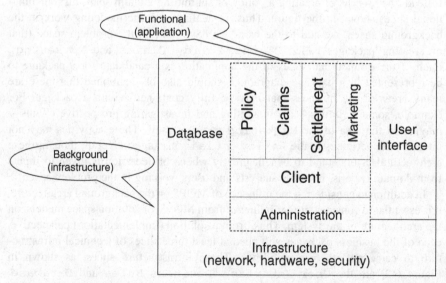

**Figure 6.3** Putting application architecture in the context of the infrastructure (background) architecture.

In medium-sized to large projects, it will also be discovered that these tiles, represented by packages, need to be further subdivided into lower-level or smaller packages. This subdivision can be based entirely on the business division or on a combination of business and technical divisions. For example, going back to Figure 6.2, the Client package can be further subdivided into a Client-Corporate package and a Client-Personal package (not shown in the figure). Alternatively, the package divisions could be Client-UserInterface, Client-BusinessRules and Client-Database. Thus, in medium-sized to large projects, each cross section resulting from the horizontal and vertical slicing of functionality and infrastructure offers a potential package. And the layering of packages, facilitated by UML's package diagrams, enables modelers to create a MOBS that reflects the conceptual layers/tiles shown in Figure 6.3.

One interesting difference between Figure 6.2 and Figure 6.3 is the way in which Client relates to other functional tiles. In Figure 6.3, the slices of Policy, Claims, Marketing and optionally Settlement are all shown as relating to Client. Thus all business functionalities depend on Client. This dependency paves the path for a typical Client relationship management system.

Also shown in Figure 6.3 is the Administration tile of the system, mentioned as a package in the discussion of MOPS in Chapter 4. More often than not, this administrative part of the system is neglected in the problem space, as it deals only with administrative functionality rather than with main business functionality. This additional administrative functionality usually appears in subsequent iterations of the project after the initial functional use cases have been documented. The additional use cases describe administrative functions such as printing of control totals, printing of reports, calculating the system data population, cleanup of data on a monthly, quarterly and annual basis, creation of backups, archiving and mirroring of data, to name but a few. These and innumerable other such functions remain in the background and form the administrative part of the system, resulting in the Administration package shown as a tile underneath Client. Both Client and Administration packages rest on the Infra structure slice of the architecture. This Infrastructure layer caters to important operational (nonfunctional) requirements such as network, hardware, security, integration, performance, scalability and volume.

Finally, Figure 6.3 also shows the User Interface and Database layers supporting business functionality. These tiles at the base of the figure indicate that the Policy, Claims, Settlement, Marketing, Client and Administration packages rest on—*depend on*—the database and user interface packages. These concepts are ready for representation in UML's package diagrams, as discussed next.

## 6.3  V&V OF PACKAGE DIAGRAMS IN MOBS

Figure 6.4 shows the LUCKY insurance system's package diagram. The high-level slices of business functionality in Figure 6.3 are represented by packages here.

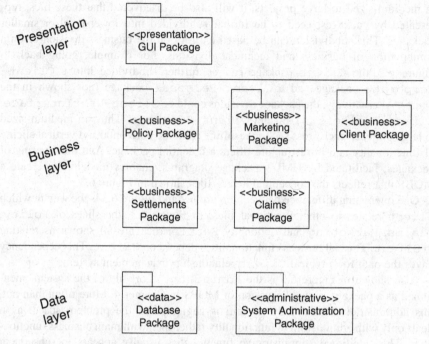

**Figure 6.4**   Insurance system package diagram.

In fact, Figure 6.4 extends the package diagram arrived at in MOPS (Figure 4.13). Here, in the background space, we additionally have the GUI package, which deals with the presentation layer; the Database package, which deals with the data; and the System Administration package. The System Administration package was briefly alluded to in MOPS. Here, it is modeled entirely in this background space, because often administration is considered a background task. If, however, the administrative aspect of the system is of interest to the user in specifying the system, then this Administration package may be modeled as part of MOPS. In other words, system administration could be split into two different types of tasks:

1. Tasks that are performed by the system automatically on a periodic basis or processes that run every night, once every week, and so on. An ideal example is a notification to the client relationship manager telling him that one of his clients is due for renewal of his policy. This is a typical background space modeling task, resulting in MOBS.

2. Tasks that are performed manually by a person—usually a system administrator. An example is that of a client who has shifted residence from one state to another. All of his details now need to be reassigned to a different branch and to a new relationship manager. As this task is performed only when clients

move from one place to another, as in this example, there may not be a need to automate this task—or, even if part of it is automated, some manual (and occasionally legal) intervention will be necessary. Therefore, this part of the system administration may be modeled under the umbrella of MOPS.

Figure 6.5 further expands the package diagram for LUCKY at the architectural level. This package diagram builds on the architectural discussion presented in previous sections. This is a detailed implementation-specific package diagram. It shows layered packages and components inside the packages. In addition to showing the components and packages of LUCKY, this diagram shows how applications are built by putting together (reusing) components which may belong to other reusable packages.

For example, the `PremiumManagement` application can be built by using the `Premium` component and the `Client` component. The `ClientManagement` application, however, depends only on the component `Client`. Furthermore, if patterns are incorporated in this architecture (see Gamma et al., 1995) then we will also be showing the `Façade` package inside each of these component packages. Further decomposition of the component `Premium` package shows an inquiry package inside it that deals with all inquiries related to a `Policy`. This package also relies on the `Transaction` package to handle the `Inquiry` transaction.

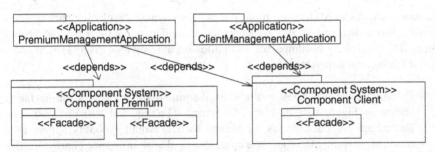

Applications would use component systems. They, in turn, are made up of components that are imported through their respective facades

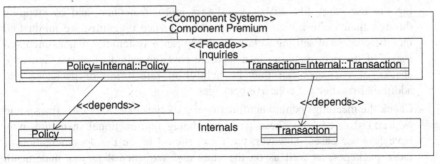

**Figure 6.5**  Package diagrams as layered frameworks.

Having described the creation of a package diagram for the LUCKY insurance system, we now proceed with the V&V checks for diagrams in MOBS.

### 6.3.1   Syntax Checks for Package Diagrams in MOBS

Syntax checks of a package diagram such as the one drawn in the previous section are not intense in the background space. This is because packages are still primarily used as organizational units. Thus, the syntactic checks of package diagrams in the background space are similar to those for the package diagrams in the problem space (discussed in Chapter 4). These checks are:

- Packages created as organizational units should be represented with a tabbed rectangle.
- The notation for a package, the stereotype of a package and, optionally, the relationship between packages should be checked for syntactic correctness.
- The relationship between packages, if shown, should be the dependency relationship (also optionally with a stereotype), as shown in Figure 6.5.
- Stereotypes on packages should use the correct stereotype notations.

### 6.3.2   Semantic Checks for Package Diagrams in MOBS

Semantic checks in MOBS are more intense than syntax checks for package diagrams. This is because MOBS packages have detailed semantic reasoning behind them. This reasoning encompasses and builds on the previous discussion of functional slicing and dependencies.

- Investigate the use cases and activity diagrams within each of the packages shown in Figure 6.4: Policy, Client, Claims and Marketing. The Settlement package, as mentioned earlier, would probably appear as a result of "stepping through" use cases that deal with insurance claims. Verifying the use cases within the context of the packages is part of the background space semantic checks for package diagrams. Thus, by inspecting and reviewing the use cases like submitsClaim more than once, and by stepping through their corresponding activity and sequence diagrams, we might find that the process of settling a claim in an insurance system has major functional issues of its own, resulting in a separate package called Claims. Semantic checks of packages can thus be helpful in refactoring of packages into additional smaller yet cohesive packages.
- Check the meanings behind nonfunctional packages like GUI, Database and Administration. These packages, being nonfunctional in nature, may have few use cases; however, the focus should be on the documentation of these packages, as well as on the class and sequence diagrams underneath these technological packages. The language of implementation and the

database used for persistence need to be understood for their capabilities and meanings while performing this check.

- Check for dependencies between the packages. As mentioned in the discussion of aesthetic checks in the next section, these dependencies can provide valuable input to the project manager in terms of scheduling the iterative and incremental development project plan.

- Ensure that if packages are shown, they correspond to layers (or stereotyped as such) and they are the correct layers. For example, in Figure 6.4, the GUI package is correctly stereotyped as <<presentation>> (alternatively, <<boundary>> or <<interface>> would also do). Similarly, the entity packages are stereotyped as <<business>>, although <<entity>> would also be acceptable.

- Check for the extent to which the package diagrams represent the slices or tiles discussed earlier. For example, do package diagrams include system integration (i.e., one system talking to another, like CRMS talking to legacy systems) models? If so, are those integration aspects mentioned on the package diagrams (through a note)? If not, are separate packages representing the legacy or CRMS systems shown on the diagram?

Additional V&V checks specifically for Figure 6.5 are as follows:

- Should the PremiumManagement application be a separate application?

- Does the PremiumManagement application genuinely depend on the component Premium and the component Client?

- What sort of interdependency there is between the component Premium and the component Client?

- What does the Facade package do?

- Is Inquiries (for example) a genuine framework or is it a high-level pattern that will need a fair amount of implementation-level detail?

- Is the stereotyping of each of these packages correct? For example, should the medium-level packages all be stereotyped as component systems?

- Are the components reusable?

- Are the application packages worth stereotyping as applications?

- Is Transaction the only package inside Inquiries that deals with the actual transaction of inquiry or are other packages needed? Are other classes needed as well? The opposite is also true, because transactions may not be restricted to Inquiries but may deal with Payments and Settlements. Has this been checked?

### 6.3.3 Aesthetic Checks for Package Diagrams in MOSS

Aesthetic checks of package diagrams in the background space deal primarily with assigning packages to teams. The project manager can use this aesthetic check to identify and assign packages to development teams, depending on their skill set and the dependencies of the packages. For example, in Figure 6.4, it is necessary to check whether these packages are assigned to individuals and/or teams? Redistribution of packages to developers will not only be a technical necessity but also a question of aesthetic balance.

In order to create an aesthetically elegant solution, the package should be assigned to people with appropriate skills. For example, packages such as GUI and Database should be assigned to technical designers and lead developers with skills in user interface development and specific database (such as ORACLE or SQL Server) development, respectively. The number of packages, the assignments of packages to teams and the extent of dependency of one package on another are aspects of the aesthetic quality of models in the background space, and they should all be checked here.

Check for reuse in package diagrams. This check deals with the number of packages and the implementation domain from which they are emanating. Balance in reusing packages is essential.

## 6.4   CLASSES AND CLASS DIAGRAMS IN THE BACKGROUND SPACE

### 6.4.1   Relational Table Representation by Classes

Classes in the background space can represent database tables. This, of course, is suggestive, and if the development environment of the databases provides a modeling mechanism, then this particular usage may not be required. Furthermore, the current discussion assumes that the backend database is a relational database. Unlike an OO database, where objects are stored directly as objects, storing objects in relational tables requires translation of classes to tables. This creates interesting challenges in terms of V&V of these models.

Classes representing database tables are called "persistent classes" and can be stereotyped as <<table>>. These classes represent objects and their states that are stored beyond a single execution of the system. It is reasonable to say that in most practical systems, more than half one the classes are persistent. This is because most business objects, such as Policy and Claim, need to store their data (values of their attributes) and their states and make them available when the system is run the next time. Persistent classes, therefore, have to incorporate in their design database issues of storage and retrieval, concurrency and security.

Identification and modeling of persistent classes is important, as it can greatly assist database modeling. Most UML-based CASE tools enable the architect to mark the classes as persistent, either by using the stereotype facility or as additional information in the class specifications. These persistent classes can then be used by the UML CASE tools to create an initial relational database schema from the class diagrams.

Representation of a table by a class is possible because, conceptually, a class considered only in terms of its first two compartments (i.e., name and attributes) is effectively a table. While the class name represents the table name, the attribute names represent the columns. The behavior of these tables is restricted to the storage and retrieval functions of the database and, as a result, may incorporate SQL statements.

### 6.4.2  Mapping ClientDetails to Relational Tables

Figure 6.6 demonstrates the mapping of class diagrams to relational database tables. The mapping between the part of the class diagram dealing with the details of a client in the LUCKY insurance system and the corresponding relational database tables is shown in Figure 6.6.

Firstly, each of the classes finds a corresponding table in the relational schema on the right side of Figure 6.6. This is followed by columns representing attributes within the classes. Note how the ClientID provides the key to access the tables and also provides the necessary links between various rows to enable creation of a complete object. The inheritance relationship between OrganizationalClient (and PersonalClient) derived from Client is translated into three tables, with a row for every type of client in the Client table and a row for each subtypes of client in the Organizational Client table and the Personal Client table. Note also how the association relationship between Organizational Client and ClientRep is managed by the common key ClientID. The ClientRep table has, additionally, PersonID, which shows its relationship with Person (the inheritance ClientRep and Person is not shown here, but was shown in Figure 4.xx in Chapter 4). Multiple addresses for an Organizational Client are shown with multiple rows. Finally, note how GUI and controller classes need not be mapped to database tables, as these classes are not persistent classes and their objects are not stored in a database.

### 6.4.3  Describing Active Classes in MOBS

Figure 6.7 is an example of another class diagram in the background space—an architectural class diagram. This figure shows three classes: ClaimManager, Claim_Form and Claim. Their stereotypes are respectively <<control>>, <<boundary>> and <<entity>>. The class <<control>> ClaimManager is an Active class, which is controlling the messages and their sequences dealing with the other two classes.

This class diagram answers the question "What happens when the system is started?" In this particular case, when the user initiates the system with a double click of an executable, the ClaimManager module is loaded in memory first. This is the Active class, shown with a thickened rectangle, in Figure 6.7. It is from this ClaimManager module that the rest of the system is controlled. Note that even though in this class diagram ClaimManager continues to remain active, the duration of its control remains outside the scope of this static-structural diagram. That additional information is provided through other diagrams, like the sequence or communication diagrams.

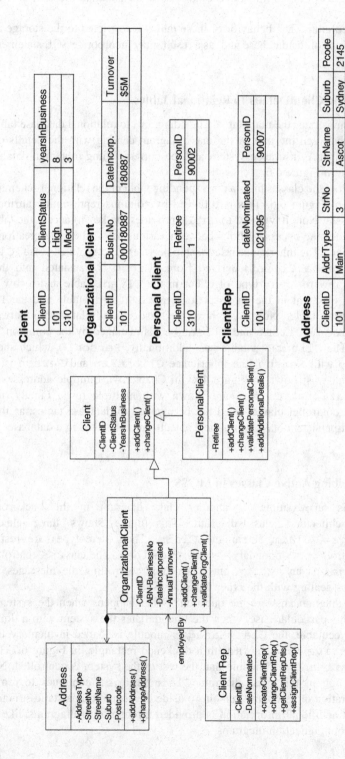

**Client**

| ClientID | ClientStatus | yearsInBusiness |
|----------|--------------|-----------------|
| 101 | High | 8 |
| 310 | Med | 3 |

**Organizational Client**

| ClientID | Busin.No | DateIncorp. | PersonID |
|----------|----------|-------------|----------|
| 101 | 000180887 | 180887 | 90002 |

**Personal Client**

| ClientID | Retiree | PersonID |
|----------|---------|----------|
| 310 | 1 | 90007 |

**ClientRep**

| ClientID | dateNominated | PersonID |
|----------|---------------|----------|
| 101 | 021095 | 90007 |

**Address**

| ClientID | AddrType | StrNo | StrName | Suburb | Pcode |
|----------|----------|-------|---------|--------|-------|
| 101 | Main | 3 | Ascot | Sydney | 2145 |
| 101 | Mail | PB 101 | Ryde | Ryde | 3124 |

**Figure 6.6** Mapping classes related to Client to the corresponding relational tables.

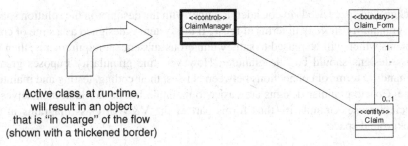

Active class, at run-time,
will result in an object
that is "in charge" of the flow
(shown with a thickened border)

**Figure 6.7** Considering active classes, processes and threads in MOBS.

## 6.4.4 Class and Granularity of Design in the Background Space

The OO concepts of inheritance and peer-to-peer interaction among classes in OO designs facilitate the *decomposition* of classes into smaller *grains*. Alternatively, many classes can be merged together to produce a big class. This is the concept of "granularity," and its application in MOBS can be a valuable ingredient enhancing quality. Figure 6.8 shows the concept of granularity as applicable in OO designs. The same functionality (represented by UML diagrams in the problem space) can be designed in the solution space with bigger classes (coarse granular) or with smaller classes (fine granular). Thus, granularity allows the designer a choice of putting a large amount of functionality in a class and making its size bigger or spreading out the same functionality over many smaller classes (Unhelkar and Henderson-Sellers, 1993; Unhelkar et al., 1996). The architect working in the

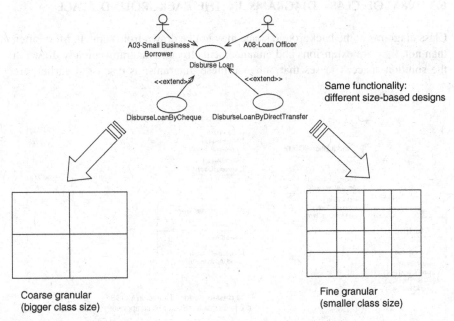

**Figure 6.8** Granularity of OO designs.

background space needs to consider, together with the designer in the solution space, the granularity strategy in terms of reuse. If the system is designed as a suite of components which will be reused to satisfy numerous subsequent requirements, then the class designs should be fine granular. However, fine granularity imposes greater demands in terms of connections between classes, their coding, testing and maintenance. Coarse granular designs are easier to maintain but do not lend themselves to efficient reuse. Granularity thus forms part of the V&V of class diagrams in the background space.

### 6.4.5   Assigning Classes to Components

Figure 6.9 shows how a suite of classes is mapped to a `Client.exe`. This mapping need not be done pictorially in practice. Most CASE tools will do this mapping implicitly once classes are related to a component by setting suitable flags in the class description. Balancing components with the number of classes—at both design time and run time—is crucial to quality. Figure 6.9 shows that all `Client` details will be implemented in `Client.exe`. It is worth mentioning here that the `Client` component can also be a `.dll` (representing a dynamic linked library) that can eventually be integrated along with other `.dll`s (like `Address.dll`), and together they would form a `.exe`. For example, in Visual Basic terms, the project would be a `Claims.exe` (if it is `Claims` system) or `Insurance.exe` (if it contains the entire insurance modules).

## 6.5   V&V OF CLASS DIAGRAMS IN THE BACKGROUND SPACE

Class diagrams in the background space may not be drawn from scratch. More often than not, they are extensions and enhancements to class diagrams already drawn in the solution space. Classes that enhance these diagrams, as discussed earlier, are

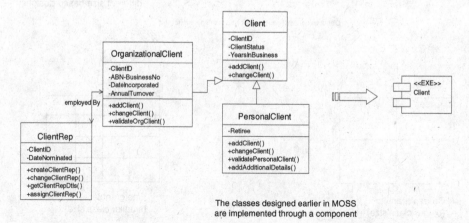

The classes designed earlier in MOSS
are implemented through a component

**Figure 6.9**   Assigning classes to components for physical implementation.

<<table>> classes and <<boundary>> classes. The <<controller>> stereotypes are discussed separately under robustness diagrams in Section 6.6. If a major database modeling exercise is undertaken, then there would be separate class diagrams dealing exclusively with persistent classes. Here we are discussing the specific use of class diagrams, such as consideration of active classes and/or mapping of classes to databases.

### 6.5.1 Syntax Checks for Class Diagrams in MOBS

- Check the representation of implementation constructs (e.g., mapping database storage tables to classes) in the class diagram here.
- Check the access keys and IDs represented in the classes that represent the tables. These would be the primary and foreign keys, and their correctness needs to be verified.
- Consider the representation of access keys and IDs from the point of view of language of implementation.
- Check for the way data are searched and sorted from an architectural viewpoint, and check how they are stored and accessed through the keys, indexes and definitions of classes in MOBS.
- Check the storage by keys and the values of the position of the record in the database.
- Check the syntactic correctness of inheritance when classes are reused from the programming language or third-party libraries.
- Check additional language representations (e.g., #hashtables in Java).
- Check multiplicities between the relationships of the classes (e.g., 1.m).
- Check link or association classes for their relationship with the association line (association classes are not directly connected to other classes but rather to their association line).

### 6.5.2 Semantic Checks for Class Diagrams in MOBS

- Check that what is being stored in the databases is correctly represented in the class diagrams.
- Check for unique responsibilities for classes. For example, Client and Policy should not be stored in the same table.
- Cross-check persistence representation with multiplicities shown on the class diagram.
- Revisit the keys and IDs, checking them for balance in terms of speed versus volume.
- Cross-check with direction of associations. This will determine the direction of access.
- Check for possibilities and correctness of semantic reuse, which will imply reuse of business classes/objects/packages.

### 6.5.3 Aesthetic Checks for Class Diagrams in MOBS

- Check for further partitioning of classes, their normalization, and creation of association classes to improve the aesthetics of the class diagram.
- Applying the concepts of granularity, discussed earlier in reusability, to class diagrams to improve not only their reuse but also their elegance.

## 6.6 V&V OF ROBUSTNESS THROUGH CLASS DIAGRAMS IN MOBS

### 6.6.1 Extending Class Diagrams to Robustness Diagrams

Robustness diagrams are an extension of class diagrams. They are considered important from an architectural viewpoint, as they enhance the robustness of the system by keeping its presentation layer separate from its business logic layer.

Robustness in the architecture of class diagrams in the background space is expressed by considering three different types of classes. Figure 6.10 describes two robustness diagrams, for policy creation and claims processing, using two different types of notation. The policy creation diagram uses the original objectory (Jacobson et al., notations, now used) as icons in many UML CASE tools, whereas the claims processing diagram uses the standard << >> stereotype notations. In both cases, three types of classes shown in Figure 6.10. They are described as follows:

- Boundary classes used by actors in communicating with the system. They are shown by a "lollypop" in the diagram marked as boundary classes.
- Entity classes derived from the domain of the problem and containing the business logic. They are shown as a circle with a flattened base and are marked as an entity class in the figure.
- Control classes serving as glue between the boundary and entity objects. They are shown as a circle with an arrowhead in the figure.

In addition to the above three types of classes, there is the association relationship on this diagram—identical to the association discussed in the class diagrams.

The rules for robustness are as follows:

- Two GUI classes cannot talk with each other.
- Two entity classes cannot talk with each other.
- A GUI class or an interface/boundary class cannot associate directly with an entity class.

The policy creation robustness diagram in Figure 6.10 starts with the boundary class called 'PolicyForm'. This class handles the responsibility of accepting the input from an actor and providing the actor with results (the actor is not usually shown on the diagram, and most CASE tools will prevent it from being shown). The

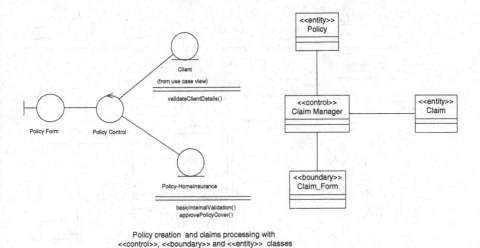

Policy creation and claims processing with
<<control>>, <<boundary>> and <<entity>> classes

**Figure 6.10** Robustness diagrams for `PolicyCreation` and `ClaimsProcessing` processes with <<control>>, <<boundary>> and <<entity>> classes.

two entity classes are `Client` and `Policy-HomeInsurance`, which contain business logic. Following the concept of robustness, it is necessary to separate the entity classes from the boundary classes. This is achieved by introducing a new control class called '`PolicyControl`' in Figure 6.10. This is similar to the well-known model view controller (MVC) pattern in Smalltalk. By introducing the controller class `PolicyControl`, changes to the GUI class will not affect the business logic, and vice versa—resulting in a relatively more stable (and hence robust) architecture. Similar rules are applied to the claims processing robustness diagram, where <<control>> `ClaimManager` is the controller class that separates `Policy` and `Claim` from each other, as well as the `Claim_Form` boundary class from the entity classes.

### 6.6.2 Robustness through Alternative Sequence Diagrams

Robustness need not be expressed by class diagrams alone. In Figure 6.11, an attempt is made to refine a sequence diagram by making sure that all the messages that go from the GUI classes to the entity classes or objects go through the controller objects. This diagram is also a good way of determining the architectural requirements in terms of the number of controllers needed in the system. For example, in Figure 6.11, we have two controller objects: <<control>> `CliamManager` and <<control>> `TransactionManager`.

### 6.6.3 Syntax Checks for Robustness Diagrams in MOBS

Syntax checks for the robustness diagram will follow the syntax checks for a class diagram in the background space. However, the focus here is on the controller class,

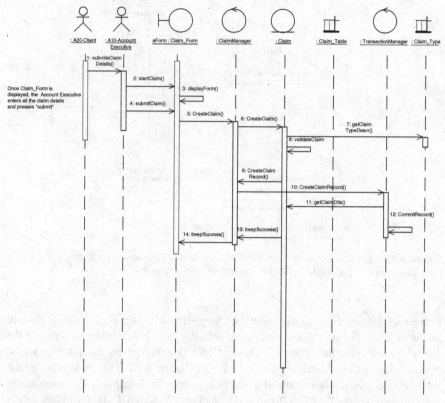

**Figure 6.11** Effect of robustness on the SubmitsClaim sequence diagram.

whose stereotype ≪control≫ should appear in the diagram. Alternatively, the icon for the controller stereotype should be visible on the diagram. It is necessary to check the syntax of the controller class, its stereotype and its multiplicity, as well as its list of operations. Furthermore, in the robustness diagram, displaying of all correct stereotypes—≪boundary≫, ≪control≫ and ≪entity≫—is mandatory.

### 6.6.4 Semantic Checks for Robustness Diagrams in MOBS

More often than not, a controller class will be a singleton class (based on the pattern literature of Gamma et al., 2000 that will ensure only one instance of that class in execution of the system. Such a class will have minimal administrative attributes but a full list of operations, which provide the interface, rather than the actual implementation of the operations. As seen earlier in the collaboration diagram, it should be possible to visualize the load on a controller class and therefore the need to either combine more than one controller classes into one or split a controller class into many. This is the semantic aspect of quality of a robustness diagram.

What does a controller class mean? Is there a transaction controller (or a "transaction manager," as it is colloquially called)? Is there a client manager or a policy manager? There have been suggestions of introducing a controller class in the first use case and then following it with as many controller classes as use cases as the first cut of adding robustness to the architecture. However, having a controller class for every use case would be excessive. A good starting point for the creation of controllers would be a controller class for every diagram.

### 6.6.5  Aesthetic Checks for Robustness Diagrams in MOBS

The aesthetic quality of robustness diagrams is ensured when the architects do not go overboard with this concept—which, in this context, means providing for one controller per class diagram. An aesthetically correct robustness concept means providing the right number of <<control>> classes, such as a `TransactionManager` and a `DatabaseManager`. The rest of the checks of the aesthetics of this diagram are similar to those of the class diagrams.

## 6.7  V&V OF COMPONENT DIAGRAMS IN MOBS

Figure 6.12 shows component diagram, where the components are shown together with their packages. For example, the component `Policy` is shown as a part of the package `Policy` subsystem. Furthermore, the relationship between policy and client is shown through the interface of ownership. Similarly, each component is shown in Figure 6.12 accessing the database through its CRUD operations interface.

Figure 6.13 clarifies Figure 6.12 by showing only the components without the packages. The relationships and interfaces are stereotyped to clarify the meaning of the diagram further. There are also notes on the diagram to increase clarification. The three levels of quality checks applied to these diagrams are discussed in the following subsections.

### 6.7.1  Syntax Checks for Component Diagrams in MOBS

Syntax checks for component diagrams focus on correctness of physical implementation of the system. As discussed during the SWOT of component diagrams in Chapter 3, the nature of these diagrams is relatively static structural. Component diagrams need to be verified for their structural representation. These checks are as follows:

- The first things to check is the correct representation of a component on the diagram. This involves using correct notation for the component. Figure 6.13

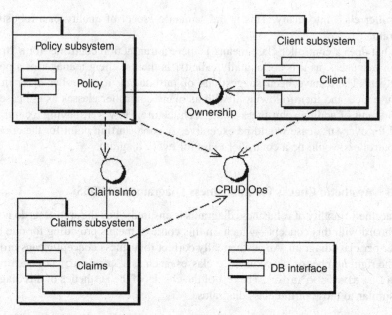

**Figure 6.12**   LUCKY insurance components, packages and interfaces.

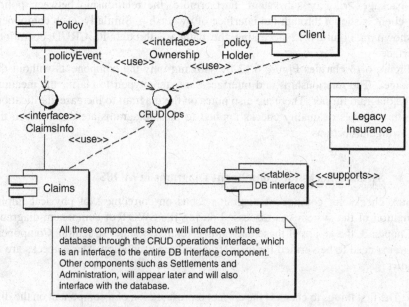

All three components shown will interface with the
database through the CRUD operations interface, which
is an interface to the entire DB Interface component.
Other components such as Settlements and
Administration, will appear later and will also
interface with the database.

**Figure 6.13**   Insurance system component diagrams.

shows only the allowable component diagram notations of component, interfaces, relationship and notes.

- Components realize interfaces. The next check therefore would be the representation of the interfaces on the diagram. Check the names of the components as well as the names of their interfaces. These are Ownership and CRUD Ops in Figure 6.13.

- If you there are components within components, then it is necessary to show the external package or another component to which an embedded component might belong. This could be done by writing the name of the parent package or parent component as `policy:: premium` or `client::address`.

- Occasionally components may have additional values or constraints shown on the component diagrams and may have their responsibilities documented. In that case, check for the correctness of this additional documentation.

- In checking the name of the component, check if there is a suffix to the name that represents either a language class, a database table or a linked library. If the suffix is nonstandard or relatively unknown, make sure that it is syntactically correct or that it represents a physical entity like a document, program or file, because there is only one notation representing various types of implementations.

- Components are usually be stereotyped. In that case, check the syntax of the stereotypes. Components can realize the interfaces. Components can also depend on the interfaces of other components. In both cases, check the relationship arrow, which is primarily a dotted line with an open arrowhead that indicates dependency. Dependency can be stereotyped again in various ways—for example, import or compile. A stereotype of <<table>> appears on the database interface in Figure 6.13.

- An important syntactic check is to ensure that the component, which is mapped to many classes, is physically implementable. More often than not, this requires not only programming knowledge and effort, which is language specific, but also creating the actual executable and running it in the given environment. Linking, building and executing a particular component are crucial syntax checks that ensure that the component is syntactically correct.

## 6.7.2 Semantic Checks for Component Diagrams in MOBS

Checking the semantics of the components in MOBS is far more involved and requires a good understanding of the technological or solution domain. Knowledge of languages and databases is important in deciding whether or not a component has been correctly modeled semantically.

- Check that the component correctly represents the class or collection of classes that is meant to represent. For example, the `Client` components contains the entire `ClientDetails` set of classes (e.g., address, contacts, telephone, fax, e-mail, banking, etc. are all part of the collection of classes that belong to

ClientDetails) that provides the realization of all these classes. Therefore, it is important to create a component showing the relationship between the component and the classes (through its specifications) and to make sure that the component provides the right number of well-defined interfaces that it realizes.

- In a component such as Client, we have an interface that provides the ClientDetails as far as insurance system administration is concerned. This interface can provide the name, address and other such administrative details. However, the Client component may have another interface that it relies on and that provides the details of the Client component with respect to the Client's past history of insurance policies, renewals and claims.

- Semantically, it is important to check whether a component has sufficient interfaces, the extent to which these interfaces overlap each other and how the component realizes these interfaces. Ideally, interfaces should not overlap. One quality of a good component is that it is easily replaceable. However, if a component has more than four or five interfaces and if they are used right through the system, then replacing one component by another will be far more involved. (This is an aesthetic check as well.)

- Use of third-party components is quite common and is encouraged. Therefore, the semantic meaning of each third-party component used in the project should be clarified. Check the meanings of any external components used on your diagram. This involves checking the interfaces and their definitions, and the specifications of the components that realize these definitions, as provided by the vendor of the components.

- Third-party components need not be only database-related technical components. They can also be business components, as would be tendered by, say, the MDA architecture. In that case, understanding the business functionality of the components is extremely important in creating a semantically complete component diagram.

- Another major semantic check involves the number of classes belonging to or implemented by a component. Mapping a class or a suite of classes to a component is an important semantic activity that needs focused verification.

- Check that a class created in either MOPS or MOSS is not floating around in those models without being realized in the background space.

- Increasing access to a legacy application in order to retrieve data is done through a legacy "wrapper" which is an interface of a component, and the entire backend code is treated as a component itself. While this does not provide a great syntactic challenge, there will be a phenomenal amount of semantic meaning behind such an interface to a legacy application. This should be checked to ensure that the legacy application is able to realize the interfaces that it provides.

- Many of the syntax and semantic checks of the component will benefit from the creation of an architectural prototype. It is therefore important to create such a prototype by using one simple business component and a corresponding solution-level component that depend on the programming language, the database and the operating environment. Check to see if the technical architectural issues are satisfied by a prototyped component.

- If a prototype is created, then it is important to trace the results of the prototype to the operational requirements. Creation of components goes hand in hand with their ability to be reused. Therefore, it is important to check that components have sufficient and crisply defined interfaces that enable them to be reused in the next project and beyond.

- Producers of reusable components have an additional responsibility, for they are unaware of specific business requirements or problem situations where their components will be reused. Therefore, the need to check all possible scenarios where the component or parts of it to be produced are likely to be reused, and to provide corresponding interfaces for these reusable components, are crucial quality criteria.

- Security architecture and security components also provide an interesting syntax and semantic challenge to quality. Therefore, components that relate to security should be checked for syntactic correctness, which involves their ability to integrate with the application that is being produced and to function correctly. The functional bit of the security component will be the part of semantic checks.

## 6.7.3  Aesthetic Checks for Component Diagrams in MOBS

- If components and component diagrams are syntactically correct and semantically complete and consistent, it is still important for the sake of reuse and for the sake of overall good quality that each of these executables components are well balanced.

- Is the component too big or too small? This is the issue of granularity, and involves the same argument discussed earlier in this chapter in terms of granularity of classes. A large, unwieldy component may not be reusable, may be out of balance and therefore may be aesthetically poor even if it performs all the functions that it is expected to perform.

- A suite of smaller components creates problems of maintenance of design and execution. While a small component may fit in various situations, it is difficult to maintain not only the component but also all of its interfaces.

- The next aesthetic check is on the interfaces provided by and/or realized by the component. For example, the number of interfaces per component and their definitions will also form part of aesthetic checks. Creation of new interfaces should be easy, provided that the component itself is well balanced.

- It is also important that these interfaces are properly documented to make the component easily accessible. Therefore, an important aesthetic check of a component diagram is to ensure that there is sufficient documentation for the interfaces and the components on the diagram.

- Components need to be put in a package once they show logical cohesiveness. For example, Client, Client Table and Client Type can be not only classes but also components in their right, and they would all form part of the Client package. Similarly, Policy may have the transaction or may have the inquiry, which would form part of the Policy package.

- If too many different types of transactions are discovered, then they need to be placed in a separate transaction component or in different types of transaction components like Inquiry, just as with class and use cases and other diagrams. Just as one element of the diagram can appear in more than one diagram, components can appear in more than one component diagram whether each diagram is blackened or not. Whether it has too many or too few components is also part of the check of the aesthetic aspect of component diagram quality. Putting components in packages and showing dependencies between packages is one more aspect of aesthetics.

- One component could affect another component, and vice versa, and other components could affect the first component. Extensive checks need to be made to avoid errors in either of these components. It is human nature to forget about something that has already been worked on, and often we have seen that fixing one error on one side can create many times the number of errors on the other side. For example, in our case, a Client changes his personal details. This change not only affects the Client component but also the Policy component.

## 6.8  V&V OF COMPOSITE STRUCTURE DIAGRAMS IN MOBS

Figure 6.14 shows a composite structure diagram dealing with a run-time scenario of the insurance system. Three run-time components are shown, together with their interfaces: aClient, aPolicy and aClaim. This diagram shows how the aClient component at run-time depends on the aPolicy component, as there is ownership from Client to Policy. Policy provides an interface, shown by a line with a semicircle at the end (seen as a semicircle on the diagram). A similar relationship is shown at run-time between Policy and Claim, where Policy needs ClaimsInfo for processing.

### 6.8.1  Syntax Checks for Composite Structure Diagrams

Check for representation of object or components at run-time. These are shown as aClient, aPolicy and aClaim in Figure 6.14.

Check for correct representation of the port symbol. This is shown as the Ownership and ClaimsInfo on the Policy and Claim components.

Check for the Interface representation—a required and realized interface. The diagram under discussion shows only required interfaces (semicircles), not realized interfaces (full circles).

Check for accuracy of the direction arrow.

Check for correctness of notes notation.

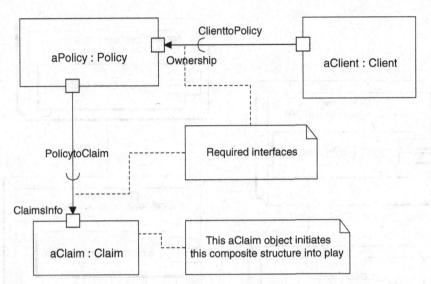

**Figure 6.14**   An example composite structure diagram for the LUCKY insurance system.

## 6.8.2  Semantic Checks for Composite Structure Diagrams

The semantic check for the composite structure diagram deals with checking whether it faithfully represents a run-time scenario. Therefore, it may be necessary to trace the meaning of this diagram back to other diagrams in the other two modeling spaces. For example, in Figure 6.14, the relationship shown between the three run-time components is true only at a particular time when Client is looking for her Policy and when Policy is looking for Claim details. This scenario could be based on the description of how claim details are accessed—and that description could appear in use case documentation, sequence diagrams or activity diagrams. Individual components and their meanings should also be checked for correct representation; however, that can be expected to follow the semantic checks for object diagrams and communication diagrams.

## 6.8.3  Aesthetic Checks for Composite Structure Diagrams

Aesthetic checks of composite structure diagrams are similar to those of communication and object diagrams. Ensure that the diagram is not overloaded with too many run-time components, and if it is necessary to show more than seven components, it may be advisable to create more than one composite structure diagram. Notes and explanatory texts enhance the aesthetic value of the diagrams.

## 6.9  V&V OF DEPLOYMENT DIAGRAMS IN MOBS

### 6.9.1  Factors Influencing Deployment of Systems

Figure 6.15 shows a deployment diagram for the LUCKY insurance system. It shows the physical positioning of the server as well as corresponding client

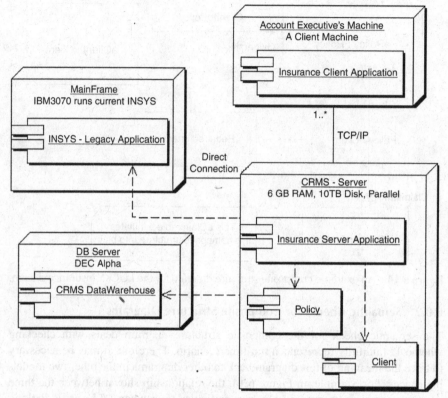

**Figure 6.15** Deployment diagram for the LUCKY insurance system.

machines from where the Account Executives will be able to access the software. The client, as in A20-Client, will also use some of these client machines. The client's access to the software is the extension of the standard client server system, where a client can log onto the system through the Internet and perform most functions, especially inquiries and some basic creation of client details, as well as creation of some standard policies. On the other hand, the server that hosts the new insurance system will need to interface with the machine that holds the existing legacy applications. Thus, it is the server that will contain the new CRMS application server-side components, which will then integrate with the legacy executables on the mainframe. This, of course, is a limited representation of the physical deployment of the system. Many more such diagrams would be needed to completely represent the physical deployment. However, the current UML standards only allow the creation of one deployment diagram that contains all the hardware. More important, though, it is the mapping between the components, as shown in the component diagrams and the corresponding nodes in the deployment diagram, that is of interest from a quality angle.

### 6.9.2   Syntax Checks for Deployment Diagrams in MOBS

Checking the syntactic correctness of deployment diagrams is relatively straight-forward. It is the semantics and now, more important, the aesthetics that play a crucial role in ensuring the quality of these diagrams. While showing the meaning of a node, as in a processing element, is also relatively straightforward, it is an important part of the architect's job to ensure that the right components are assigned to the right processors.

### 6.9.3   Semantic Checks for Deployment Diagrams in MOBS

Deployment diagrams are heavily influenced by the operational requirements of the system—that is, the nonfunctional, nonbehavioral requirements. Therefore, a deployment diagram will incorporate requirements related to performance, scalabil-ity, security, volume, operational environment, networking, integration, bandwidth and other such issues.

One of the limitations seen in the SWOT of deployment diagrams is that standard UML does not provide a large number of appropriate icons to represent the different nodes and processors—understandably, because UML does not claim to be a hardware-specific language. However, because of the availability of only simple notation, much of the responsibility for semantic correctness of a deployment diagram depends on stereotyping of the nodes and processors. This means that almost all nodes must be stereotyped to indicate whether they are a server or client machine or whether they are a printer or any other such device. More often than not, a good deployment diagram will move away from the basic UML notation in order to create a more substantial architectural picture of how the hardware and the physical network of the solution will look. This means not only representing the client and server but also the Internet cloud, the security checkpoints like firewalls, and so on.

A typical deployment environment together with some aspects of remote or outsourced development is shown in Figure 6.16. The quality of such a deployment diagram depends on how accurately it represents the required physical environment and also how faithfully this diagram is eventually translated into a real deployment network. Thus, once again, prototyping will play a crucial role, especially in trying to determine the ability of the hardware to support the necessary operational requirements.

### 6.9.4   Aesthetic Checks for Deployment Diagrams in MOBS

The aesthetic quality of a deployment diagram depends on operational needs as well. Unlike a class diagram or a use case diagram, the architect in the background space will have few choices in terms of the number of nodes and processors needed for the system. If the operational requirements dictate a need, then that need will have to be satisfied by as much hardware as is required. However, the architect will use her skills to distribute and redistribute the load on the hardware. The aesthetic quality of the diagram can be improved by improving the load sharing by the processing nodes. For example, a small project handling a small system will need only a

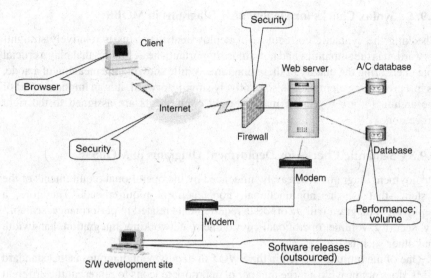

**Figure 6.16** Web Infrastructure in development and deployment of systems.

single server, whereas a large system will need to balance its server load by providing additional servers to handle security and databases. For Internet-based systems with global reach, it is necessary to consider mirroring of server databases to ensure speed.

## 6.10 CROSS-DIAGRAM DEPENDENCIES IN MOBS

The UML diagrams in the background space that relate to each other (and therefore exhibit some dependency) are as follows:

*Package and Component Diagrams.* When components are shown within packages, there is a dependency between the two. This was shown in Figure 6.5. Semantic checks relating to the meaning of the packages and the components within them, as well as aesthetic checks focusing on the number of components within a package, should be performed here. Although technically there is no limitation on the number of components on a package, the size of the package must be kept in mind. If a package is made up of a large number of components (e.g., 20 components in a typical Java or C++ implementation), then further layering of packages must be considered.

*Class and Component Diagrams.* Components realize classes. Therefore, there is a certain mapping between classes and components. This is not shown visually in most CASE tools. However, components to class mapping must be investigated at both semantic and aesthetic levels in V&V in MOBS. A component can realize 7 to 10 <<entity>> classes. Additional stereotypes of classes can appear in a component. However, separate components realizing the user interfaces and the databases must be considered to enhance the quality of the architecture.

*Composite Structure and Object/Communication Diagrams.* As composite structure diagrams become increasingly used, their closeness to object and communication diagrams will be discovered. This is because the run-time components shown on communication diagrams (here, Figure 6.14) are also run-time objects for all practical purposes (although in theory objects and run-time components are different). Furthermore, the communication diagram is a close representation of run-time objects and messages being passed between them. In composite structures, dependencies between run-time components are shown, as against the messages in component diagrams. Also, composite structure diagrams show interfaces, which are not shown on communication diagrams. Still, a cross-diagram check between communication/ object diagrams and the corresponding composite structure diagrams should be considered valuable in improving the semantic and aesthetic quality of MOBS.

*Component and Deployment Diagrams.* Components eventually execute on processors represented in the deployment diagrams. Therefore, it is important to investigate, again at the semantic and aesthetic levels, the number of components executing on a processor. This can lead to interesting discussions about the load and distribution of components at run-time. It also leads to enhancement of security and connectivity in the architecture, as shown in Figure 6.16.

## DISCUSSION TOPICS

1. Why is architectural work placed in the background space?

2. What are the most important architectural diagrams of UML?

3. Why is robustness an architectural issue?

4. Why is granularity an important concept in OO designs?

5. Which of the UML diagrams considered in this chapter is distinctly different from the other diagrams?

6. Why is a component diagram called a physical implementation diagram?

7. What is the minimum number of components required in implementing a system fully designed in class diagrams? Why?

8. Compare the syntax checks of robustness diagrams with those of class diagrams. How are they different from the semantic and aesthetic checks of those two diagrams?

9. What is the concept of layering in architecture? Differentiate the fundamentals of horizontal and vertical layering. Further, explain how they relate to an iterative and incremental process.

10. Outline in detail the additional considerations in modeling a Web application.

11. How is a database schema similar to a class diagram? How does it differ?

12. What is the importance of a composite structure diagram in the background space?

## REFERENCES

Fowler, M. *Analysis Patterns: Reusable Object Models.* Boston: Addison-Wesley, p. 225.

Gamma, E., Eriksson, H., and Penkar, M. *Business Modelling with UML: Business Patterns at Work.* OMG Press, 2000, p. 73.

# Chapter 7

# Managing the V&V Process

> Product is like light at the end of the tunnel; Process, however, is like that guide rail, that rope you grope, while transiting through the tunnel.[1]

## CHAPTER SUMMARY

The checks used for V&V of UML models need to be encapsulated within a process that forms part of an overall process of software development. In this chapter, we discuss this process aspect of V&V.

## 7.1 PROCESSES AND UML

V&V, on its own, comprises a comprehensive suite of checklists to enhance the quality of UML-based models. However, we must still discuss the approach that is needed to conduct V&V. In fact, creation of the models in the three modeling spaces also requires a well-thought-out approach. The approach we take in creating good-quality models, and the accompanying approach used to verify and validate their quality, is a process. This chapter briefly delves into this process aspect of quality.

The first thing to note is that sometimes UML is confused with a process. However, UML is not a process. Earlier, during the development of UML, its

---

[1]Source: Bhuvan Unhelkar (author).

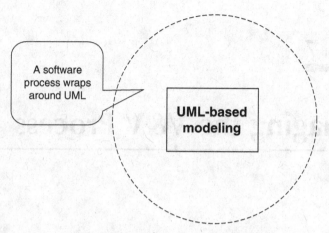

**Figure 7.1**   Process wraps around UML.

creators (Booch, Rumbaugh and Jacobson) had combined process and modeling notations. This is how UML was presented—as Unified Method 0.8—during the OOPSLA conference in Austin (OOPSLA, 1995). The modeling notations remained unified and were ratified by OMG in 1997. However, the approach to development is still not a unified standard. This is acceptable in practice, as development projects (like the six different types and three different-sized one discussed in Chapter 1) may require their own approach. The accompanying quality processes may also vary, depending on the project.

UML, which is not a methodology or process, requires a process to be wrapped around it, as shown in Figure 7.1. As a result, it is important to consider the process aspect of UML.

## 7.2   UNDERSTANDING THE PROCESS AND PROCESS COMPONENTS

### 7.2.1   A Simple Process Architecture

When a process is discussed, it is always helpful to have a theoretical background for it. This background may be considered the architecture of the process itself and is shown in Figure 7.2, which presents the architecture of a process component. A process component is a small part of a process. Depending on the requirements of the project, various process components can be put together to configure a process. Unhelkar (2003) has described in detail 18 such process components that can be used in all three modeling spaces.

The architecture of a process-component is made up of three major parts:

*Deliverable*—what is produced at the end of a process. It can be a suite of UML diagrams, programs, databases or quality checks. The deliverables comprise the "what" of a process component.

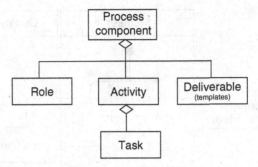

**Figure 7.2** Architecture of a process component.

*Activity-Task*—the step-by-step guide to how a particular process component is created. They are analogous to the guide rail in a tunnel that one holds while traveling. Activities are at a higher level of description, whereas tasks are the smallest units of work carried out in a project. Together they form the task list in a project plan and can be described as the "how" of a process component.

*Role*—the person carrying out the activities and tasks. This is akin to the person traveling through the tunnel to reach the light. The role defines the people who carry out the tasks. That definition is within the environment or the organizational context in which those tasks are carried out. The role comprises the "who" of a process component.

Process components form the building blocks of the process. This process component is made up of activities, deliverables and roles. Activities associate with tasks. The process-components are configured to create a process, which is then enacted in a real software development project.

## 7.2.2 A Process Component for V&V of Class Diagrams

How do we apply process components in conducting V&V of software models? Figure 7.3 shows a simple example of the three elements of a process component, as applicable in V&V of classes and class diagrams. This diagram is effectively an activity diagram. It is made up of the following elements of a process component:

*Roles:* modeler and quality analyst

*Activities:* create classes, apply syntax checks, create class diagrams, apply semantic checks, create MOPS, apply aesthetic checks

*Deliverables:* Since the end result of this process component is improvement in quality, the actual deliverable is identical to the class diagram already produced. Hence it is not shown separately.

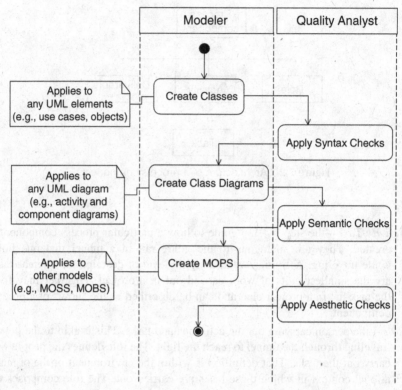

**Figure 7.3** A process component for V&V of classes and class diagrams in MOPS.

Based on the above description, is should be possible to create a suite of process components that will guide the application of V&V checks on UML diagrams.

## 7.3 ITERATIONS AND INCREMENTS IN A PROCESS

### 7.3.1 Iterations and Increments

Before concluding the discussion on processes, it is worthwhile to highlight the nature of a good process. All good processes that guide the development of UML-based projects are iterative and incremental in nature. Iterations and increments imply that one does not produce and sign off on a deliverable in one attempt. In practice, it is advisable to produce a deliverable in three iterations. This can then be followed by incremental addition of newer deliverables.

***7.3.1.1 Iterative Development*** The iterative aspect of a process facilitates repetition of tasks, resulting in addition to and improvement of the deliverable. For example, in Figure 7.4, when we iterate to produce the client package, the first

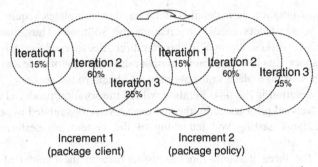

**Figure 7.4**   Iterations and increments (a high-level example).

iteration results in creation of use cases and classes related to the problem space. The second iteration is a major iteration resulting in completion of all use cases and class diagrams, as well as development of the solution in the design space. The third iteration completes the implementation as well as the testing and readies the deliverable for deployment.

***7.3.1.2  Incremental Development***   The incremental aspect of a process enables addition of new elements and diagrams to an existing deliverable. For example, in Figure 7.4, a new policy package is shown as being incrementally added to the system. The iterative aspects of a process described above now apply to this increment.

***7.3.1.3  Parallel Development***   Two or more parts of a system can be developed in parallel. This is possible if the interfaces of the packages are finalized beforehand. Parallel element is possible because properly encapsulated classes and components interact with each other only through their interfaces. Once these interfaces have been defined and remain unchanged, the development of these classes and components can proceed in parallel.

### 7.3.2  Project-Level Iterations

What is shown in Figure 7.4 at the package level can also be applied at the project level. At this level, the three iterations are performed.

The first iteration is rapid, ensuring that all project participants and stakeholders develop a good understanding of the project. Some project management–related activities are performed in this iteration, including creation of early use cases and use case diagrams, cost estimations based on the overall expected requirements of the project, and project planning including resources, prototyping and quality planning. Also, in the first iteration, identification and documentation of the increments of package development take place. Thus, most of the activities in the first iteration occur in the problem and background spaces.

The second iteration is a detailed iteration that completes requirements and applies the requirements model in creating the solution. Thus, most process components are worked through in this iteration. Because of extensive work in the solution space, this iteration results in major development of code and databases. The activities thus take place in the solution and background spaces.

The third iteration is the final iteration, where the solution produced is tested at the system level and pilot tested by the end users. Activities related to performance testing, acceptance testing and launching of the system are performed in this iteration.

Although the three iterations are discussed here in the context of a project, iterations and increments are intertwined concepts. As a result, a good software development process will display both iterative and incremental characteristics. What is more pertinent to this discussion is that UML is likely to succeed only when it is supported by a carefully thought out process. Such a process will not only facilitate the creation of good-quality UML diagrams and models, but will also help business analysts, system designers, architects, project managers and quality analysts to understand when and where to apply the V&V checks we have discussed in this book.

## DISCUSSION TOPICS

1. Discuss why the UML is not a process (refer to Chapter 1 as well).

2. What are the three major elements of process architecture?

3. What is an iteration? How does it differ from an increment?

4. Why is parallel development possible in OO projects?

## NOTE

For further detailed discussion on processes and process components and a configurable process, see *Process QA Assurance for UML-Based Projects* (Boston: Addison-Wesley, 2003), by this author.

## REFERENCE

Unhelkar, B. *Process Quality Assurance for UML-Based Projects*. Boston: Addison-Wesley, 2003.

# Appendix A

# LUCKY Insurance Case Study

Show me by example.[1]

## A.1 DESCRIBING AN INSURANCE EXAMPLE

This appendix contains *half-baked* requirements statements for a hypothetical organization called LUCKY INSURANCE. They are purposely kept incomplete and unpolished to provide true representation of problem statements in practice. There are areas in this problem statement that good modelers will have to sidestep, depending on the needs of their users. This case study is based on a real CRMS implementation project in which the author was involved. It provides opportunities for application of quality, testing, modeling and design in software projects. The description of the business situation in this case study also opens up the possibility of its application in studying globalization and mobilization (dealing with application of mobile technologies to businesses) projects.

### A.1.1 Background Information on the Project

LUCKY INSURANCE has grown rapidly by acquisition and has a large customer base. However, it now finds that the lack of appropriate and sufficient customer service is causing it to lose many clients. Competition from rivals is intense. Many

[1] Source: Unknown.

*Verification and Validation for Quality of UML 2.0 Models*, by Bhuvan Unhelkar
Copyright © 2005 John Wiley & Sons, Inc.

competitors have implemented the latest technologies, including sophisticated customer call centers fully integrated with CRMS. LUCKY INSURANCE realizes that it must now catch up, and the board of directors has decided to install an off-the-shelf Internet-enabled new CRMS package. The board considers the following to be major issues in this project:

LUCKY's insurance system is a typical 25-year-old legacy system written in COBOL using an ISAM database. This software system has provided the necessary support for LUCKY's business without any major technical flaws. Experienced users are able to navigate through it easily. During the Y2K saga, this insurance system underwent detailed corrections of both its Date-Logic and Date-Storage systems at a substantial cost to the organization. Therefore, despite its future-oriented viewpoint, LUCKY's board is not keen to give up the old system. Thus, the new CRMS software project will have to consider integration with the existing system

Since LUCKY's board has decided to proceed with a third-party developed CRMS system. The major part of this project will include capturing and documenting detailed requirements that can be satisfied by the CRMS package rather than instituting major in-house development. A certain amount of customization is envisioned to ensure that the package is tailored to LUCKY's needs. Thus, there is a need for a detailed, quality-conscious software development process that will handle the issues of both integration and package implementation. It is recognized that the information technology (IT) department of the organization still uses the old mode of thinking. The IT department has only read and briefly discussed processes such as QSP, RUP, OPEN, MeNtOR, ICONIX and XP. There is a general awareness that these processes are beneficial, but how and when they should be deployed and used is not clear. Therefore, LUCKY's board wants to consider not only these new processes of software development and maintenance but also the transition to them. The sociological factors related to this transition are matters of concern. The level of maturity of software processes that can be achieved after the transition (particularly the CMM process maturity levels) is also of interest to this technology-savvy board.

As mentioned earlier, the existing legacy application that supports LUCKY's current business contains a large amount of data that are stored in an ISAM format. Handling of these data is crucial to LUCKY's business. Therefore, the board is eager to consider the issues related to data integration, including both existing primary data that may continue to remain in the legacy system, as well as new data that will be needed to perform additional analysis and to provide additional functionalities demanded by the business users. Eventually, issues related to data conversion will also have to be considered. The overall development, as well as conversion, will need a disciplined approach for data conversion and testing.

### A.1.2 LUCKY Insurance Business

**A.1.2.1 Clientele** The primary business of LUCKY is to provide insurance. Having been in business for several decades, and having acquired new and established businesses over the past few years, LUCKY has a suite of customers that range from individuals who take out vehicle, home, contents, life cover and hospital insurance to large businesses, medical practitioners and hospitals who also take out professional indemnity and worker's compensation insurance. Furthermore, new types of insurance products are being continuously conceived by LUCKY's marketing department, resulting in new types of clients.

While individuals deal directly with LUCKY for the most part, organizations that deal with LUCKY do so through their representatives. These representatives are usually the employees of the client organization dealing with LUCKY. Individuals can also nominate their representatives—especially in cases of life insurance, where representations are required for clients who may not be physically capable of representing themselves or who may be dead. There are thus people who play a variety of roles in dealing with LUCKY—most representing themselves as personal clients and others representing their organizations.

### A.1.2.2 Insurance Policies and Risk Categories

Whatever is insured by LUCKY is called a "risk" in insurance parlance. Therefore, all insurance policies are taken out by clients in order to insure themselves against a particular risk.

Potential clients (including existing clients who are buying a different type of insurance) need to provide complete and correct details of the risk item for which they are taking a quote (e.g., a vehicle insurance quote involves the make, model, registration, and other details, as well as details of the driver, including age, driving experience, claims history, etc.). The existing legacy application is able to provide this information. In that application, all the details provided in response to a query are stored separately from the details of an actual paid policy. Therefore, when the time comes to convert a given quote into a real policy, there is a certain amount of avoidable duplication of data and procedure. One of LUCKY's needs is that the software support for inquiries should be provided in such a manner that the quotes can be converted into policies and all the information provided for quotes is reused and not lost. At the end of a detailed quote, clients are provided with a premium amount. This is the amount they have to pay if and when they decide to proceed with the insurance cover.

There are additional terms and conditions under which a policy is issued. As mentioned earlier, a policy is provided for a particular item, which is also called a risk. Thus, a policy insures a risk. A policy can cover more than one risk (e.g., a car and a home). Policies are also issued for part of a risk (e.g., only for the stereo system in a car or jewelery in a home). Policies are issued on monthly, quarterly, half-yearly and yearly bases. They are governed by regulations, requiring details of the insurance to be documented formally and provided to the respective government organization through an interface to its software system. This information includes what is being insured, the sum for which it is insured, excess payments and details of the conditions under which excesses have to be paid, and, most important, the terms and conditions under which LUCKY is obliged to cover the item even if premiums have not been paid. For example, in a life cover, the person is covered even if premiums are not paid for a quarter, provided that the arrears premiums are paid in the event of a claim. Another example concerns a motorcycle whose risk is covered with a cover note even if the premium is not yet paid. It is also necessary to interface with other government departments that help deal with legal issues, as well as departments that interact with hospitals and the police. This interaction becomes important if a claim runs into dispute and especially if the claim is related to worker's compensation for injuries on work sites.

**A.1.2.3 Payment Types** Insurance premiums can be paid in various ways—by credit cards, checks, cash, or BPAY. The client can also determine the frequency of payment—weekly, fortnightly, monthly, quarterly, half-yearly or yearly. Premium payments can be automatically renewed or may need a signature for renewal.

**A.1.2.4 Interactions** Clients, both personal and organizational, continue to interact with LUCKY by traditional face-to-face contact, phone calls and faxes. LUCKY's board believes that this interaction should be better supported by providing the staff with detailed information on the caller, especially if the caller is known to the organization. This would first require software support in identifying the caller, followed by detailed information on the caller to be flashed on system screens in front of the staff once the caller has been identified. Furthermore, the traditional means of contact can no longer suffice. There is a need to facilitate client contact with LUCKY through e-mail, on the company's Internet website, and very soon through mobile technologies. This need to enhance interaction through the new technologies is important not only for LUCKY's staff, but also for its clients—especially large corporate clients who want to automate the process of inquiries, payment of premiums and lodgements of claims with LUCKY.

Business managers at LUCKY realize the acute need to free their crucial sales staff from the work of answering routine inquiries so that they can pursue new leads. Therefore, they want a sophisticated inquiry facility on their Internet website that will not only provide regular information to clients and potential clients, but also basic calculations on quotes for premiums. A quick market survey indicates that existing clients as well as many potential clients prefer Internet-based access to information, doing basic calculations and comparisons, and making routine payments of premiums (e.g., through BPAY or periodic charges to credit cards).

**A.1.2.5 Growth** While the business is continuously coming up with new ways of insuring clients and new ways of packaging insurance, it is eager to utilize the potential of the new software support to create additional cross-sell and up-sell opportunities. (For example, when home contents insurance is provided, building insurance should be offered; when motor vehicle insurance is provided, additional insurance to cover injuries should be suggested.) Currently, these opportunities are created by the skills and perseverance of individual sales staff. System support is considered vital in improving the offerings and scaling them up. Essentially, the business is looking for proactive system support.

**A.1.2.6 Employee Portal** In addition to dealing with clients, LUCKY's management wants the substantial spin-off benefit of putting the employee details of

LUCKY on the potential CRMS package. This would include the name and address of the employees and other contact details, as well as workers' compensation details. Leave accrued, salaries, tax and other such details, once placed in the employee portal, will substantially reduce LUCKY's administrative overhead of and improve the information flow among employees. LUCKY also uses many contract staff and wants to be able to manage their timesheets effectively. Using the employee portal would free management from routine timesheet management, and an interface with the accounting department would speed up processing of invoices and payments. Eventually, the software package's human relations management module can be tailored to handle internal career tracking and management of employees.

**A.1.2.7  Thinking Ahead**  LUCKY's management is keen to consider all new technologies in this project. For example, mobile technologies remain a serious consideration in this new CRMS project. The ability to provide on-the-spot insurance (especially for travelers) by simply dialing a number from their mobile phones and having a one-time premium appear on their mobile phone bills is a new concept that LUCKY feels will provide a great advantage over its competitors. LUCKY is also eager to explore the concept of "e-services" when the new application is implemented. This is because LUCKY believes it can provide insurance service from system to system, thereby eliminating the overhead of dealing with insurance manually. The concept of e-services transforms the business of providing insurance into a suite of interactions between two systems representing the client and the insurance organization rather than two people representing these organizations.

# Appendix **B**

# UML CASE Tools

This appendix is divided into two parts: the criteria that can be used to evaluate CASE tools and a list of some UML CASE tools. Needless to say, both of these lists can be improved upon; here they are provided as a starting point for practitioners.

## B.1  CRITERIA FOR EVALUATING UML-BASED CASE TOOLS

| | Check |
|---|---|
| Compliance with UML: ensure that the tool complies with the UML standard | |
| Support of the development environment | |
| Support of multiple users (teamwork) | |
| Information generation (document and Web publishing) | |
| Support of reusability (patterns) | |
| Integration with other products | |
| User friendliness of the tool | |
| Costs of licensing and deployment | |
| Ability to suit a process: the tool selected should be able to follow the process being used | |

*Verification and Validation for Quality of UML 2.0 Models*, by Bhuvan Unhelkar
Copyright © 2005 John Wiley & Sons, Inc.

Check

Tool support in the region
Performance
IDE compatibility
References from other users of the tool
Tool friction factor: ability of the tool to co-exist with other tools
   such as document management, configuration management
   and testing tools

## B.2   SOME UML-BASED CASE TOOLS*

TauG2 v2.4 from Telelogic

| Information | www.telelogic.com |
|---|---|
| Comments | Of the many products offered by Telelogic, I have investigated TauG2 for UML 2.0, particularly with their document management tool called DOORS. I found TauG2 extremely helpful in creating UML 2.0-specific good-quality diagrams. The ability to integrate with other configuration management and testing tools was impressive, as was its ability to work with the quality software process (QSP). |

Together v5.0 from TogetherSoft

| Information | www.togethersoft.com |
|---|---|
| Comments | I have used TogetherSoft controlcenter, and I find its architecture and its sleek user interface excellent. It is aimed at the high end of the market and does an excellent job in large projects with multiple teams. The availability of patterns within the tool promotes reuse and quality. Furthermore, as well-known author Peter Coad's tool, it has the necessary personality "blessings" that help it challenge other UML-based tools that enjoy similar celebrity. |

*Disclaimer: I am a user and adviser but not a reseller of any of these UML-based CASE tools, and I do not have any vested interest in recommending one tool over another. My priority is always what is in the best interest of my client. The order of presentation of these tools is random.

## ROSE from IBM Rational

| | |
|---|---|
| Information | www.rational.com |
| Comments | Rational's Object Software Engineering (ROSE) remains the most well-known tool in the UML modeling arena. In addition to the awesome influence of Jacobson, Booch, and Rumbaugh on this CASE tool, it is important to note the comprehensive suite of other tools that go with ROSE (configuration management, testing and process). |

## Component Modeller (Earlier, ParadigmPlus v4.0) from Computer Associates

| | |
|---|---|
| Information | www.ca.com |
| Comments | While I have had a brief look at Component Modellers, I have used its earlier versions, called ParadigmPlus, in practice and in conducting industrial training. The configurability of this tool to suit the needs of modelers is excellent. |

## COOL Suite from Computer Associates

| | |
|---|---|
| Information | www.ca.com |
| Comments | The COOL suite of products (COOL:Plex, COOL:Joe, COOL:Gen, and others) cannot be called UML modeling tools, but they do use UML notations for their development work. The suite is worth investigating for UML-based projects. |

## ArgoUML 0.9 from Tigris

| | |
|---|---|
| Information | www.tigris.org |
| Comments | I have not had the opportunity to investigate this product in great detail. However, many of my colleagues have done so, and they recommend that I mention it. (Note the.org.) |

## VisualUML 2.70 from Visual Object Modellers

| | |
|---|---|
| Information | www.visualuml.com |
| Comments | VisualUML is aimed at the medium to low end of the market. It is ideal for small to medium-sized projects. However, the tool can scale up and relates to various development environments. I have used this product, and I find it excellent for the purposes mentioned here. |

## SimplyObjects v3.2.3 from Adaptive Arts

| | |
|---|---|
| Information | www.adaptive-arts.com |
| Comments | SimplyObjects is a "techie" UML product that goes directly to the heart of architecture and design. This is a definite advantage when starting your modeling work in the background space (creating MOBS). Integration with other products enables the creation of code. |

## MagicDraw v4.1 from NoMagic

| | |
|---|---|
| Information | www.nomagic.com |
| Comments | NoMagic, which created MagicDraw, is not a tool vendor but more of a technology partner. MagicDraw also provides excellent support for UML-based modeling, particularly in the problem space (creation of MOPS). |

## Ectoset Modeler

| | |
|---|---|
| Information | www.ectoset.com |
| Comments | Simplicity and affordability are the hallmarks of this tool. It is extremely valuable to small projects or pilot projects that are trying to inculcate methods discipline. There is no reason why this tool should not scale up to large projects, but I do not have that direct experience. |

## Enterprise Architect

| | |
|---|---|
| Information | www.sparxsystems.com |
| Comments | A very simple, practical tool of immense value, especially to starters with UML. And, also extremely cheap compared with most other UML tools. |

## Visio

| | |
|---|---|
| Information | www.microsoft.com |
| Comments | Occasionally, modelers have used Visio, but the general impression is that it is more of a UML (and other) documentation tool than a design tool. |

# Appendix C

# Summary of Checks for V&V of the Quality of MOPS

The following table provides a summary of the quality checks for the UML diagrams used to express MOPS. This table can be used as a reminder of what needs to be checked. Readers are encouraged to add to this list their own specific checks, which may arise out of internal project standards, preproject discussions, or their specific need to use UML. For example, a data warehousing project will need additional checks for the class diagrams that specifically deal with data tables, primary and foreign keys, and so on, but that project may not need the extensive checks needed for, say, the use case diagrams.

Checks for V&V of the Diagrams in MOPS

| Syntax Checks for Use Cases* | Yes | No |
|---|---|---|
| 1. Does the use case have a proper name? | | |
| 2. Optionally, have you considered numbering use cases? | | |
| 3. Is the use case name verb-like? | | |
| 4. Is the use case named from the point of view of the actor? | | |
| 5. Does the use case have an actor? (This is not mandatory if it is an included or extended use case.) | | |
| 6. Is the use case stereotyped? | | |
| 7. Is the use case stereotype from the predefined set of project stereotypes? | | |

*Verification and Validation for Quality of UML 2.0 Models*, by Bhuvan Unhelkar
Copyright © 2005 John Wiley & Sons, Inc.

| Syntax Checks for Use Cases* | Yes | No |
|---|---|---|

8. Is the use case documented?
9. Does the use case documentation follow a predefined template?
10. Does the use case documentation have proper pre- and postconditions?
11. Does the use case documentation have a text or a flow describing the interaction between the actor and the system?
12. Does the use case documentation have possible alternative and exception flows?

*We check use cases at the ground level first, before moving to use case diagrams

| Semantic Checks for Use Cases | Yes | No |
|---|---|---|

1. What is the objective of the use case? (This will depend on the project type and project size as well.)
2. Is this a business use case?
3. Is this a system use case?
4. Does the use case documentation correctly represent the interaction between actor and system?
5. Have the users helped in creating and naming the use case?

| Aesthetic Checks for Use Cases | Yes | No |
|---|---|---|

1. Is the use case too long (to become unwieldy)?
2. Is the use case too short?
3. Have you considered cross-diagram dependencies?
4. Have you considered activity diagrams for this use case?
5. Have you considered sequence diagrams for this use case?

| Syntax Checks for Use Case Diagrams | Yes | No |
|---|---|---|

1. Check that use cases are correctly represented by their notation (bubble).
2. Check that actors are correctly represented by their notation (stickman).
3. Check actor and use case stereotypes.
4. Are all the actors correctly named (singular noun, representing a role)?
5. Are all the use cases correctly named (verb-like fashion)?

| Syntax Checks for Use Case Diagrams | Yes | No |
|---|---|---|

6.  If the use cases have been numbered (optional for local projects), check to see if they satisfy the project standard.
7.  If a boundary is present, check that all use cases are inside the boundary and all actors are outside it.
8.  Check the actor-use case relationship (including its optional direction).
9.  Ensure that the line showing the communication between the actor and the use case is correctly shown as a thin, continuous line.
10. Check that the arrowhead on the communications (or associates) line drawn between the actor and the use case is an open arrowhead.
11. If an external system or device is interacting with the current system, ensure that the arrowhead is not a closed hollow arrowhead (inheritance arrowhead).
12. When use case A is meant to include use case B, check that the arrowhead on the relationship points from A to B.
13. When use case C extends to use case B, the arrow should point from C to B.
14. When use case D represents a concrete form of use case B, check that the arrowhead points from D to B and that the arrow is a thick line with a closed arrowhead.
15. Check the abstract (unimplementable or uninstantiable) notation for use cases and actors. If the use case is abstract, ensure that its name case is written in italics.
16. If there are notes on the diagram, check that they are in a dog-eared rectangle as per the UML standard.

| Semantic Checks for Use Case Diagrams | Yes | No |
|---|---|---|

1.  What is the objective of the use case? (This will depend on the project type and project size as well.) What does each use case represent?
2.  Check what each actor represents in the problem space. Does each actor have a real semantic meaning in the problem space?
3.  Perform another semantic check of the actors to ascertain if they represent a human user, a device, an external system, an interface, etc.
4.  Check for flow and make corrections (use case diagrams should not have flow).
5.  Check for alternative and exception flows within the use case specification.
6.  If the use cases have pre- and postconditions, check to see if those conditions have been documented.

| Semantic Checks for Use Case Diagrams | Yes | No |
| --- | --- | --- |

7. Have you considered use case refactoring?
8. Have you considered actor generalization?
9. Check to see if the use cases have been ranked.
10. If one use case <<includes>> another, ensure that the meaning of the inclusion is clarified.
11. Have sufficient notes been added to the diagram to clarify issues? Are the notes correctly linked to elements on the diagram?
12. Check to see if the use case represents a logically cohesive set of requirements or whether it is just a collection of incoherent use cases and actors. In other words, what is the meaning behind the entire use case diagram?

| Aesthetic Checks for Use Case Diagrams | Yes | No |
| --- | --- | --- |

1. Are there sufficient use cases to cover all requirements? (Are all requirements covered by the use cases? These will be functional.)
2. Are there sufficient actors to cover all users of the system?
3. Are there sufficient actors to cover all other remaining external entities to the system?
4. Is there a time actor to represent use cases initiated by time?
5. Check how many use cases and actors appear on each diagram and ensure that they adhere to the classic span of control principle of management.
6. Check that the ratio of actors to use cases on one diagram is approximately 1:3.
7. Ensure that the use case documentation is not too long and unwieldy.
8. If an iterative process is being followed, start considering the completeness and correctness of the diagrams during the second iteration.

| Syntax Checks for Activity Diagrams | Yes | No |
| --- | --- | --- |

1. Check that all the elements on the activity diagram are allowable elements. Ensure that a use case or a component is not shown on an activity diagram.
2. Check that there is a start activity—and is only one.
3. Check the number of stop activities. These are used to indicate where the suite of activities will finish.

| Syntax Checks for Activity Diagrams | Yes | No |
|---|---|---|

4.  Check that the notation for activity is correctly used. Ensure that the activity notation has not been confused with the notation of a state.
5.  Check that the notation for transition (an open arrow pointing to the transition from one activity to another) is correctly used.
6.  Check that the notation for sync points (forks and joins) is correctly used to represent the forking of multithreads and then their joins.
7.  Check that for every fork there is a join.
8.  Check that the notation for the decision points (hollow diamond) is correctly used.
9.  Check that whenever partitions are introduced, the partition notation, as well as the corresponding actor notation for that partition, is correctly used.
10. If objects are used on activity diagrams, check for object notation.

| Semantic Checks for Activity Diagrams | Yes | No |
|---|---|---|

1.  What is the objective of the activity diagram? (This will depend on the project type and project size as well.)
2.  Check to ascertain the names of the activities and their corresponding meaning within the business domain.
3.  If partitions exist, check their meanings.
4.  Check for semantically correct dependencies between activities.
5.  Check to see if forking is semantically correct. Also check to see if joining is correct.
6.  Check that activities that are supposed to be in parallel are indeed so.

| Aesthetic Checks for Activity Diagrams | Yes | No |
|---|---|---|

1.  How many activities are there on a diagram? Check to see that in most cases there are more than 14.
2.  Check to see if the decision points are confusing. (More than four decisions [flows] coming out of a decision point makes the activity diagram inelegant.)
3.  If partitions are shown, ensure that there are no more than approximately four for the sake of elegance.
4.  Check to see how many activity diagrams are associated with a use case. If there are more than three, consider factorizing the use case itself.
5.  In MOPS, check how many activity diagrams are representing an overall flow of a business process.
6.  If objects are represented, ensure that the creators of the activity diagrams are not playing the role of business analyst.

| Syntax Checks for Package Diagrams | Yes | No |
|---|---|---|

1. Check package notation for UML compliance.
2. Are package names correct?
3. If the package diagram shows the relationship between packages, check the dependency relationship arrow.
4. If packages are shown with a stereotype, check that the stereotype is UML compliant.
5. If present, check for notes explaining the packages.
6. Check if the packages are more than just subsystems.

| Semantic Checks for Package Diagrams | Yes | No |
|---|---|---|

1. What is the objective of the package diagram? (This will depend on the project type and size as well.)
2. Are packages correctly leveled?
3. Do the levels appear in the package name?
4. Are packages correctly stereotyped?
5. Are the dependencies necessary? Dependencies between packages should be shown only if necessary.
6. Check the manner of package creation (bottom up or top down).
7. Do the packages belong to the right team of modelers and developers?
8. Are notes added to clarify diagrams?

| Aesthetic Checks for Package Diagrams | Yes | No |
|---|---|---|

1. Check the size of the package. There should be a right balance of the number of packages in a good model.
2. Check to see if packages have been leveled. Creating more than three levels of packages will lead to comprehension problems.

| Syntax Checks for Classes | Yes | No |
|---|---|---|

1. Check that the classes are named correctly (the name is a noun).
2. Check that all class names start with a capital letter.
3. Ensure that class names are singular.
4. If a stereotype is used to classify the class further, check that it is correctly represented using the stereotype notations.
5. If the class description has attributes, ensure that they are also singular common nouns describing the characteristics of the class.
6. Check that the responsibilities of a class are clearly described.
7. If the class is abstract, is it represented by its name shown in italics?

| Semantic Checks for Classes | Yes | No |
|---|---|---|

1. Check that a class represents one and only one logical concept.
2. Check that a class is given a cohesive set of responsibilities.
3. Check that a class represents the intended meaning of the class in the problem space.
4. Check to see if there are opportunities for generalization and/or specialization of classes.
5. Go through the additional documentation, comments and business rules for the class as a semantic check for each class.

| Aesthetic Checks for Classes | Yes | No |
|---|---|---|

1. Check the size of the class. A class should be comprehensible as a single entity (well balanced).
2. Check to see if the class has the right number of attributes.
3. Ensure that the class is not overloaded or underloaded in terms of the number of operations or methods it contains.

| Syntax Checks for Class Diagrams | Yes | No |
|---|---|---|

1. Check the allowable elements on a class diagram.
2. Check the notation for a class.
3. Check the relationship notations.
4. Check all the association relationships.
5. Check to see if the association relationship line has an (open) arrowhead.
6. Check to see if the inheritance relationship (one class inheriting from another class) line has an arrow with a closed, unfilled arrowhead.
7. Check to see if aggregation appears on the class diagram.
8. If an aggregation line appears, does it show an open arrowhead?
9. Check if multiplicity is shown on the class diagram.
10. Check if constraints are shown.
11. Check if tagged values are shown.
12. Are stereotypes shown for classes? Are stereotypes shown on relationships? Check the notational correctness of the stereotypes.
13. Are notes added to the diagram using the notation of a bent-dog ear box?

| Semantic Checks for Class Diagrams | Yes | No |
|---|---|---|

1. Check the meaning of each class on the class diagram.
2. If already defined, check the attributes and operations for each of the classes.

| Semantic Checks for Class Diagrams | Yes | No |
|---|---|---|

3. Check the meaning of each relationship—does association mean that one class uses another class?
4. Check the semantics of inheritance.
5. Does the aggregation represent a genuine "has a" relationship.
6. Check the meanings of multiplicities.
7. Check the meanings behind constraints and tagged values.
8. Check the reasoning behind stereotypes.
9. Check to see if multiple inheritance is appearing on the diagram.
10. Check to see if roles are shown on association relationships. If so, are the roles correctly representing the role played by the class in a particular relationship?

| Aesthetic Checks for Class Diagrams | Yes | No |
|---|---|---|

1. Check the size of the class diagrams.
2. Check the relationships on the class diagrams.
3. Check that classes are repeated sufficiently, ensuring that their relationships and the roles they play are clear.
4. How many diagrams are there?
5. Check the depth of inheritance.

| Syntax Checks for Sequence Diagrams | Yes | No |
|---|---|---|

1. Ensure that only allowable elements are present.
2. Check for the syntactic correctness of an actor.
3. Check the correctness of the object representation.
4. Check the representation of anonymous objects.
5. Check the messages of the sequence diagram.
6. Check preconditions and postconditions.
7. Check notes for their syntactic correctness.

| Semantic Checks for Sequence Diagrams | Yes | No |
|---|---|---|

1. What is the overall purpose of the sequence diagram? What is its meaning, and what does the set of sequences represent?
2. Is the diagram free from unnecessary objects like GUI objects? (They will appear in MOPS.)
3. Is the diagram free from unnecessary objects like <<control>> objects? (They will appear in MOBS.)

| Semantic Checks for Sequence Diagrams | Yes | No |
| --- | --- | --- |

4. Is the diagram free from unnecessary message types? (Only simple message types should be used at this stage.)
5. Check that the objects on sequence diagrams correspond to classes in the model.
6. Check that each object shown here belongs to the corresponding class and make sense in this particular sequence.
7. Ensure that each method (message) is in the right sequence.
8. Check for completeness in whatever has been represented in the sequence diagrams.
9. Check that it is indeed a business system diagram.


| Aesthetic Checks for Sequence Diagrams | Yes | No |
| --- | --- | --- |

1. Check that the sequence diagram is not trying to show every conceivable sequence on a single diagram.
2. Check to see that the system contains a sensible sequence or a sensible snapshot of some steps occurring in the system.
3. Check to see if text descriptions and notes have been judiciously added.
4. Check the number of objects, messages and notes.


| Syntax Checks for State Chart Diagrams | Yes | No |
| --- | --- | --- |

1. Are the states clearly shown on the diagram? Are the objects to which the states belong marked?
2. Are there avoidable nestings on the state chart diagram?
3. Are avoidable historical states shown on the state chart diagram?
4. Are the states correctly represented by the rounded rectangle notation on the state chart diagram?
5. Is a start state shown on the diagram? Ensure that there is only one start state. Also, if they are there, are the stop states correctly shown?
6. Check that the diagram includes transitions, events and guard conditions and that they are correctly represented.


| Semantic Checks for State Chart Diagrams | Yes | No |
| --- | --- | --- |

1. Check to see whether the states are well defined or fuzzily defined.
2. If a transition occurs from one state to another, check to see if it is driven by a business need or if it is a technical transition.
3. Check to see if the value of the flag is changing.
4. Check to see if the transition is occurring because of a combination of changes in attributes.

| Aesthetic Checks for State Chart Diagrams | Yes | No |
| --- | --- | --- |
| 1. Is the state chart diagram representing messages and transitions to only one object? If messages to other objects are involved, have they been kept to a minimum?<br>2. Are multiple flows of states involved? If so, have you considered more than one state chart diagram for one object? | | |

| Syntax Checks for Interaction Overview Diagrams | Yes | No |
| --- | --- | --- |
| Checks described on p. 155 | | |

| Semantic Checks for Interaction Overview Diagrams | Yes | No |
| --- | --- | --- |
| Checks described on p. 155 | | |

| Aesthetic Checks for Interaction Overview Diagrams | Yes | No |
| --- | --- | --- |
| Checks described on p. 155 | | |

# Appendix D

# Summary of Checks for V&V of the Quality of MOSS

Checks for V&V of the Diagrams in MOSS

| Syntax Checks for Classes (Advanced) | Yes | No |
|---|---|---|
| 1. Check class names. | | |
| 2. Check class stereotypes. | | |
| 3. Check the type of the class itself. | | |
| 4. Check attributes. It is important to subject the attributes to syntax checks that are language specific. | | |
| 5. Check attribute types. | | |
| 6. Check attribute initial values. Ensure that the types of value initialization and the attribute types are compatible. | | |
| 7. Check attribute visibility. | | |
| 8. Check attribute stereotypes. | | |
| 9. Check operations to ensure that their format compiles with the language of implementation. | | |
| 10. Check operation signatures. | | |
| 11. Check operation visibility. | | |
| 12. Check operation stereotypes. | | |

*Verification and Validation for Quality of UML 2.0 Models*, by Bhuvan Unhelkar
Copyright © 2005 John Wiley & Sons, Inc.

| Semantic Checks for Classes | Yes | No |
|---|---|---|

1. Check the meaning of the class.
2. Check the meanings of the attributes.
3. Check attribute initial values.
4. What does an operation mean?
   Ensure that the meaning of the operation is reflected in
   its name and format.
5. Check the pre- and postconditions of operations.
6. Check the signature of the operation.
7. Check the stereotypes of operations.
8. Check the scope of operations.
9. Check to see if the operations of a class are overloaded.
10. If overriding operations exist, ensure their correctness.
11. Check for overriding variables.
12. Check for encapsulation.

| Aesthetic Checks for Classes | Yes | No |
|---|---|---|

1. Check the number of attributes.
2. Check the number of operations.
3. Check the load on operations.
4. Check the load on the class.

| Syntax Checks for Class Diagrams | Yes | No |
|---|---|---|

1. Check that the multiplicity on an association is correctly
   represented on the class diagram.
2. Ensure that stereotypes are represented by $\ll \gg$ on classes,
   attributes, operations and relationships on a class diagram.
3. Check the association of classes with language libraries.
4. Check to see if the class is an exception class.
5. Check how error handling is modeled and implemented in the class.

| Semantic Checks for Class Diagrams | Yes | No |
|---|---|---|

1. Check directions of association.
2. Check the meaning of the relationships on a class diagram.
3. Check for collection classes.
4. Check the roles of classes.
5. Check the business rules behind the multiplicity.
6. Check for association classes.
7. Check if the operations of a class that has been specialized
   (inherited from) are overloaded.
8. Check for encapsulation.
9. Ensure that language constructs subject to interpretations are
   checked for their implied meaning.

| Aesthetic Checks for Class Diagrams | Yes | No |
|---|---|---|

1. Ensure that technical classes are represented only by their names rather than by their entire qualifications.
2. Improve the aesthetics by letting the entity classes appear in more than one diagram.
3. Improve the aesthetics by redistributing the classes and their associations across more than one class diagram.
4. Ensure that sufficient explanatory notes are provided.

| Syntax Checks for Sequence Diagrams | Yes | No |
|---|---|---|

1. Check the correctness of all objects on the sequence diagram.
2. Check the correctness of actors on the sequence diagram.
3. Check object-object interaction.
4. Check the message types shown in the sequence diagram.
5. Check the syntax of the message signatures and return values.
6. Check the syntax of multiple messages.
7. Check for multiple objects on the sequence diagram.

| Semantic Checks for Sequence Diagrams | Yes | No |
|---|---|---|

1. Check the meaning behind the sequence diagram.
2. Check the meaning behind the focus of control.
3. Check to see if the sequence diagram depicts creation and destruction of objects.
4. Check to see if the sequence diagram is based on a pattern.
5. Check to see if there are alternative flows and create separate sequence diagrams for them.

| Aesthetic Checks for Sequence Diagrams | Yes | No |
|---|---|---|

1. Ensure that the sequence diagram shows a cohesive set of interactions between collaborating objects.
2. Ensure that the sequence diagrams have sufficient notes and other annotations to explain the technicality of the diagrams.
3. Check the number of objects.
4. Check the number of messages.

| Syntax Checks for Communication Diagrams | Yes | No |
|---|---|---|

1. Check the correctness of all objects.
2. Check the correctness of all messages.
3. Ensure that all messages are correctly numbered.
4. Check object-object interaction.
5. Check the message types shown in the communication diagram.

| Syntax Checks for Communication Diagrams | Yes | No |
|---|---|---|

6. Check the syntax of the message signatures and return values.
7. Check the syntax of multiple messages.
8. Check for multiple objects on the communication diagram.

| Semantic Checks for Communication Diagrams | Yes | No |
|---|---|---|

1. Check the meaning behind the communication diagram.
2. Check the meaning behind the focus of control.
3. Check to see if the communication diagram depicts creation and destruction of objects.
4. Check to see if the communication diagram is based on a pattern.
5. Check to see if there are alternative flows and create separate communication diagrams for them.

| Aesthetic Checks for Communication Diagrams | Yes | No |
|---|---|---|

1. If an object is overloaded, ensure that its work is distributed among other objects by introducing a new object and its corresponding class.

| Syntax Checks for Object Diagrams | Yes | No |
|---|---|---|

1. Check the objects and links.
2. Ensure that there is only one object per rectangle.
3. Ensure that no attributes or operations are shown.
4. Ensure that no multiplicity is shown.
5. Ensure that notes are correctly represented on the diagram.

| Semantic Checks for Object Diagrams | Yes | No |
|---|---|---|

1. Ensure that example object diagrams are drawn whenever needed to clarify the links.
2. Relate the objects on the object diagram to other diagrams (like class diagrams) whose meanings the object diagrams are supposed to clarify.

| Aesthetic Checks for Object Diagrams | Yes | No |
|---|---|---|

1. Ensure that there are not too many object diagrams.

| Syntax Checks for State Chart Diagrams | Yes | No |
|---|---|---|

1. Check transitions.
2. Check events.
3. Check guard conditions.
4. Check entry conditions.
5. Check exit conditions.
6. Check activity states.
7. Check action states.

| Semantic Checks for State Chart Diagrams | Yes | No |
|---|---|---|

1. Check messages going out to other objects.
2. Check messages being received from other objects.
3. Check nested states.
4. Check historical states.
5. Check parallel states.
6. Check to see that state chart diagrams map with
   objects—shown for a class within a class diagram.

| Aesthetic Checks for State Chart Diagrams | Yes | No |
|---|---|---|

1. Ensure that the number of states on a diagram and
   their complexity are understandable.

| Syntax Checks for Timing Diagrams | Yes | No |
|---|---|---|
| Checks described on p. 188 briefly. | | |

| Semantic Checks for Timing Diagrams | Yes | No |
|---|---|---|
| Checks described on p. 188 briefly. | | |

| Aesthetic Checks for Timing Diagrams | Yes | No |
|---|---|---|
| Checks described on p. 189 briefly. | | |

# Appendix **E**

# Summary of Checks for V&V of the Quality of MOBS

| Checks to verify and validate the diagrams in MOBS | Yes | No |
| --- | --- | --- |
| Syntax Checks for Package Diagrams | | |
| 1. Ensure that packages created as organisational units are represented with a tabbed rectangle | | |
| 2. Check the notation for a package | | |
| 3. Check the stereotype of the package | | |
| 4. If relationships between packages are shown, ensure that it is a dependency relationship | | |

| Semantic Checks for Package Diagrams | Yes | No |
| --- | --- | --- |
| 1. Check packages for their meaning | | |
| 2. Check the meaning behind the GUI | | |
| 3. Check the meaning behind the database | | |
| 4. Check the meaning behind the administration package | | |
| 5. Check whether the premium management application should be a separate application | | |
| 6. Check whether the premium management application genuinely depends on the component premium and component client | | |
| 7. Check what sort of inter dependency is there between the component premium and component client | | |
| 8. Check what does the façade package do | | |

*Verification and Validation for Quality of UML 2.0 Models,* by Bhuvan Unhelkar
Copyright © 2005 John Wiley & Sons, Inc.

| Semantic Checks for Package Diagrams | Yes | No |
|---|---|---|

9.  Check whether it is genuine frame work or is it a high level pattern that will need a fair bit of implementation level detail
10. Ensure that the stereotyping of each package is correct
11. Check to see if they are reusable components
12. Check to see if the application packages are worth stereotyping as an application
13. Check to see if other packages are needed
14. Check to see if other classes are needed

| Aesthetic Checks for Package Diagrams | Yes | No |
|---|---|---|

1.  Ensure that packages are assigned to people and teams
2.  Check the number of packages
3.  Check the assignment of packages
4.  Check the extent of dependency of a package on another package
5.  Ensure that reuse, in terms of packages is balanced

| Syntax Checks for Class Diagrams | Yes | No |
|---|---|---|

1.  Check the representation of implementation constructs
2.  Check the access keys and IDs represented in the classes
3.  Check for the way in which data is searched and sorted
4.  Check the storage by keys and the values of the position of the record in the database
5.  Check syntactical reuse through language libraries
6.  Check additional language representations (e.g. #hashtables in Java)

| Semantic Checks for Class Diagrams | Yes | No |
|---|---|---|

1.  Ensure that what is getting stored is correctly represented in the class diagrams
2.  Check for unique responsibilities for classes. For example, Client and Policies should not be stored in the same table.
3.  Crosscheck persistence representation with multiplicities shown on the class diagram
4.  Crosscheck with direction of associations. This will decide the direction of access.
5.  Check for possibilities and correctness of semantic reuse—which will imply reuse of business classes/objects/packages

| Aesthetic Checks for Class Diagrams | Yes | No |
|---|---|---|
| 1. Check the partitioning of classes | | |
| 2. Check the normalisation | | |
| 3. Check the association classes | | |
| 4. Ensure application of granularity to class diagrams | | |

| Syntax Checks for Robustness Diagrams | Yes | No |
|---|---|---|
| 1. These checks will follow the syntax checks for class diagrams. | | |

| Semantic Checks for Robustness Diagrams | Yes | No |
|---|---|---|
| 1. Upon visualising the load on a controller class ensure that you combine more than one controller class into one or split a controller class into many | | |
| 2. What does the controller class mean? | | |
| 3. Check to see if there is a transaction controller (transaction manager) | | |
| 4. Check to see if there is a client manager or a policy manager | | |

| Aesthetic Checks for Robustness Diagrams | Yes | No |
|---|---|---|
| 1. Ensure that a controller is provided per diagram | | |
| 2. Check the partitioning | | |
| 3. Check the normalisation | | |
| 4. Check the association | | |
| 5. Ensure application of granularity to robustness diagrams | | |

| Syntax Checks for Component Diagrams | Yes | No |
|---|---|---|
| 1. Ensure the correct representation of a component on the diagram | | |
| 2. Check the representation of the interfaces on the diagram. Check the names of the components as well as the names of their interfaces | | |
| 3. If there are components within components, ensure that external packages or another component to which an embedded component might belong is shown | | |
| 4. Check the additional values of components and their responsibilities for correctness | | |
| 5. Check the names of the components | | |
| 6. Check the stereotypes | | |
| 7. Check the relationship arrow and ensure that it is primarily a dotted line with an open arrowhead | | |
| 8. Check the linking, building and executing of a particular component | | |

| Semantic Checks for Component Diagrams | Yes | No |
|---|---|---|

1. Ensure that a component correctly represents a class or collection of classes that it is meant to represent
2. Check the class to component tracing
3. Check the component interfaces
4. Check the mapping of components to nodes on the deployment diagram
5. Check for reusable components
6. Check the meaning of any external components used on your diagram
7. Check that a class created either in the MOPS or MOSS is not floating around in those models without being realised in the background space
8. Check to see that the legacy application is indeed able to realise the interfaces that it provides
9. Check to see if the technical architectural issues are satisfied by a prototyped component
10. Check the security components

| Aesthetic Checks for Component Diagrams | Yes | No |
|---|---|---|

1. Ensure that all executable components are well balanced
2. Check to see if the component is too big or too small
3. Check the number of interfaces and their definitions for each component
4. Ensure that there is sufficient amount of documentation for the interfaces and the components on the diagram
5. Ensure that components are put in a package once they are showing logical cohesiveness

| Syntax Checks for Deployment Diagrams | Yes | No |
|---|---|---|

1. Ensure that the right components are assigned to the right processors
2. Ensure that right notations are used to represent the nodes and processors on the deployment diagrams

| Semantic Checks for Deployment Diagrams | Yes | No |
|---|---|---|

1. Check that all operational issues that are capable of being represented on the deployment diagrams have been represented.
2. Ensure use of stereotypes and notes to enable clear understanding of the semantics behind the deployment diagram

| Semantic Checks for Deployment Diagrams | Yes | No |
|---|---|---|
| 3. Map the diagram to the prototypes created, to ensure that the diagrams reflect what was conceived in the prototypes | | |

| Aesthetic Checks for Deployment Diagrams | Yes | No |
|---|---|---|
| 1. Check to see if the load sharing by processing nodes can be improved<br>2. Optionally, consider mirroring of databases and nodes to improve performance | | |

| Syntax Checks for Composite Structure Diagrams | Yes | No |
|---|---|---|
| Checks described on p. 218. | | |

| Semantic Checks for Composite Structure Diagrams | Yes | No |
|---|---|---|
| Checks described on p. 219. | | |

| Aesthetic Checks for Composite Structure Diagrams | Yes | No |
|---|---|---|
| Checks described on p. 219. | | |

# Templates for Actors, Use Cases and Classes in MOPS

These downloadable templates can be used to jump start your documentation work. It is recommended that you modify this template to suit your project type and size and your individual requirements of documentation. These documents can then be linked to the corresponding UML elements on the diagrams.

## F.1  ACTOR DOCUMENTATION TEMPLATE

**Actor Thumbnail**
<This is the name and, optionally, a prefixed number of the actor>

**Actor Type and Stereotype**
<Actors can be of various types, such as primary versus secondary, direct versus indirect, abstract versus concrete, person versus external system or device, etc.>

**Actor Description**
<A one- or two-line description of the actor and what he/she/it does>

**Actor Relationships**
<Thumbnails of relevant use cases and/or other actors with whom this actor is interacting. If there is an inheritance hierarchy, thumbnails of generalized/ specialized actors will be documented here>

---

*Verification and Validation for Quality of UML 2.0 Models*, by Bhuvan Unhelkar
Copyright © 2005 John Wiley & Sons, Inc.

| **Interface Specifications**
<Since, by definition, the actor has to interact with the system, we note here the details of the interface through which the actor performs this interaction>

**Author**
<Original author and modifiers of this actor description>

**Reference Material**
<Relevant references, as well as sources> |

## F.2 TEMPLATE FOR DOCUMENTING USE CASES

**Use Case Thumbnail**
<Number and name of the use case and, optionally, a version number>

**Use Case Description**
<A one-line description of the use case>

**Stereotype and Package**
<Description of the stereotype and the package to which this use case belongs>

**Preconditions**
<Preconditions are conditions that must be met before the execution described by the use case can commence>

**Postconditions**
<Postconditions are conditions that must be met at the end of the use case>

**Actor-Goal Table**
<A list of the actors involved in the use case and the corresponding goals that the actors aim to achieve in interacting with the system in the context of the particular use case>

**Use Case Relationships**
<Thumbnails of other use cases that are included, extended or inherited>

**Use Case Text** (flow within the use case)
1.0 <description of step>
2.0 <description of step> (A1, E1, E2)
3.0 <description of step> (A2, E3)
INCLUDES <thumbnail of use case(s) included>
EXTENDS <thumbnail of use case(s) extended>

*Another format for documenting the flow within the use cases is the following:*

| User Intentions | System Response |
| --- | --- |
| 1. | |
| 2. | |
| 3. | |

*Here is another format that may be appropriate for the project/role.*

| User Actions | System Response |
| --- | --- |
| | |
| <<include>> AcceptPremium | |

**Alternative Flow**
<A1>

**Exceptions**
<E1>

**Constraints**
<The documented special constraints and/or limitations relevant to the use case>

**User Interface Specifications**
<Number and name of UI specifications related to the use case, including Web screen specifications>

**Metrics**
<Anything that needs to be measured in relation to the use cases>

**Priority**
<The importance of the functionality described by this use case: high/medium/low>

**Status**
<The state of the documentation of this use case: initial/major/final>

**Author and History**
<Original author and modifiers of the use case>

**Reference Material**
<Relevant references, as well as sources>

## F.3   DOCUMENTING A CLASS-SUGGESTED CLASS TEMPLATE

| | |
|---|---|
| <<Stereotype>> Class Name | <A one-word name for the class. The name is prefixed by the optional stereotype. The stereotype indicates, for example, whether this class deals with interface, persistence or control> |
| Description | <A one-line description of the class> |
| Relationship | <A list of other classes and their relationship with the class> |
| Attributes | <A list of all attributes of the class> |
| Responsibilities | <The main responsibilities of the class> |
| Business Rules | <Special business rules and constraints that are not easily listed under responsibilities> |
| Complexity | <Simple/medium/complex> |

# Index

Activity diagrams, 33
  Nature, 33
  Specifications, 34
Analysing MOPS for MOSS for a
    Solution, 163
  Analysis of use cases in MOSS, 163
  Analysis of business class diagrams in
    MOSS, 165
  Analysing activity diagrams in MOSS, 165

Background of Lucky insurance
    case study, 231
Background space, 257
  V&V quality checks Summary, 257
  Working in Background space, 194
  V&V of Component diagrams, 213
  V&V of class diagrams, 208

Class diagrams, 35
  Nature, 35
  Putting together class diagrams, 36
  Specification, 36
  Class diagram to sequence dependency,
    quality, 157
  V&V of Robustness in MOBS, 210
Communication diagrams, 39
  Nature, 39

Putting together communication
    diagram, 40
Composite structure diagrams, 44
  Nature, 44
  Putting together, 44
Component diagrams, 45
  Nature, 45
  Putting together, 46
  Specifications, 46
  V&V in MOBS, 213
  SWOT of Component diagrams, 78
Converting Models into Systems, 189
Cross-Diagram dependencies MOSS, 189
Cross-Diagram dependencies MOBS, 222
Classes and class diagrams in MOBS, 204
  Relational table representation by
    classes, 204
  Mapping ClientDetails to relational
    tables, 205
  Active classes in MOBS, 205
  Class and granularity in MOBS, 207
  Assigning classes to components, 208
Component diagrams in MOBS, 213
  Syntax checks for Component diagrams
    MOBS, 213
  Semantic checks Component diagrams
    MOBS, 213

Component diagrams in MOBS (*Continued*)
Aesthetic checks for Component diagrams
MOBS, 213
Composite structure diagrams, 218
Syntax checks composite structure
diagrams, 218
Semantic checks composite structure
diagrams, 218
Aesthetic checks composite structure
diagrams, 218
V&V in MOBS, 218
Criteria for evaluating UML case tools, 237

Deployment diagrams, 46
Nature, 46
Putting together, 47
Syntax checks in MOBS, 221
Semantic checks in MOBS, 221
Aesthetic checks in MOBS, 221
V&V in MOBS, 219
SWOT of Deployment diagrams, 79

Employee portal, 234
Lucky Insurance case study, 234
Elasticity in UML diagrams, 28
Extending class diagrams robustness
diagrams, 210
E-commerce applications and Use case, 62

Functional slices and Relation to
infrastructure, 198

Growth Lucky insurance case study, 234

Iterations and increments in Process, 228
Iterative development, 228
Incremental development, 229
Parallel development, 229
Project-level iterations, 229
Interaction overview diagrams, 41
Nature, 41
Putting together interaction overview
diagrams, 41
Interaction overview to sequence
and use case dependencies, 157

Lucky insurance case study, 231
Description, 231
Background, 231
Insurance business, 232
Policies and risk categories, 233
Payment types, 234
Interactions, 234
Growth, 234
Employee portal, 234

Levels of quality checks to UML
diagrams, 20
Syntax checks and UML elements, 21
Semantics checks and UML elements, 22
Aesthetic checks and UML models, 22

Model driven architecture and quality, 23
Modelling and quality, 2
Modelling advantage, 2
Modelling caveats, 2
Model quality context, 3
Model quality, 4
Modelling spaces in software, 7
Modelling spaces and UML, 7
UML diagrams and models, 8
UML diagrams and modelling spaces, 9
Model of problem space, 10
UML diagrams in MOPS, 10
Model of solution space, 11
UML diagrams in MOSS, 12
Model of Background space, 12
UML diagrams in MOBS, 13
Managing V&V Process, 225
MOPS Summary of V&V quality checks, 241
MOSS Summary of V&V quality checks, 251
MOBS Summary of V&V quality checks, 257

Nature of UML diagrams, 27
Elasticity, 28
Structural and behavioural nature, 28
Static versus dynamic nature, 29

Object diagrams, 41
Nature, 41
Putting together object diagrams, 42

Prototyping and modelling spaces, 23
Positioning UML for modelling, 4
Package diagram, 47
Nature, 47
Putting together, 48
Specifications, 48
SWOT of Package diagrams, 80
Process and UML, 225
Process and process component, 226
Simple process architecture, 226
Process component for V&V class
diagrams, 227
Iterations and increments, 228

Quality aspects of UML, 5
Visualizing, 6
Specifying, 6
Constructing, 6
Documenting, 6

Quality checks and skills levels, 19
Quality of Activity diagrams, 122
   AddsClientDetails description, 122
   CreatesHomeInsurancePolicy, 124
   Syntax checks for Activity diagrams, 126
   Semantic checks for Activity diagrams, 126
   Aesthetic checks for Activity diagrams, 126
Quality checks of Package diagrams, 129
   Lucky Package description, 129
   Syntax checks for Package diagrams, 130
   Semantic checks for Package diagrams, 131
   Aesthetic checks for Package diagrams, 132
Quality checks of classes and class
      diagrams, 129
   Documenting class and template, 133
   Client class description, 135
   Syntax checks for Classes, 137
   Semantic checks for Classes, 138
   Aesthetic checks for Classes, 138
   Class Diagrams, 139
   ClientDetails description, 139
   PolicyDetails description, 142
   Syntax checks for Class diagrams, 142
   Semantic checks for Class diagrams, 144
   Aesthetic checks for Class diagrams, 144
Quality of Sequence diagrams
      in MOPS, 145
   CreateClient Sequence description, 145
   CreateClientOnInternet description, 146
   ApprovePolicy description, 147
   Syntax checks for Sequence diagrams, 148
   Semantic checks for Sequence
      diagrams, 148
   Aesthetic checks for Sequence
      diagrams, 150
Quality of State Machine diagrams in
      MOPS, 150
   Client State Machine description, 150
   Policy description, 151
   Syntax checks for State Machine
      diagrams, 152
   Semantic checks for State Machine
      diagrams, 153
   Aesthetic checks for State Machine
      diagrams, 153
Quality of Interaction Overview
      diagrams in MOPS, 154
   CreateClient Interaction Overview
      description, 154
   Syntax for Interaction Overview
      diagrams, 155
   Semantics for Interaction Overview
      diagrams, 155
   Aesthetics Interaction Overview
      diagrams, 155

Quality of classes and class diagrams in
      MOSS, 166
   Syntax for classes, 166
   Semantics for classes, 170
   Aesthetics classes, 155
   Syntax for class diagrams, 175
   Semantics for class diagrams, 176
   Aesthetics class diagrams, 177
Quality of Sequence diagrams in MOSS, 178
   Submission Claim Sequence description, 178
   Syntax checks for Sequence diagrams, 180
   Semantic checks for Sequence
      diagrams, 181
   Aesthetic checks for Sequence
      diagrams, 182
Quality of Communication diagrams in
      MOSS, 182
   SubmitsClaim Communication
      description, 182
   Syntax checks for Communication
      diagrams, 183
   Semantic checks for Communication
      diagrams, 183
   Aesthetic checks for Communication
      diagrams, 184
Quality of Object diagrams in MOSS, 182
   Policy Claim Object diagrams
      description, 182
   Syntax checks for Object diagrams, 185
   Semantic checks for Object diagrams, 185
   Aesthetic checks for Object diagrams, 186
Quality of State Machine diagrams
      in MOSS, 186
   Syntax checks for Object diagrams, 186
   Semantic checks for Object diagrams, 187
   Aesthetic checks for Object diagrams, 188
Quality of Timing diagrams in MOSS, 186
   Policy claims timing diagrams
      description, 188
   Syntax checks for Timing diagrams, 188
   Semantic checks for Timing diagrams, 188
   Aesthetic checks for Timing diagrams, 189

Robustness diagrams, 210
   Extending class diagrams robustness
      diagrams, 210
   Robustness through sequence diagrams, 211
   Syntax checks robustness in MOBS, 211
   Semantic checks robustness in MOBS, 211
   Aesthetic checks robustness in MOBS, 213

Sequence diagrams, 37
   Nature, 37
   Putting together sequence diagrams, 38
   Specification, 39

State machine diagrams, 43
  Nature, 43
  Putting together, 44
SWOT of UML diagrams, 57
  SWOT of use case diagrams, 59
  Strengths of Use case diagrams, 59
  Weakness of Use case diagrams, 60
  Objectives of Use case and Use case
    diagrams, 61
  Use case and E-commerce applications, 62
  Use case and contract management, 63
  Use case diagrams and education, 63
  Traps of use case diagrams, 63
  SWOT of activity diagrams, 65
  Strengths of activity diagrams, 65
  Weakness of activity diagrams, 66
  Objectives of activity diagrams, 66
  Traps of activity diagrams, 67
  SWOT of classes and class diagrams, 67
  Strengths of classes and class diagrams, 67
  Weakness of classes and class diagrams, 68
  Objectives of classes and class diagrams, 69
  Traps of classes and class diagrams, 69
  SWOT of Sequence diagrams, 70
  Strengths of Sequence diagrams, 70
  Weakness of Sequence diagrams, 71
  Objectives of Sequence diagrams, 71
  Traps of Sequence diagrams, 72
  SWOT of Communication diagrams, 73
  Strengths of Communication diagrams, 73
  Weakness of Communication diagrams, 73
  Objectives of Communication diagrams, 73
  Traps of Communication diagrams, 74
  SWOT of Interaction Overview
    diagrams, 74
  Strengths of Interaction Overview
    diagrams, 74
  Weakness of Interaction Overview
    diagrams, 74
  Objectives of Interaction Overview
    diagrams, 74
  Traps of Interaction Overview diagrams, 75
  SWOT of Object diagrams, 75
  Strengths of Object diagrams, 75
  Weakness of Object diagrams, 75
  Objectives of Object diagrams, 75
  Traps of Object diagrams, 76
  SWOT of State Machine diagrams, 76
  Strengths of State Machine diagrams, 76
  Weakness of State Machine diagrams, 76
  Objectives of State Machine diagrams, 76
  Traps of State Machine diagrams, 77
  SWOT of Composite Structure diagrams, 77

  Strengths of Composite Structure
    diagrams, 77
  Weakness of Composite Structure
    diagrams, 77
  Objectives of Composite Structure
    diagrams, 77
  Traps of Composite Structure diagrams, 78
  SWOT of Component diagrams, 78
  Strengths of Component diagrams, 78
  Weakness of Component diagrams, 78
  Objectives of Component diagrams, 78
  Traps of Component diagrams, 79
  SWOT of Deployment diagrams, 79
  Strengths of Deployment diagrams, 79
  Weakness of Deployment diagrams, 79
  Objectives of Deployment diagrams, 80
  Traps of Deployment diagrams, 80
  SWOT of Package diagrams, 80
  Strengths of Package diagrams, 80
  Weakness of Package diagrams, 81
  Objectives of Package diagrams, 81
  Traps of Package diagrams, 81
  SWOT of Timing diagrams, 82
  Strengths of Timing diagrams, 82
  Weakness of Timing diagrams, 82
  Objectives of Timing diagrams, 82
  Traps of Timing diagrams, 82
Summary V&V of quality checks
  in MOPS, 241
Summary V&V of quality checks
  in MOSS, 251
Summary V&V of quality checks
  in MOBS, 257

Timing diagrams, 49
  Nature, 49
  Putting together, 49
  SWOT of Timing diagrams, 82
Templates for actors, use case and
  classes in MOPS, 263

Use case diagrams, 30
  Nature of use case diagrams, 30
  Use case diagrams specification, 32
  SWOT of use case diagrams, 59
  Use case to activity dependency, quality, 156
  Use case to class diagram dependency,
    quality, 157
UML extensibility mechanisms, 50
  Stereotypes, 50
  Notes, 51
  Constraints, 52
  Tagged values, 53

UML meta-models and quality, 53
UML diagrams in MOPS, 86
UML diagrams in MOSS, 161
UML diagrams in MOBS, 194
  Layers in software architecture, 196
  Relating the functional slices to
    infrastructure, 198
UML case tools, 237
  Some case tools, 238

Verification and validation, 14
  Quality models syntax, 15
  Quality models semantics, 17
  Quality models aesthetics, 18
  Quality checks and V&V, 18
V&V of Quality of MOPS, 85
V&V of Quality of MOPS, 161
V&V of Quality of MOBS, 193
  Syntax checks for package diagrams
    MOBS, 202
  Semantic checks for package diagrams
    MOBS, 202
  Aesthetic checks for package diagrams
    MOBS, 203
V&V of Use case and use case diagrams in
  MOPS, 88
  List of Use case diagrams, 90
  Policy creation and maintenance, 100
  Claims Processing, 113
  Sales campaigning, 114
  Actor class confusion, 95
  Actor documentation and quality checks, 96
  Use case documentation and quality
    checks, 103
  Use case documentation examples, 108
  Syntax checks for Use case diagrams, 115
  Semantic checks for Use case diagrams, 118
  Aesthetic checks for Use case diagrams, 120
  Acceptance testing and documentation, 121
V&V of class diagrams in MOBS, 208
  Syntax checks for class diagrams is
    MOBS, 209
  Semantic checks for class diagrams is
    MOBS, 209

  Aesthetic checks for class diagrams is
    MOBS, 209
V&V of Robustness through class
  diagrams MOBS, 210
V&V of Component diagrams in MOBS, 213
V&V Composite structure diagrams
  MOBS, 218
V&V Deployment diagrams MOBS, 219
  Factors influencing system
    deployment, 219
V&V of quality checks in MOPS
  Summary, 241
V&V of quality checks in MOSS
  Summary, 251
V&V of quality checks in MOBS
  Summary, 257
Validating Entire MOPS, 156
  Use case to activity dependency,
    quality, 156
  Use case to class diagram
    dependency, quality, 157
  Class diagram to sequence
    dependency, quality, 157
  Interaction overview to sequence
    and use case dependencies, 157
  Quality of documentation MOPS, 158
  Aesthetics of MOPS, 158
V&V of Package diagrams in MOBS, 199

Working in Background space, 194
Weakness of Timing diagrams, 82
Weakness of Package diagrams, 81
Weakness of Deployment diagrams, 79
Weakness of Component diagrams, 78
Weakness of Composite Structure diagrams, 77
Weakness of State Machine diagrams, 76
Weakness of Object diagrams, 75
Weakness of Interaction Overview
  diagrams, 74
Weakness of Communication diagrams, 73
Weakness of Sequence diagrams, 71
Weakness of classes and class diagrams, 68
Weakness of activity diagrams, 66
Weakness of Use case diagrams, 60

## WILEY SERIES IN SYSTEMS ENGINEERING AND MANAGEMENT

Andrew P. Sage, Editor

ANDREW P. SAGE AND JAMES D. PALMER
**Software Systems Engineering**

WILLIAM B. ROUSE
**Design for Success: A Human-Centered Approach to Designing Successful Products and Systems**

LEONARD ADELMAN
**Evaluating Decision Support and Expert System Technology**

ANDREW P. SAGE
**Decision Support Systems Engineering**

YEFIM FASSER AND DONALD BRETTNER
**Process Improvement in the Electronics Industry, 2/e**

WILLIAM B. ROUSE
**Strategies for Innovation**

ANDREW P. SAGE
**Systems Engineering**

HORST TEMPELMEIER AND HEINRICH KUHN
**Flexible Manufacturing Systems: Decision Support for Design and Operation**

WILLIAM B. ROUSE
**Catalysts for Change: Concepts and Principles for Enabling Innovation**

LIPING FANG, KEITH W. HIPEL, AND D. MARC KILGOUR
**Interactive Decision Making: The Graph Model for Conflict Resolution**

DAVID A. SCHUM
**Evidential Foundations of Probabilistic Reasoning**

JENS RASMUSSEN, ANNELISE MARK PEJTERSEN, AND
LEONARD P. GOODSTEIN
**Cognitive Systems Engineering**

ANDREW P. SAGE
**Systems Management for Information Technology and
Software Engineering**

ALPHONSE CHAPANIS
**Human Factors in Systems Engineering**

YACOV Y. HAIMES
**Risk Modeling, Assessment, and Management, 2/e**

DENNIS M. BUEDE
**The Engineering Design of Systems: Models and Methods**

ANDREW P. SAGE AND JAMES E. ARMSTRONG, JR.
**Introduction to Systems Engineering**

WILLIAM B. ROUSE
**Essential Challenges of Strategic Management**

YEFIM FASSER AND DONALD BRETTNER
**Management for Quality in High-Technology Enterprises**

THOMAS B. SHERIDAN
**Humans and Automation: System Design and Research Issues**

ALEXANDER KOSSAIKOFF AND WILLIAM N. SWEET
**Systems Engineering Principles and Practice**

HAROLD R. BOOHER
**Handbook of Human Systems Integration**

JEFFREY T. POLLOCK AND RALPH HODGSON
**Adaptive Information: Improving Business Through Semantic Interoperability,
Grid Computing, and Enterprise Integration**

ALAN L. PORTER AND SCOTT W. CUNNINGHAM
**Tech Mining: Exploiting New Technologies for Competitive Advantage**

ANDREW P. SAGE AND WILLIAM B. ROUSE
**Handbook of Systems Engineering and Management**